BEARDED TIT

Praise for *Bearded Tit*

'McGrath's tale of fumbled romance and birding evangelism is ultimately a sweet and elegiac read' *Mail on Sunday*

'There is far more to Rory McGrath than meets the eye. Yes, he can be very funny, basic and boisterous, but beneath the stubble is a countryman and birdwatcher ... lyrical and beautiful' *Daily Telegraph*

'With great warmth and his trademark wit, he recounts his love affair with birding. A real pleasure to read' *Sunday Express*

'I rapidly consumed Rory McGrath's Bearded Tit, about his time at Cambridge. He trod an almost identical path there to me, and his recollections of fancying a girl like crazy, who then disappeared into the ether, I could identify with all too easily. It makes me want to be a student again and fancy a girl who works in the bookshop' **Bill Oddie**

'I've just seen Rory McGrath's Bearded Tit talk and I really enjoyed it, although I couldn't understand all of his words' **Jimmy Carter**

BEARDED TIT
RORY McGRATH

EBURY
PRESS

5 7 9 10 8 6

Published in 2009 by Ebury Press, an imprint of Ebury Publishing
A Random House Group Company
First published in the UK in 2008
This edition published 2009

The Random House Group Limited Reg. No. 954009

Addresses for companies within the Random House Group
can be found at www.randomhouse.co.uk

A CIP catalogue record for this book is available from the British Library

The Random House Group Limited supports the Forest Stewardship
Council (FSC®), the leading international forest certification organisation.
Our books carrying the FSC label are printed on FSC ® certified
paper. FSC is the only forest certification scheme endorsed by the
leading environmental organisations, including Greenpeace.
Our paper procurement policy can be found at
www.randomhouse.co.uk/environment

Printed and bound by CPI Group (UK) Ltd, Croydon, CR0 4YY

ISBN 9780091924607

To buy books by your favourite authors and register for offers visit
www.randomhouse.co.uk

A message to my readers

Many thanks to both of you.

For Nicola

Another message to my readers

There is nothing quite like the sentence 'And this is a true story' to make you instantly doubt all that you are about to hear. And 'This is no word of a lie' invariably precedes a tale of palpable mendacity. 'I kid you not, hand on heart', you just *know* heralds a pile of arrant bullshit. With all this foremost in my mind, I nervously say to you now that what follows is a true story.

Hand on heart. Hand on heart.

Some of it anyway.

A lot of this happened a long time ago. Strange, is it not, that most of the things that happen in our life seem to happen in the past?

This is a love story; well, some of it is a love story.

It is a love story with, and without, feathers.

It is no ordinary love story, though. It has 'boy meets girl' and 'girl meets boy' elements to it, but, as far as I know, it is the only love story in which the scientific name for a Caspian snowcock plays a significant part.

The truth is that I have only recently become interested in birdwatching in a truly dedicated way: six or seven years maybe. But I realized, as I came to write this book, that birds have been with me all the time, singing in the background of my growing up, hovering over key events of my past and shitting, from time to time, on the windscreen of my life.

I hope you find in these pages something to titillate you, tickle your fancy, amuse you, inform you, irritate you or perhaps even offend you.

I hope you like it, of course, but if you do not, if you think it's a piece of garbage, if you think it's the worst book you've ever read and a total waste of money, just go out and watch a kestrel for a few moments and you will glimpse the beauty and the joy of the world, the enormity of nature, the brush-strokes of God and you will realize how microscopic and insignificant you are in the history of the universe … And, at least, you'll be off your arse for five minutes and out in the fresh air.

SCARY

Lizards don't scream with pain. They don't have the mechanisms for making noise. They can't purr or growl or bark or sing. The one we were watching was not screaming. It should have been. Its mouth gaped dumbly. Its eyes were blank. Its claws twitched and its tail flicked occasionally from side to side. We knew it was in pain though. It must have been.

It was impaled on a metal spike. The point of which was freshly and moistly red.

I felt scared.

Not for the lizard; not for me; but for the girl next to me. What did she make of this? She, who seemed to be made for compassion and humanity. Made *from* compassion and humanity, even. The girl whose eyes were green, bottomless pools of love and sympathy.

Would she be appalled by this?

And the lizard was not alone. A few inches further along the fence, a grasshopper was stuck on a wire barb.

Perched next to it was the bird.

A beautiful, cleanly marked grey and white bird with black wings. Its bill broad and heavy with a fine hook on the end. A bandit's black mask failing to conceal two dark eyes, lively with mischief.

The great grey shrike.

The butcher bird.

Lanius excubitor according to the textbooks. *Lanius* from a Latin word *lanio*, which means 'to mangle, tear, rip or mutilate'.

Like an *excubitor* – that is, a vigilante or sentinel – this bird perches high up on branches or telegraph wires alert to any movement on the ground: an insect, maybe, or a reptile or small mammal. Whichever, it will soon disappear in a feathery flurry of black and white death. The shrike will eat it there or take it off to its 'larder', where it will be kept for later, stuck on a thorn or a spike.

I turned to the girl. 'Pretty gruesome, eh?'

She looked surprised.

'Why gruesome? It's only doing what a shrike does best.'

'Lizard-torturing?'

'What a very human interpretation. All it's doing is being a shrike. In fact, when it comes to being a shrike, you can't beat a shrike. I think it's quite impressive.'

Her matter-of-factness was scary.

'You don't like it, though, do you?'

She looked at me with a puzzled expression. 'There's nothing to like. Or dislike. It's nature. You're being too human.'

Was this a bad thing, I thought?

'Sorry, I was born human.'

She tutted.

'My parents were human. In fact, there've been humans in our family for generations. Mind you, there's always been a question mark over my great-uncle Daisy.'

She was ignoring me. 'Listen, nature is neither likeable nor dislikeable. Nature is just … er, well, natural.'

And so was she. So natural. And so wise. That was scary.

And I was totally in love with her.

That was scary too.

Part One: Falling From The Nest

THE BEAUTIFUL STRANGER

The seventies rose, ashes-like, from the phoenix of the sixties. With the 'midi' replacing the 'mini', and the 'maxi' replacing 'the midi', hemlines dropped like the shutters being pulled down on the age of carefree hedonism. I was eighteen, the age when you are the universe and the universe is you. The real world happened in an incoherent blur of meaningless names, unknown places and vague headlines. The narcissism of being an adolescent shielded me from the constant, grey drizzle of strikes, the Yom Kippur war, three-day weeks, power-cuts, inflation and Nixon's impeachment in something I think was called the 'Watership Down' scandal. It was a low, nondescript and dispirited decade with the bleak tawdriness of 'glam-rock' as its embarrassing background music.

They were a decade-long morning-after headache, but, significantly, they were also the most formative years of my life.

In fashion, hair was huge and good taste was tiny. I don't think the phrase 'big hair' existed then, but it was the best way to describe mine: its curliness meant that it grew outwards rather than down. All the clothes then were made of too much material: three-piece suits, double-breasted jackets, wide ties and expanses of lapel.

And so in 1974, dressed in a dark maroon version of one such fabric nightmare, I arrived, virginal and awkward, in Cambridge to study modern languages: Spanish and French. I was to attend a college called Emmanuel.

The cinema across the road was showing *Emmanuelle*. It seemed only appropriate that I should go and see it. Nine times in the first week, in fact. I saw it so often that for years afterwards I was terrified of bumping into Sylvia Kristel in the street in case she recognized me from the end seat of row W. That said, it was the only meaningful relationship I had in my first year; a sorry state of affairs that I intended to rectify at the beginning of my second.

It was 1975, a few days before the official start of the new academic year, and a friend of mine, Richard McShee, and I were discussing the lamentable condition of our love-lives over a coffee in the market square.

'Too many blokes, Mack. The odds are stacked against us,' I said.

He agreed. 'Six male students to one female student, apparently.'

'She's not complaining though!' I said with half-hearted humour, realizing that comments like that magnified, rather than relieved, the bleakness of our situation.

A pigeon landed on the table and pecked at Mack's sandwich. I attempted to punch it and missed.

'Oi, that's not nice!'

'Bloody things,' I said. 'Flying rats, you know.'

'Well, actually,' said Mack, reminding me that he was studying zoology, 'they're more like flying reptiles. Birds are descended from reptiles, not mammals. The feather is an evolution of the scale.'

'No shit!'

'Plenty of shit actually,' Mack was pleased with this in a 'science student makes joke – hold the front page' sort of way.

I reminded him of our agenda. 'Girls, Mackie!'

'But you've no need to complain about lack of women, Ror. You had no problems last year!'

This came as big news to me.

'Didn't I?'

'Yes, you had loads of girls. In fact, we didn't think it was fair. You should have shared them round.'

I cast my mind back over the previous twelve months and struggled to think of a single romantic or sexual episode that included another person. Apart from Sylvia Kristel.

'Who were you thinking of?'

'That lovely waitress from the college canteen. With the amazing red hair. The South African one.'

Oh yes, Brigid. What a nightmare that was! And I think I speak for both of us …

Brigid served dinner in what was laughingly called Formal Hall. First-years had to attend dinner in Formal Hall for at least the first term. You had to wear a gown. An academic gown, of course, not an evening dress. (Though I do recall a chap called Adrian who turned up once in a glamorous, velvet number with a daring neckline and a slit up the side. I think he now works in children's television.)

Each evening, an undergraduate scholar was chosen by the senior tutor to read a Latin grace before the meal. If he did it well enough he was given half a cider in a pewter tankard – if Rex the Chaplain hadn't already necked it. I think by some ancient college law the scholar could opt for a brass farthing or a bale of hay instead of the cider, though I don't recall anyone taking this up.

The young South African waitress did look stunning with her huge blaze of red hair and breasts that could only be described as massive and freckly. And to me, back in those innocent days, quite alarming.

'Enjoy your dinner, guys.' This was a refreshingly friendly

comment. The English waitresses could never quite put a plate on the table without some grunt or hand gesture which seemed to say, 'Don't know why *I'm* serving *you*. You're no better than me. Just coz you've read a few books and talk posh.'

'What's your name?' I asked.

'Me? I'm Brigid. What's yours?'

'Rory.'

'Rory? That's a bit queer, isn't it?'

The downside was that she had an impeccably unpleasant accent, even by South African standards.

'Hey, I love your accent!' I said. 'Where are you from?'

'Guess!'

'The moon?'

'No, but thanks for not saying Australia. I really hate that. Everyone says Australia. Aussies make me puke.'

A spunky girl but with real possibilities if you could just deal with the voice.

After a few formal dinners of casual banter with the golden Boer, I ended up meeting her after her shift in the pub across the road, where I gradually became aware of subtle cultural differences. I brought the drinks, a pint of Guinness and a dry white wine, over to our table. She tucked into the Guinness. I noticed she had taken a packet of cigarettes out of her handbag and put them on the table in front of her.

'Cheers,' I said and we clinked glasses. Things were going well.

'I'd love a cigarette,' she said impatiently.

'Go ahead. Don't mind me!'

She sighed deeply and raised her eyes to heaven.

'I said, I'd love a cigarette.'

'By all means. You just go right ahead.'

She fixed me with her eyes. 'The packet's on the table!'

I looked at the cigarettes and then back at her and realized I was supposed to open the packet and offer it to her.

'Oh sorry!' This I duly did. She didn't take one. She looked at me with contempt. I was puzzled.

'Well, light one for me then. What's wrong with you?'

Clearly South African girls were used to a higher degree of chivalry from their menfolk than I would have expected. I struck a match and put it to the cigarette I was holding between my index and middle fingers. Never having smoked in my life, it did not occur to me that you had to put the object in your mouth and suck on it to ignite it.

'Stick it in your mouth, you moron!'

The coughing stopped eventually. With the help of most of Brigid's Guinness, the scorched patch of my throat settled down and I was able to manage a rudimentary form of speech.

Despite this setback, we were back in my room at midnight and snogging was under way.

'Mmm, this is good,' she said encouragingly, adding, with mock regret, 'I'm afraid we're not going to get much sleep tonight, babe.'

Snogging resumed. Hands and arms acquired a life of their own. Brigid's lively and adventurous tongue seemed engaged in licking my brain clean.

So this was it then. The Games had commenced. It was going to happen at last. But something troubled me. Yes, I was sexually frustrated. Yes, I was a virgin. Yes, these were both personal features I wished to change. But I was more nervous than expected. When I had got this far with girls in the past, I knew that something would stop us. 'I've got to go home!' or 'My parents'll be back soon' or 'I'm not on the pill' or 'What if the bus conductor comes up?' It was easy for me, in those circumstances, to be the one in the driving seat. To be the keen one, the more insistent one, the pesterer. It was clear I wouldn't actually have to 'do it', to 'perform'.

But tonight was different. I looked down the long and lonely highway that stretched out ahead of me and could see nothing but green lights. What if I couldn't do it? I knew in theory *what* to do, but in practice, I'd had no practice. And this girl was clearly well practised. Did I actually *want* to do it with her? Or did I feel I *should* do it with her? Was there an invisible peer pressure forcing me on? A bloke needs to lose his virginity as soon as possible with whomever and carry on having as much sex as possible for the rest of his life. That's the received adolescent male wisdom, isn't it? Was it *expected* of me to do this thing, whether I wanted to or not? Was it expected of me by *me*? Brigid was a fit, healthy, immensely physical girl and as I imagined the bio-mechanics involved in making love to her, they seemed suddenly daunting. This is no time to get cold genitals, I thought. It's got to happen sooner or later, so let's get it over with. I returned her next kiss with as much passion as I could manage.

'Hey, let me get a bit more comfortable,' she said detaching her tongue from the inside of my cranium. She kicked off her boots and stretched out alluringly on the bed. She giggled in the South African version of coquettish and then decided it was time for another cigarette. (This one she lit herself, having worked out that this was the least time-consuming procedure for the task.)

'Tell me something about yourself,' she said. My body was beginning to respond as I steeled myself for the job ahead, and now she wanted to talk. This just brought home to me the fact that she was very much in control. Yes, we would have a sleepless night of hot sex, but clearly on her terms, in her time. The conversation that then unfolded consisted mainly of me rambling as endearingly as I could about a huge range of subjects like sport, food, cinema, books, family, history, sunbathing, Tchaikovsky and *Sooty and Sweep*. She listened intently, stopping me occasionally when I was getting 'Really boring, man!'

Eventually she was driven to interject.

'What about big things? You know, death!' An abrupt change of subject, it has to be said, as I was talking about fish fingers at the time. 'I mean, listen. What happens when you die? And what about God? Do you believe in God?' she asked earnestly.

Now, I don't know why I said what I said next. Perhaps I needed to know a bit more about her upbringing or background. She evidently had issues on this subject whereof I knew not and perhaps I should have trodden more carefully, but I replied dramatically, 'Of course I believe in God. How could I not? Because if God doesn't exist, then I don't exist.' I turned off the overhead lights, leaving the room in the gloom of a single reading lamp, looked her in the eyes, grabbed her hand and said, 'For the truth is, my child, I am THE DEVIL!'

Her scream was deafening. She grabbed her coat and boots and slammed the door as she fled into the night.

She left her cigarettes. I kept them for a while in case she came back for them.

She didn't.

I guess she bought a new packet.

'She was a hell of a feisty girl,' Mack was saying. 'Reg the Hedge said he heard her screams from his room.'

I smiled a dismissive smile as if to say, 'Oh, it was nothing!' And I knew that it *was* nothing, but I was building on the lie. I did not say that I had fabulous sex with Brigid, but I was not denying it either. A reputation was being born. A reputation based on a pack of feeble lies.

'Well, what about that girl from the posh school in Shelford? She was a bit special!'

'Oh her. Charlotte.' I recalled another bleak encounter.

Charlotte was a very well brought-up, 'nice' girl, with rich parents and lots of blonde friends called things like Pongo, Baggers and Smell. Things had progressed well with Charley and I found myself at the end of our third evening out back in my room, nervously unbuttoning her shirt.

'You seem nervous,' she said. 'Your hands are all shaky.'

'Nervous? No! Excited. Eager!' More lies. I had decided that if I just ignored my nerves and misgivings I might end up having the bawdy one-night stand students were supposed to be having all the time; in fact, the sort of night I presumed every student in the world, except me, had already had. Again it was the girl who saved me from the brutal interior fight I was having.

Charlotte had a boyfriend. He was called Dusty. Just as I was faking lusty impatience and undoing her belt buckle, she put her hand on mine to stop me, saying, 'I don't know if I can do this. What would Dusty say?'

'Sorry?'

'What would Dusty say?'

'What would Dusty say?' was not one of the questions I was expecting to be asked that night, nor indeed at any time during my university career, so I was at a loss to know how to answer it. Dusty was her 'sort-of' boyfriend but they hadn't been getting on well lately and she was beginning to think there was 'no future' in it, especially as he was about to go off to agricultural college.

I saw Charley on three further occasions. On each occasion we got back to my room and I managed to remove one more piece of clothing before the business was halted by the 'what would Dusty say?' moment. It had a feel of pass the parcel to it, though increasingly I felt that when the music finally stopped, I would not be the one holding the prize.

The fourth occasion did involve total nakedness. And we spent the whole night cuddling and snuggling together. The total nakedness was mine only and the night was as chaste as you'd expect in bed with a girl wearing T-shirt, jumper, jeans, boots and an Afghan coat.

But the truth is I enjoyed the closeness. I actually enjoyed the lack of sexual pressure, and because the constraints were entirely hers, I could continue with the flimsy myth of me as philandering alpha male pestering her for sex.

Incidentally, about a week after that fourth night I found out exactly what Dusty *would* say. It was: 'This is for sleeping with my girlfriend, you silly arse!' followed by a serious punch in the jaw. He had evidently turned up at the college bar one night and asked who was Rory McGrath and been directed to the one with the ludicrous hair.

To be honest, I still feel a bit sorry, and guilty, for Furry Frank Evans's fat lip. He didn't even look *that* much like me.

'She was lovely,' Mack reminded me. 'You lucky thing!'

I smiled non-committally once more. 'Yeah, she was sexy. Never quite hit it off with her, though. Our backgrounds were too different I suppose.' So The Lie limped on, and Mack reminded me of another non-conquest from the previous year.

'Cathy from Newnham. She was a corker. I remember the night she came to the bar. She couldn't wait to whip you back to Newnham!' Mack chuckled. 'And "whip" was probably the right word!'

Enter, from very wide left, Cathy Daniels. Newnham was an all-girl college, with a reputation for being fairly straight and academic. I too remembered the night distinctly. There was something a little unsettling about Cathy Daniels right from the beginning. After an encouraging start, her small talk, I recall, strayed towards famous serial killers. Witchcraft got a mention or two. As did the arrow-poison frogs of the Amazon jungle.

She was certainly original. I didn't even mind her chalk-white make-up and teardrops drawn with purple eyeliner. Her room in college looked like it could be the torture annexe in the Museum of Satanism. She offered me a shot-glass filled with a volatile, viscous green liquid that I took to be methylated washing-up liquid.

'Cheers,' I said, gulping down the flames.

I sensed a hot night could be in prospect and decided I'd better use the toilet.

'Oh, I'm afraid there aren't many gents' loos in college. The nearest one is down two flights of stairs and right at the end of the corridor on the left through the third set of swing doors.'

'Cheers.' She'd clearly given those directions out a few times. The gents was surprisingly clean and well maintained but, then, I suppose, in a place like this it didn't get much use. As I relieved myself, I read the one bit of graffiti that had made it on to the walls. It was a depiction of a skull and cross-bones, in scarlet broadline marker, under which was written, 'CD bad news. Leave now, while you still have that in your hand!'

It was enough. Ungallantly, I left through a firedoor in the side of the building and disappeared. I ran all the way back to college, half expecting to be greeted at my door by a severed goat's head and a note saying, 'No escape!'

Eleven failed encounters in my first year. I had left a college room in the morning with eleven different girls over the nine months and had not had a sniff of sex. Friends would wink knowingly as they saw me with a new girl. 'Good ol' Ror!' It was a sham. A half-drunken, fumbling, grappling sham. A sham that was only adding to the pressure.

Eleven failed one-night stands. But had they failed? Or had I failed? Did I want them to fail? I still had not grasped that what I wanted was not to found in the bleakness of casual encounters, it was to be found somewhere else. Somewhere, at that precise moment, that was very, very close.

'I'll tell you what, Macko. Let's go and find us both a girl-friend. Today! Let's be brave. Let's wander about town a bit. Go into a few shops, cafés and pubs and chat to some girls. Not just anyone. Nice ones. Ones we like the look of. No pressure. Let's not look too eager. Too desperate. Let's try to be cool and laid-back. Let's just go with the flow.'

'OK. Where shall we start?'

'We'll start …'

A divine vision walked past our table. Good God. She is incredible.

'… with her!'

I don't know if I thought at that moment, my life will never be the same again, but if I didn't, I should have done.

JACKDAW

The jackdaw has a blue eye. A pale blue eye. Amazing. How come I've never noticed that before? That's one I've drawn dozens of times. Just outside the classroom window a jackdaw is pecking around in the grass. There's loads of them round the school buildings. Perhaps they nest here. They're really noisy too when they get together; like all crows. Jackdaws don't 'caw' in a crow-like way; they make a strange, sharp, 'chack' noise. It is almost a dog-like yelp. That is supposedly how they get their name. But I didn't actually know this when I was a schoolboy staring out of the window, letting Dismal Desmond's physics lesson wash over me. Back then, I didn't know that the scientific name was *Corvus monedula*, which is Latin for 'jackdaw crow'. I didn't then know that the Romans had another word for jackdaw, which was *graculus*. The Romans did many great things, they gave so much to arts, to science, to language, to civilization, but I can't for the life of me work out why they'd need two words for 'jackdaw'. *Monedula* and *graculus*. Most people don't know one word for a type of bird in their own language. I had heard of Graculus, the wise and sardonic bird in the children's cartoon series *Noggin the Nog*, though. But *that* Graculus was 'a great green bird' and was probably, therefore, a cormorant … or maybe even a shag.

I knew that the bird distracting me from the lesson was a jackdaw. I knew it was in the crow family. A nice crow, though. Not big and ragged with an alarming bill like a rook or a raven. Handsome. Greyish neck and breast, black face, glossy blue-black everywhere else. And a pale blue eye. Or is it white? Maybe it's white and the glossy blue-black plumage makes it appear blue. I'm calling it blue, anyway. Yes, the jackdaw has blue eyes.

'Gravity, McGrath!'

The voice of Dismal Desmond.

'Sorry, sir?'

'We're talking about gravity, McGrath, and you appear to be looking out of the window.'

Sniggering 4B's eyes were all on me.

'Sorry, sir.'

'So tell us, Mr McGrath, what do you understand by "gravity"?'

I had been so involved in not listening to the teacher that I was struggling to remember what lesson I was in.

'Er … seriousness, sir.'

More sniggers.

'Seriousness? What are you on about?'

More sniggers.

'Er … gravity … seriousness … the gravity of the situation, sir.'

'So, McGrath, you're telling me that in 1665, Sir Isaac Newton discovered "seriousness"?

Mocking laughter now.

'Yes, sir. Er … up till then everything had been quite amusing.'

Some laughter on my side now.

'Your mouth is going to get you into a lot of trouble one day, McGrath. I hope I can be there. As well as your homework, McGrath, you can write one hundred times, "All particles attract each other with a force whose magnitude is directly proportional to the product of their masses divided by the square of their distance from each other."'

Ironic applause from my classmates.

That seemed a very long line to write one hundred times. And thinking about it now, it was probably far too advanced a definition of 'gravity' for the level of physics we were studying. I'm sure we were still at the 'gravity is what makes apples fall out of trees' level. And supposing it hadn't been an apple tree that Sir Isaac Newton was sitting under when he was pondering the forces of the universe. Supposing it had been a coconut tree! That would have delayed the advance of physics considerably. Einstein's ideas might not have existed if Newton hadn't given us a mechanical model of the universe. After all, more people are killed worldwide by falling coconuts than by sharks. But I didn't know that then.

'Could you repeat that, sir, while I write it down?'

Dismal repeats it. I write it down.

'Could you repeat it ninety-nine more times, sir, while I write it down?'

There is a loud bang as Dismal thumps his desk.

The jackdaw outside the window takes off. An effortless jump and flap and the bird is in flight. And what a flight. High, fast and straight, then tumbling acrobatically to join others on the roof of the language lab. Is that why it's so easy to watch birds? They fly. We aspire to that; we want it; we envy it. Anyone, birdwatcher or not, must admit that deep down it's more fun watching a bird flying than a flightless bird. Penguins are fascinating and the ostrich is quite remarkable in its way, but surely we all want to watch an eagle soaring, a hawk diving or a swift racing over the rooftops at over 100 mph. So much for gravity. The jackdaw's flight was an open defiance of Dismal Desmond and his dull lesson, of gravity, of weightiness, of heaviness and of seriousness. All the stuff that keeps our feet on the ground, ties us down, attaches us to the daily grind of the planet. Like all birds, the jackdaw can do without gravity when he feels like it. It can leave planet Earth, humans and all their filth; birds can rise above it.

It was as if the jackdaw was saying, 'Gravity? What the hell is gravity!'

Well, I'll tell you: it's the attraction that particles mutually exert with a force whose magnitude is directly proportional to the product of their masses divided by the square of their distance from each other.

THE GIRL IN NATURAL HISTORY

'Hi,' I said, as neutrally as I could, hoping that nothing in my words gave away the fact that I wanted to make love to her, run away with her, have her children, look after her sheep on a remote Hebridean island and die with her in a magical suicide pact and then roam the earth forever holding hands with her in spiritual ecstasy.

'Hi,' she said neutrally back. I think I'd got away with it. She was stunning. All life and sunshine was compressed into her petite frame, her bewitching smile and her infinitely twinkling eyes.

Mack and I had tracked her down to Blackwaters bookshop. This could be very handy. Students spend a lot of time in bookshops. Buying books, of course. These may often end up getting read. Though that was of secondary importance. You couldn't read a book you didn't have, therefore having them was an important first step.

She was working in the natural history section and I noted that, from my lurking position in the Mammalian recess, she seemed to be rearranging the bird books. This was good. As a boy, I used to draw birds. Back home I had about a dozen bird books. This was familiar territory. We were three floors away from the Modern Languages section where I should be buying most of my study books, but no matter, it's always good to broaden one's horizons.

'Can I help you?' she said stunningly.

I jumped but, thank God, she didn't notice.

'Sorry to make you jump!'

'No, it's OK ... er, actually, I was looking for a book.'

'Well, you're in a bookshop, that's not a bad start. You Cambridge students really are bright!'

'Ha, yes ... very good!' I said, as un-feeling-like-a-twatly as possible. I went on treading carefully.

'A bird book.'

She nodded stunningly.

'A book about birds,' I went on.

'Yes, I know what a bird book is. What sort? We have a few.'

'Well, it just needs to have pictures in it really.'

'Can't you read then?' she said cheekily but still stunningly. But not quite as stunningly. The cheekiness had used up some of the stunningness.

'Well, I just need a reference really. I draw birds, you see.'

'Oh wow. You're an artist?'

'Well, yes and no!'

'Meaning?'

'Well, *no* ... I'm not strictly speaking an artist but; *yes*, I am ... '

'You are what?'

'Yes, I am not strictly speaking an artist!'

She laughed charmingly, which at least indicated that she did not think I had mental health problems.

'Oh, I know just the book. It's up there on the top shelf. Hang on, I'll get the stool.' She proceeded to get the stool, stand on it and stretch up to get the book. I whistled to myself, indifferent to her short skirt riding up, her T-shirt riding up, the firm curve of her calf muscles, the dainty, balletic, inward arching of her back.

'Here.'

'It's just what I want.'

'You haven't looked at it yet.'

'It's fine. I'll take it.'

'Lovely colour photo on the front. I suppose you know what bird that is?'

I looked casually. It was a jackdaw. If I was editing a bird book full of glossy photos I might put something more exciting than a jackdaw on the front, I thought.

'It's a jackdaw.'

'Yeah, aren't they lovely-looking birds?' she asked. 'There's something cheeky about them. Look at that bright eye.'

Of course, I agreed. 'Yes, lovely. Some people think they're boring. Good choice for a front cover!'

'Well, they're ignorant then!'

'Well, exactly,' I said, taking out my account card. 'I'll pay with this.'

'Right,' she said, walking over to the cash desk and sitting down. 'Blimey, it's pricey – £24.99.'

I flinched and dropped my account card. This was not going 100 per cent according to plan. I was now rummaging around on the floor for the card, on my knees under her desk, face to face with the chair she was sitting on. Oh dear. Don't look. Get out of there. I had to get up quickly but not bang my head on the under-side of the desk. Hear that, NOT bang my head on the desk; she clearly thought I was a big enough imbecile already. I got up and banged my head on the desk. She laughed. I stood up red-faced and breathless, hating myself for dropping the card. If only Isaac Newton had been hit by a coconut, this probably would never have happened.

'Sorry about that. Here's the card.'

She looked up my account details.

'So this is the first book you've bought this term!'

'Yes, I always buy my first book of the term … er, first. Er … before I buy any others.'

'I bet you buy your second book of the term next!'

I laughed. I think she was probably taking the piss out of me but was doing it in a friendly enough way to help me out.

'No, I'll buy my third book next. I've already read the second book.'

'Hey,' she said looking my 'purchase history'. 'Last year all the books you bought were on Spanish, French and linguistics!'

'Yes, I'm a language student but I'm thinking of changing my degree.'

'I didn't know they did a BA in bird-drawing,' she said, completing the administrative bits of buying the book, which she put in a bag and handed to me. My heart was beating abnormally fast and I think I probably held the bag fractionally too long, enjoying the moment. We were, but for a plastic bag and a ludicrously overpriced book, touching each other.

'Are you OK?' she asked.

'Er … yes, I'm just recovering from the shock of paying nearly £25 for a book!' This was in fact true. It was the most expensive object I had ever bought. More expensive than my superb, second-hand guitar, which I had spent nearly a year saving a colossal £20 for. I could not afford this book and was already working out whom I could sell it to or which other bookshop I could return it to, saying it was bought for me by mistake.

'Yes, it is a hell of a lot of money.' She looked me straight in the eye sympathetically. It was a wonderful feeling. I started trembling.

'Especially for a book with a jackdaw on the front!'

'Aaah,' she said, biting her bottom lip and touching my arm. 'I forgot to give you your discount: twenty-five per cent off! Give me your card back.' This I did, and the book suddenly cost £18.74.

'Er ... what was the discount for?'

She smiled the best smile available in the world that day and said, 'The changing-your-degree-to-bird-drawing discount.'

'But ...' I started to say something and she stopped me with a wink. She winked at me! Suddenly we were connected. We had a secret. It was the rest of the world and us. Me and the girl whose name ... er, I didn't know.

BACK TO THE DRAWING BIRD

'An artist' would be an exaggeration, but then so would 'not an artist'. When I was about seven, I was good at drawing. No, I was good at drawing birds.

Well, I was good at drawing *some* birds. The passerines. Though I'd never heard the word when I was a five-year-old drawing robins, blue tits and blackbirds. Passerine is a perching bird. From the Latin *passer*, meaning 'sparrow'. You'll all, no doubt, remember this from the famous poem by Catullus. Don't pretend you don't know what I'm talking about. The one that goes:

Passer, deliciae meae pullae,
Quicum ludere, quem in sinu tenere ...

The poet is jealous of his girlfriend's pet sparrow. We've all been there. She's playing with her sparrow in her lap and he wishes she was playing with *him*.

Because I was good at drawing birds like sparrows, people assumed I was 'interested in birds'. They would buy me bird books, on my birthday and at Christmas, and I would painstakingly copy the pictures, unwittingly learning to recognize and name most British birds. My first and favourite was the *Observer's Book of Birds*. Small and handy and one bird per page. The trouble with the *OBB* was that colour pictures alternated with black-and-white. So pages one and two would be beautiful sharp colour plates and then pages three and four would be dull monochrome. And so on throughout the book. Now, even at the time, I thought this was not a great scheme for learning how to identify birds. Not quite so bad for those of us who just wanted to draw them. Since most of the fun of my schoolboy 'bird art' was the colouring-in, I ended up only drawing the coloured ones. These I knew off by heart, and by the age of ten I could identify each and every one of half the birds in Britain. Years later when I became a more 'serious' birder, I realized this meant a legacy of embarrassing ignorance. I'd heard of, and could easily identify, the moorhen and the coot, but not the oystercatcher and the avocet. (The gorgeous avocet should definitely be in colour. It is the only way you can appreciate how beautifully black and white it is.) I could recognize the swallow and the swift but not the house martin and the sand martin. 'Yes!' to cormorant and shag; 'No!' to gannet and bittern. A buzzard but not a goshawk. A mallard but not a wigeon. A dunlin but not a sanderling. I mean, take it from me, these are serious omissions, heinous gaps in general bird knowledge. For this I thank the *Observer's Book of Birds*.

So, a bird artist, of a crude kind, yes; but a birdwatcher? Never. What is the point of that? Birds are part of the outside world and young people only live in an inside world. I would see birds occasionally. Obviously. And, more than my friends, I'd know what they were. But the birdwatching gene was definitely not twitching. The simple fact was I could draw birds.

Though, actually that's not true either. I wasn't so good at drawing that I could decide in advance what bird it was going to be. If you said to me, 'OK, draw a jay,' I could certainly start drawing a jay. In fact, the first two or three pencil strokes would be a hundred per cent jay, but as the bird neared completion it may have morphed into an eagle or a spoonbill.

I remember one rainy holiday in particular, when I drew one of my best ever lapwings. For Christmas I'd got a new set of pencil crayons. One of my childhood joys – still a delight, in fact, as well as a happy memory – was opening a new set of pencil crayons. The clean smell of wood and crayon-lead. The smart arrangement of similar colours: blacks, greys and blues segueing nicely into greens which paled neatly into yellows which darkened richly into oranges, reds, purples and browns. Then there was always a white one, which you would use once or twice and realize it was never quite as white as the paper you were drawing on. Anyway, it eventually got smudged with other colours and rather than pure white it would just leave browny streaks on what you were colouring. And I loved the pristine needle-like points. I savoured a long look at the points and even jabbed myself with a few to enjoy the pointiness of them. I knew that before long the ends would be rounded, blunt, broken off or stuck annoyingly for ever in the deep bit of a pencil sharpener.

'I bet you're going to draw a bird,' sneered one of my family.

'Well, as it's a new box of pencils, I thought I'd do an easy one. A chaffinch.'

Before starting the black outline, I took out the crayons I'd probably use: pink, pale blue, olive green, brick orange, and a couple of light browns. As the outline proceeded I realized this was going to end up as un-chaffinchy a chaffinch as was possible. Well, I supposed it looked more like a chaffinch than if I'd been attempting a Mexican red-kneed tarantula, but for 'someone who was good at drawing birds', it was not good enough.

'How's the chaffinch coming along,' asked my younger brother, who was turning shapeless blobs of plasticine into shapeless blobs of plasticine.

'It's a lapwing,' I said, hastily adding a long black crest to the back of its head. 'I decided that chaffinches are too boring!'

And so that was it. I would start drawing the bird and I would eventually name it after the bird it most closely resembled. It could start off a blackbird but if the beak was too hooked or the wings too broad then it would become a buzzard. Or a black kite. I found it was useful not to colour the bird in too early. That would have been a give-away. One day in class I was drawing a robin. It was a disaster. Neck too long. Legs too long. Eyes too big. But I had stupidly already coloured it in like a robin. The finished article did not look too bad. The teacher said it was the best picture in class and I got a bar of chocolate even though she had never heard of a 'red-breasted ostrich'.

I had begun learning early how much of life depends on fraud, pretence and falsehood. Or was it just *my* life?

A PAIR OF JAYS

'Call me JJ,' she said. Of course, I thought. JJ. What else? I should have known. It was perfect. It was her. But I suppose I would have thought that whatever she'd said.

'Susan.' Ah, yes, of course. So simple, so English, THE girl's name, almost.

'Sophie.' Yes, from the Greek for wisdom but a sweet diminutive.

'Jasmine.' Ah yes, exotic fragrant flower. Perfect. It was her.

'Brenda.' Ah yes, a little bit Celtic; boldly old-fashioned but so individual in 1975.

'Ron.' Yes, of course. Energetic, powerful, manly abbreviation of the twee and flowery Veronica, and amusingly monosyllabic.

This was a game I was to play many times later in life. A sort of party game, an ice-breaker. You have to find a reason why someone's name is the most appropriate name for that person. It was a game I became very skilful at over the years. Though I was once stumped by a girl called Fanny.

It was nice to know she was called JJ. I was beginning to learn the importance of knowing the names of people and things.

'So, JJ, do you have to be interested in natural history to work in the natural history department of a bookshop?'

I was scratching around for small talk as we sat on the banks of the Cam on a mild September day. After a week of bumbling, mumbling, red-faced, desultory chit-chat in the bookshop, I had eventually asked her if she wanted to spend her lunchtime with me down by the river.

It had been an ordeal for me to come up with the acceptable wording for the invitation, nothing too timid or clumsy, but I'd ended up settling on something like, 'If you want to we could go out together, I mean ... er, not go out with each other but go out at the same time as each other ... er, be together just in your lunch hour, if you wanted to, but if you're doing something else, we don't have to or you may not want to anyway and ... er, a sandwich down by the river. Or another day, perhaps?' An irresistible offer and she had amazingly accepted. We sat next to each other, but not very next to each other, on a bench overlooking the river. I was mesmerized by her eyes, smile, brain, voice and even the tomato seed on her shoe. What is it about tomato seeds? Whenever you eat anything with a tomato in it, however careful you are, somewhere on your clothes or body there will be a tomato seed. Even in the middle of the back of your shirt.

'I mean, did you study natural history?'

I was trying to be neutral and cool in that embarrassingly uncool way young men have when they're trying to be neutral and cool.

'No, my degree is philosophy.'

'Well, what do you know! And how do you know that you know it? And what is knowledge anyway?'

She laughed pleasantly.

Phew.

'You've got a tomato seed on your shoe.'

She lifted her foot up and scraped it off, showing amazing flexibility in her well-toned leg. My mesmerization needle was trembling by the red area of the dial.

'What is it about tomato seeds?' she said. 'Whenever you eat anything with a tomato in it, however careful you are, you always get a seed on you!'

I laughed. 'Yeah, worse than that, your sandwich didn't have any tomato in it!'

'It must be from last night,' she said pulling a silly but mesmerizing face. 'I was in a tomato-crushing competition.'

I liked this girl. Quirky, bright, gorgeous. And she seemed to like me. What was wrong with her? What was her dark secret?

'Do you like birds, then?' she asked me.

'Very much so.'

'The feathered sort, I meant.'

'Ha ha ha. Well, I like both sorts actually.'

'What's that over there?' She was pointing at a small, brightly marked bird flitting among the weeping willows.

'That's a blue tit.'

'Very good,' she said, giving me a cheeky thumbs-up in a mesmerizing way.

'That's easy.'

'Are you a tit man, then?' she winked.

This girl is just amazing. She was moving the conversation down paths I was frightened to go down.

'I do like tits,' I said, laughing enough to acknowledge the ambiguity.

'Have you ever seen any penduline tits?' she asked with too much mischief. I was struggling to keep up.

'Er ... don't think so. Blue, obviously, coal, long-tailed ...' I left great tits off the list. I was not ready for the conversational direction their mention might entail.

'I love long-tailed tits. They're my favourite. Probably my favourite of all birds.'

'Really? Aren't they a bit sweet and girly?'

'Yes!' she said rather sharply and left me floundering.

'It's one of those words though, isn't it?' I said, hoping to regain my unconvincing coolness. 'Tits, you know, easy gag!'

'Well, there're a few bird names like that. Shag. What about a shag?' She laughed and mockingly put her hand over her mouth. 'So to speak!'

'Yeah, it's like a cormorant, isn't it? Greener though.' I was lost but struggled on. 'But I've never seen one in colour. Only black and white.'

She looked puzzled but went on, 'Chough is another one.'

'Oh yes,' I said. 'It's not spelled c-h-u-f-f, though, is it?'

'Have you ever seen a chough?'

'No.'

'I could show you one.'

I'd now lost track of the conversation, I was too busy being besotted. My mesmerizedness was full so I'd moved on to being besotted. Besotted with this spiky, feisty, cheeky, bright and beautiful thing who knew about all things bright and beautiful.

'You could show me a chough?'

'Not now though. We'd have to go to a clifftop in Wales.'

'You should ask for a longer lunch break. Oh and there's ruff.'

'Oh yes,' she said and then added in a silly cockney accent with which I was, needless to say, besotted, 'Yer, like a nice bit of ruff.'

'Yes, a few rude birds around, aren't there? Tits, chough, ruff, shag, and what about the purple-headed ox-pecker!?'

She laughed out loud at this. I would have been in big trouble if she hadn't. She looked at me kindly. 'You like that humour, don't you? You do it a lot.'

'What?'

'Going one step further. Going slightly too far with an innuendo. Turning the innuendo on its head.'

'If you say so.'

'Oooh look,' she said, pointing at a robin that was boldly hopping by our feet pecking at the billions of tomato seeds we'd dropped, '*Erithacus rubecula.*'

'Oh, so you know the scientific names as well?'

'A few. You just pick them up.'

'Are you into birdwatching then?'

'No, I'm into walking in the countryside and looking at things and wanting to know what they are.'

'Here's one for you,' I said, desperately trying to think of a Latin bird name. '*Passer domesticus.*'

'House sparrow. That's just about the easiest one. What about *Puffinus puffinus*?'

'Well, that's dead easy too. Puffin, of course.'

'No, Rory,' she said, like a disappointed schoolteacher. 'Manx shearwater, I'm afraid. Easy mistake to make.'

This irritated me. And besotted me. She hadn't finished exposing my ignorance.

'What about *Emberiza citrinella*?'

'Er ... *citrinella* ... sounds a bit fruity.'

'Well, you're on the right lines.'

'Something lemony?'

'Keep going.'

'Er ... is it lemon meringue pie?'

'It's a bird, stupid!'

'Oh, lemon meringue mag-pie.'

'Ha ha.' She mocked. 'No. Yellowhammer.'

Of course, yellowhammer. The bird of my childhood. A small bird with a lemon-coloured breast. I loved talking to this girl. I loved being with her. I was hooked. There was no escape. She was in my bloodstream. A tiny creature had sneaked into my veins and was about to multiply and take over my whole body, my whole life. And we hadn't even touched each other.

All too soon the hour was over and we were walking back up the high street towards the shop.

'See you again, then?' I said as neutrally as I could.

'Yeah, be nice,' she said back, neutrally. But I felt that her 'neutral' was really 'neutral'. My 'neutral' was 'pretend neutral'.

'Next time I need a bird book I'll call in the shop and see you.'

'When will that be?'

'In about half an hour.'

She laughed. 'See you!' She turned her back on me and went into the shop.

Occasionally in your life you think: something big has happened. You don't always realize it, though. This time I had. If only skipping gleefully hadn't been so uncool in the seventies, I would have skipped gleefully back to college. Instead I slouched back with a moody frown ... but in a gleeful skipping kind of way.

And I'd made a decision. I was going to go straight back to my room and learn the scientific names for all British birds.

Puffinus puffinus. Manx shearwater, indeed.

YELLOWHAMMER

Yellow was different back then. Back then was before the intensive planting of oilseed rape. Now the countryside is chequered with unearthly slabs of sulphur, the landscape glows with a radioactive yellow mist and a sweat-scented cloud of allergy creeps across the fields. The yellow of my Cornish childhood summers was the yellow of dandelions, buttercups, celandines, cowslips, broom and, of course, gorse. Ah yes, gorse. Every clifftop hedge was topped with this dark spiky shrub, its small yellow pea-like flowers stunning against the impossible blue background of sea and sky. And on every other gorse bush was a bird. A lemon-yellow bird. A yellowhammer. A small bird, streaked brown on the back and wings and with a bright yellow head and breast. The thin, tinkling song, with its unmistakable drawn-out final note, falling and rising, carried for miles through the strawy heat-haze of Cornish farmland.

This bird, which, I was later to learn, is *Emberiza citrinella*, became part of my life one particular summer. I was fifteen and I'd made a discovery. A big discovery. Like most children that age I'd discovered what was wrong with the world. People. *That* was what was wrong with the world. More specifically, other people. Yes, they were the problem. Actually, even more specifically, the other people in your family. Yes, they were the root of the world's problems. If it weren't for them, the world would be perfect.

There were six in my family. Myself plus two brothers, one sister and two parents. And, in the comforting simplicity of those days, we were the children of the same two parents. One of whom was our mother and one of whom was our father. It was neat. As we all grew up I realized that the house was not really big enough for six people. Whichever room you went into, there'd be somebody else there already or arriving just after you. That was so annoying. But at that age everything was annoying. Everyone was annoying. And if people chanced not to be annoying briefly, you'd be annoyed anyway. Sometimes a parent would liken our house to 'Piccadilly Circus in the rush hour'. This expression baffled us Cornish youngsters, who had no concept of a 'rush hour' or of Piccadilly Circus, which we presumed was a travelling show.

It was apparently a substantial misfortune to be an only child. Like Eric down the road.

'Poor Eric. So lonely. And spoilt. Well, only child, you see!'

It was hard for me to grasp what was so unfortunate about Eric or what was so sad about being spoilt. 'Spoilt' seemed to mean you got what you wanted. You never had to have the 'which TV channel', 'which music', 'how much food' and 'how long are you going to be in the bathroom and don't leave a smell' discussions and their attendant punch-ups.

Birds, of course, do things differently. Overcrowded or not, brothers and sisters have reason to be afraid. The brown pelican, for example, has a chick. It is happy and well fed and grows strong for a while. Then, what's this? Another egg appears. And it hatches and, lo and behold, there is another chick. A competitor for food and attention. But a small, weak competitor for food; one that can quite easily be forced out of the nest into the river of waiting crocodiles. The same for the next chick and the next. What a ruthlessly black-and-white world they live in. A frightening and seductive simplicity. Not something I was about to propose as a solution to overcrowding in my nest. Not as a weedy second-born, anyway.

As the summer of that year approached, I took to leaving the house and going for long walks on my own. Particularly on Sundays when tempers were always a bit frayed from having been forced to go to church and when the weekly blockbuster roast lunch had put people into a tetchy stupor. St Agnes was about seven miles from our house. A small town with a pretty beach. A great walk on a spring day along the coast road lined with gorse bushes, every few yards a male yellowhammer singing. And most important, I was on my own. And going nowhere in particular. After a few weeks, people began to ask questions, of course. Why would you choose to walk fourteen miles for no particular reason? 'I want to be alone' is always going to sound ludicrous and melo-dramatic whoever says it, an ageing filmstar or a fifteen-year-old schoolboy.

Eventually I told them I was visiting a girl. That was the easi-est excuse, and it meant I had a part of my life that was just my own and nobody else's. And the girl herself was perfect. Quiet when necessary; chatty when necessary. She was funny and serious, energetic and peaceful. She was tall, small, thin, plump, blue-eyed, brown-eyed and, best of all, non-existent. I have had some fine relationships with girls in my life, and I have few complaints, but I learnt early there's something very special about a non-existent girl. They are who you want them to be, they do what you want them to do and you don't have to explain the rules of Rugby Union to them.

I did this long and, mercifully, lonely walk about a dozen times, and other than the ecstatic moments spent with my non-existent girl, whom I had christened Nema, from the Latin for a female nobody, my most vivid memory of those times was the yellowhammer and his song. This is a series of fast and high repeated notes followed by two longer notes at the end, rising and falling, 'Ti ti ti ti ti ti ti ti tyeeeuuuw.' The traditional country rendition of this is 'a little bit of bread and no cheese'. I have repeated 'a little bit of bread and no cheese' to myself a hundred times and have yet to make it sound anything like the tinkling song of the yellowhammer. I would love to meet, and have some severe words with, the slightly deaf man who decided that the yellowhammer was singing 'a little bit of bread and no cheese'. But this energetic bird starts its song in early spring and goes on daily into late autumn. It may not be a great song but it was always there in the warm fields, meadows and clifftops of my growing up. So many Cornish summers of my teens can be shrunk down into the faint, metallic, fragile and persistent song of a yellowhammer, perching on a branch of gorse, starkly bright, lemon-yellow against the infinite blue.

KRAMER VERSUS McGRATH

'What the fuck are you doing in here?' Kramer was lying on my bed, reading one of my bird books. 'Give that to me!'

Kramer shook his head and tutted. He was playing the part of the village elder about to impart a nugget of wisdom to an impetuous youngster.

'You're up to something. I don't know what it is. You disappear at strange but regular times each day and you have a load of bird books in your room. It'll end in tears, my child,' he intoned rabbinically. 'No good will come of it, whatever it is.'

'You're turning into a parody of a lugubrious Jew!' I said, trying to hide my irritation.

'Turning into? How dare you! I was born a parody of a lugubrious Jew. My parents are parodies of lugubrious Jews, my—'

'Yeah, yeah. I don't like you snooping around my room.' My anger had subsided but I had already revealed too much. I was studying languages; I had eleven bird books. I had snapped. I'd given too much away. We were always in each other's rooms. I'd once turned his upside-down looking for the *Razzle Readers' Wives Christmas Special*. I couldn't find it, but he was eaten away with embarrassment when I'd found stuffed under his bed a four-gallon catering pack of powdered chicken soup; a present from Aunty Sadie.

'So what has changed about the teaching of Spanish, French, linguistics and phonetics that they are concentrating on the birds of Britain and Northern Europe?'

'I'm interested in birds.'

'Bollocks, are you. Is there a girl at the bottom of this?'

'None of your business!'

'Aha! Tell me about her!'

I tried to wrong-foot him, 'How's Miranda?' In below-the-belt-ness, this comment was subterranean. Miranda had been the love of Kramer's first few months at college who after one night of passion with him had gone off with the captain of the ladies' rugby team.

Kramer paused so he could lower his downtrodden-ness a notch. A deep breath, then, 'Such cruelty, my son, betrays desperate tactics. So defensive!'

'Well, what's anything got to do with you?'

'I care about you, my friend. And you are in danger!'

'You know nothing.'

'OK, let's think about this.'

Carl Kramer was my closest friend at college. His room was directly below mine on N staircase. The other six occupants of N were, bizarrely, all members of the Christian Union. Kramer and I were regarded with suspicion on weekdays and contempt on Sundays. Branfield, Kramer's neighbour, and the rest of the flock held a prayer-breakfast on Sundays before chapel. Kramer and I were not invited. Branfield had ill-advisedly referred to Sunday as the Sabbath, which had given Carl a juicy opportunity to lecture him on Judaeo-Christian history and the Hebrew language. Branfield was reading divinity and had hoped to join the clergy. 'I intend to be a man of the cloth,' he told Kramer.

'Hey, what a coincidence,' Kramer had said. 'My family were tailors in Pozen!'

But Kramer was always going to be a barrister and missed no

opportunity to snap into character. 'So, Mr McGrath, the modern language student, is defensive about the eleven expensive bird books by his bed. Is he involved, do we think, with a young lady who works in the natural history department of a bookshop and needs various excuses to hang around there during the day and perhaps arrange his timetable around her tea-breaks?'

I decided to tell him a little. 'She's lovely and she's interested in birds and so am I!'

'Since when have you been interested in birds?'

'A long time, as a matter of fact.'

'What do you know about her?'

'She's stunning.'

A tut. 'What's her name?'

'JJ.'

Another tut. 'What does that stand for?'

I didn't actually know. I didn't know anything about her really. Except that she was phenomenal and I would probably be hopelessly in love with her soon and she was called JJ.

'I don't know what JJ stands for!'

'So, you're not even on first-name terms with her. Has she got a boyfriend? Husband? Girlfriend? Children? Terminal illness?'

'Next time I see her I'll give her the questionnaire.'

'Have you kissed her?'

'There's just me and her. I know it. I feel it. I've never been so sure.'

'But have you kissed her?'

'None of your business.'

'That's a no, then.'

Kramer was getting on my nerves, but he persisted.

'So you haven't had it off then?'

'What sort of question is that? That question is an insult to the relationship me and JJ have. I'm certainly not going to dignify it with an answer.'

'So that's another no, then.'

'We are in the process of getting to know each other; the physical side will emerge in its own time, it cannot and will not be rushed.'

With three tuts and a portentous shake of the head, Kramer went on, 'I don't like it. I see pain on your horizon.'

'You're the only pain on my horizon at the moment.'

Kramer picked up the *Atlas of European Breeding Birds* (was £10, now only £7.50).

'OK, then,' Carl flicked through the pages. '*Lanius collurio.*'

'Red-backed shrike.'

'Ha,' he jeered, 'it must be love – he's doing scarce summer visitors. Here's one but I don't think you'll be familiar with it: *Phalacrocorax aristotelis?*'

'Shag.'

'He's heard of it!'

BANG! The door slammed open and an ashen-faced Branfield stood there shaking and fuming and holding a milk bottle. It was a truly frightening sight. I'd never seen a Christian look so un-Christian. If I'd been a lion in a Roman amphitheatre I might well have avoided Branfield in this mood and gone for en elderly nun.

His measured staccato speech underlined the difficulty he was having controlling his temper.

'This … milk … bottle … is … half … empty.'

Carl and I looked at each other and sniggered.

'That's a very pessimistic outlook,' said the lugubrious one. 'Some people would see that as half-full.'

'Each landing has a communal fridge … the property therein is not communal …' Branfield trembled on.

'You've read this on a form somewhere,' I said jovially. 'Do people say "therein" in real life?'

'The items marked with a crucifix are the property of the Christian Union.'

'Oh,' I went on, 'we thought they were for non-vampires only.'

'We are buying … twice as much milk … as we use!'

A sentence that effortlessly ushered in Kramer's unhelpful comment, 'Well, why don't you buy half as much?'

BANG went the door as Branfield swept out leaving a life-size outline of rage in the air.

'Oh dear, I feel a religious war coming on,' I said.

'Excellent. Death, pain, evil, misery, fear, filth, poverty, disease. It'll take your mind off this ill-advised love affair you're embarking on.'

'A word of warning, Mr Kramer. You're beginning to sound jealous.'

He took one last look in the bird book. '*Diomedea exulans.*'

'Eh?'

'Come on, Rory, you've got one hanging round your neck. Albatross.'

'Piss off. Anyway, that's not a British bird. Just get the felt-tip pens. We're going to do the fridges.'

'Star of Davids?'

'No, four little strokes and we can turn the crucifixes into swastikas.'

HUMILIATION IN THE WORKPLACE

You cannot talk about a Cornish childhood without mentioning seagulls. Seagulls in this context are, of course, herring gulls. Evil-eyed robbers to some, but to me they are the sound of the sea. Not that seagulls need the sea any more. When I moved from the south west to Cambridge, it was the sea I thought I would most miss, and the laughter and tears of the herring gull's call first thing in the morning. But I had reckoned without the expanses of East Anglian farmland. When this is ploughed the black earth becomes flecked white with seagulls.

Flocks of herring gulls used to keep me amused in my very first 'proper' job. This was also about the time that I had my first life-threatening encounter with a bird.

I had decided to take a summer holiday job to earn a bit of pre-further education cash. Some friends of mine had got general unskilled labouring jobs on the site of a bypass construction near my home and they seemed to be making decent cash digging holes and moving earth and rearranging traffic cones, so I thought I would offer my services to the project.

I turned up at the site office to declare my general unskilled abilities. The foreman asked me what my long-term career plans were. I told him I was awaiting my A level results and if they were OK then I would be going to Cambridge to study modern languages.

'Oh are you brainy, then?' he asked.

'Well, it depends what you mean by "brainy",' I replied, latching on to a useful academic device I had learnt from a few of my schoolteachers. If you want to sound knowledgeable when asked a question, one of the first things you have to do is question the question.

He was unimpressed. 'I mean "brainy". You know, have you read books and things.'

'I've read books but I haven't read *things*. Except, of course, that books are things and therefore, I suppose, I *have* read things. I've read other things as well as books: pamphlets, comics, newspapers, cereal boxes, sweet wrappers, road signs …'

He looked at me as if to assess whether or not I was taking the piss out of him. He didn't say anything so I carried on. 'I read someone's palm once. Oh, and—'

'Shut up and come with me!' he said abruptly, and I thought I was going to lose my first job before I got it. He marched me along the corridor of one of the Portakabins that made up the site office to what was known as the 'chief's' office. The 'chief' was very 'chiefy': he was wearing a suit, unlike everyone else I had met on the site, and he had glasses on.

'Mark, this guy's going to university and all that,' said the foreman. 'He's here for a labouring job but I thought, you know, if he's brainy, what about a supervisory role?'

The boss looked at me very briefly. 'Which university?'

'Cambridge,' I said, adding quickly, 'If I get the right grades. I mean, it's not definite.'

'I'm going to put you on earthwork compaction. It's better money than labouring and you won't get your hands so dirty.'

I had not intended to go straight into earthwork compaction

so early on in my working life. Indeed, earthwork compaction, I feared, might be beyond my civil engineering abilities.

'Er, I'll be studying languages at university. French and Spanish and possibly phonetics and Latin American history ...'

'Don't worry; you won't need any of those,' he said dismissively. That was the end of the discussion.

The foreman explained what was required of me. The bypass was to cross a valley, but because of the shape of the valley it was decided that a bridge or a flyover would be too expensive, so the plan was to fill the valley with a sort of embankment of earth along the bottom, allowing the road to continue straight and flat on its way to Penzance, which is roughly the last place any road can go to in England. I would be sitting on the top of a steep ridge high above one side of the valley and watching as lorries came and tipped loads of soil. On a sheet of paper I was to put a mark for each lorry-load of earth. After the earth was dumped a machine called a scraper would come and I was to put a mark on another piece of paper. After the scrapers came the rollers, and I was required to put a mark on the 'roller' sheet. So it looked as if, for the next six weeks, my day would consist of clocking on, collecting my paperwork, walking up the side of the valley to my vantage point, counting things, returning my paperwork and clocking off. And all beneath the gentle Cornish sun. This could be the job from heaven.

'Oh, one more thing,' said the foreman conspiratorially as I was leaving the office. 'Let me give you a serious bit of advice.'

I was expecting something along the lines of 'You're a cocky little shit like all students and you'd be very wise to keep your mouth shut and keep your comments to yourself.'

But it was nothing like that.

'Listen,' he said taking out a pencil and a piece of paper. 'When you're counting things, do it in fives.'

'OK.'

'I'll show you. Put a horizontal mark for the first four loads,' he said, drawing four vertical lines on the paper.

He obviously had not read very many books and things.

'And when the fifth load comes, don't put another mark like the other four, but put a line *through* the first four. Like you're crossing them out. And you'll know that little set is five. Then you just count those up at the end of the day and you'll know how many loads you've done.'

It was now my turn to look at him to assess if he was taking the piss. He wasn't.

'Thanks, I hadn't thought of that. That's really useful.'

'You see, you think you know it all, you fellas, but you can still learn a thing or two from us peasants.' He clapped me on the back in an angry way which he wanted me to think was friendly, and gave me my earthwork-compaction sheets.

Followed by a huge cloud of cackling seagulls, the first lorry sped on to the site and dumped its load of soil. I duly marked this event with a single upright stroke on the lorry sheet. My career as an earthwork-compaction supervisor had begun. Then came a scraper and did something to the soil. (To this day I don't know what the scraper actually did. I assume it 'scraped' the soil but it seemed a large and complex machine for such a simple operation.) Anyway, the scraper did whatever it was it did, also to the accompaniment of screeching gulls. I marked the appropriate sheet appropriately and awaited the roller. This soon arrived with its attendant gulls. I'd never seen seabirds in these numbers so far from the sea; not that you are ever that far from the sea in Cornwall. It was an impressive sight: the wild birds exploiting man's progress. I lay on the grassy knoll in the sun and looked over the valley. What a great job this is, I thought, as I made my marks on the worksheets.

Occasionally a driver would stop his vehicle and shout up at me, 'What are you doing up there, boy? Time and motion is it?'

I had no idea what 'time and motion' meant but it seemed to exercise some of the operatives.

'No. Earthwork compaction!' I shouted back reassuringly.

'What the fuck's that?'

'I've no idea.'

The only drawback about the job was that once I was 'clocked on' and sitting up on the ridge above the site, that was it, until I clocked off. I had not thought through the implications of this, so on the first day I had to go without food and drink from eight in the morning till six at night. I hasten to add this is something I have not repeated since. And no toilet facilities had been laid on specially for me. So the afternoon of the second day found me squatting indelicately between two gorse bushes, hoping that no one could see me.

As I squatted, something hard and sharp hit me on the back of the head. Clearly I had been seen and was being shot at. Something fluttered past. Then a bird flew directly at me and I ducked as it struck out with its feet. A vulture? A condor? An eagle? No, this was the most nondescript of nondescript small brown birds. Well, it could have been a rock pipit, tree pipit or water pipit, but as I had only ever seen those in black and white I decided it was a meadow pipit. I hadn't realized I was near its nest, which it was defending vigorously. No matter how small the bird, they will attack as best they can if they think their eggs or chicks are being threatened.

There is something ignominious about being strafed by a small bird when you have your trousers down. But this was the only unpleasant incident, probably for the meadow pipit as well, that took place during my time as an earthwork-compaction supervisor. It was proving to be a most agreeable employment. The weather was improving too. So much so that I decided perhaps I should spend the Friday of my first week at the beach. I had noticed after four days that the number of lorries, scrapers and rollers was virtually the same each day. There were slight variations but they seemed negligible and no one seemed to be in a position to check up. So at 7.55 a.m. on the Friday, I clocked on and got the day's worksheets, then went off to beach about three miles in the other direction.

A disappointingly misty start to the day but, as always on the coast, the weather cleared to give a fabulous day which I spent on the sand, in the sea or in the pub, stopping periodically to tick the boxes on the worksheets. I cycled back to the site for six o'clock. The day's earthwork compaction seemed fairly average. Not a great deal different from the previous days, in fact. Almost identical to Tuesday.

'What the hell's this?' said an unexpectedly irate foreman.

'It's today's earthwork-compaction report,' I replied breezily.

'There's been a thick fog in the valley that hasn't cleared all day. They haven't done any work down there today.'

Oh dear.

I cannot remember the foreman's exact words but 'lazy', 'irresponsible', 'student' and 'clever dick' were in there somewhere among some choice bits of vernacular. Just recovering from the humiliation of being caught with my trousers down by an irate meadow pipit, I was now sacked from my first ever job. After only five days.

For being a smart-arse.

BINOMIALS

Late September was doing all sorts of late-Septemberish things to the trees. Autumn colours were all the rage again. JJ and I sat in the Orchard Café by the Meadows having a full English cream tea, complete with the inevitable side order of wasps.

'I love this season,' I said, leaning back on the rickety deckchair and pretending I was comfortable. 'It's my favourite time of year.'

'Last week you said spring was your favourite time of year.'

'I thought this *was* spring!'

'It's late September.'

'Damn, I must have overslept! No, what I meant was: my favourite time of the year is the time that I'm with you.'

She laughed. 'Ah, sweet.'

Oh no, she said 'sweet'. Such a nasty word. Such a dismissive word. Such a sexless word. 'Sweet', such a bitter word. Not the compliment you want from someone who is the object of your life-shattering passion. This was about the sixth time I'd met up with JJ. Increasingly I was taking over her lunch-hour and her morning and afternoon coffee-breaks. She had taken over my whole life but I hadn't broken this terrifying news to her just yet. I was playing it as cool as a pathologically uncool person could. I was feeling more relaxed with her, less submissive and dribbling. I'd even said my first critical thing to her, half joking, of course.

'That's a nice bright skirt you're wearing!'

'Thank you.'

'Sorry? I can't hear you over the colour of your skirt.'

'Ha ha ha,' she said. I breathed a huge internal sigh of relief that she understood the feeble joke and was not offended by it. 'Anyway, it's a dress, not a skirt.'

'When I used to wear one, I called it a skirt.'

We hadn't quite done anything physical yet. Well, I had inadvertently brushed my hand against the side of her left breast when I was reaching over to get a teaspoon. In my mind, I reeled with fear and shame and guilt and embarrassment. *Oh no, I've grabbed her breast. In public! Out of the blue I've lunged at her and grabbed a dirty great handful!*

She either didn't notice it or thought, quite rightly, it was too insignificant to mention. Oh, and I'd come up with a ruse to get a little more snuggly with her: we'd compared heights.

'You're quite tall, aren't you?' she'd mentioned.

'Average, I'd say. Taller than you. But you're microscopic. I know – stand up and we'll compare heights.'

We stood up and momentarily we were almost touching each other from head to toe. I could feel her warm breath against my chest.

'Er, I don't think you're supposed to do this face to face. You don't get such an accurate comparison.' She turned round with her back to me. It felt very pleasant.

'I think *you're* supposed to turn round as well.'

Oh, of course. We stood back to back and came to the anticlimactic conclusion that I was taller than her. And not only that, she was shorter than me. I think that was the sum of comparative height data that could be extracted from the experiment but I had touched her and that, funnily enough, had done nothing to diminish the unutterable utterness of my utter desire for her.

Her hand was resting on the table very close to my hand. I took a risk. I moved my hand on top of hers. A chaffinch arrived at the next table and started clearing up the crumbs. She moved her hand from under mine and pointed at the bird.

'Hey, that's very tame for a chaffinch!'

'Yes,' I agreed. Bloody chaffinch.

'Go on then. What is it? Chaffinch?'

'What do you mean?'

'I thought you'd learnt them.'

She was talking about scientific names for birds – how off-putting! And I *had* made a serious stab at learning them but they definitely weren't uppermost in my mind at this point.

'Er … oh. Yes, it's got "celebrity" or something in it. Er, *Celebs* something. *Coelebs fringilla.*'

'Actually it's *Fringilla coelebs.*'

'Well, it had its back to me.'

Once the commonest bird in Britain and still up there with the frontrunners, certainly still one of the most abundant birds in Europe, and an early winner for newcomers to birdwatching. You'll see a chaffinch every day. Yes, you will. They perch openly and are less timid than most birds. And they have marvellous plumage. The adult male has a blue-grey head, pink breast, brown back, an olive-green rump and two unmissable bright white wing bars on dark brown to black wings.

The long loud song, once you learn to recognize it, will seem to be the only thing you ever hear in spring as the male tirelessly attempts to attract a female. The song starts as a slow chirrup, speeding up and getting louder and ending with a long, loud fading note. Some twitchers find it reminiscent of a fast bowler, lumbering up to the crease, getting faster then climaxing with the long pitch of the ball. A better birder than I has transcribed the song as 'chip chip chip chiri chiri chiri cheep tcheweeeoooo'. That may be quite accurate, but all I can say is that I've never succeeded in attracting a female chaffinch by singing it. The female chaffinch is, incidentally, a rather dull, buffy-brown version of the male, retaining the striking black and white of the wings. *Fringilla coelebs* means 'bachelor finch'. *Coelebs* or more often *caelebs* is the root of the English word 'celibate'. Yet, inexplicably, you invariably see chaffinches in pairs. Mr and Mrs Chaffinch always look like an advert for marital stability. Has some Victorian scientist cocked up here?

'Give me another one.' I'd run out of physical proximity manoeuvres. It was time to show off my revision.

'Starling.'

She was being kind to me.

'*Sturnus vulgaris* ... which is, let's face it, Latin for "common starling".'

'Robin.'

'*Erithacus rubecula*. That's the first one you taught me. Here's one for you. *Erithacus fidus*?'

'Er ... No idea. Don't know what *fidus* is.'

'*Fidus* is dependable and loyal.'

'Still don't know.'

'Reliant Robin.'

'Oh I see. I didn't realize the game had veered off down a puerile side road.' She laughed affectionately and put her hand on mine.

Did you hear that? She put her hand on mine!

'*Anas platyrhynchos?*' she asked.

'Well, I think *Anas* is a duck, so I'll plump for mallard.'

'Spot on.'

I thought for a moment. 'How about this? *Anas lavatorius?*'

'Toilet duck.' She pulled a long-suffering parent face in my direction. 'Oh, I think I've just found your level now. What's thrush?'

'*Candida albicans.*'

She laughed and put her hand over her mouth with mock modesty. She was giggling and relaxed now. I think she likes me.

I finished with 'aquila slapheadii' (bald eagle) and she had to go back to work. This girl is the best, I thought.

She is the absolute tops.

She is, to use the scientific binomial, the *Testiculi Canis*.

FANTASTIC WORD,
FANTASTIC BIRD

Word-watching, as opposed to birdwatching I suppose, has been my constant, passive, background hobby. The bird world is a fertile breeding ground for strange technical and non-technical terms.

'Dihedral' is a great one. This is the angle formed by two meeting or intersecting planes. You might wonder what that has to do with birds. Well, it is what the experts use to describe the shallow 'V' with which some larger birds of prey glide or soar. Marsh harriers have a beautifully clear 'dihedral'.

'Supercilium' is a must. It is the Latin for eyebrow, but any bird book will be quick to describe a bird's pale or dark supercilium. The yellow-browed warbler has a peach of a supercilium: yellow, of course.

'Speculum' is a metal device beloved of doctors and, I suppose, anyone else who wants to inspect a bodily orifice. It can also be a small mirror or reflector. In the avian world it is usually a bright, lustrous mark on the wings. You need go no further than the commonest duck of all, the mallard, to find a fab speculum: a flash of purply-blue on its wing.

'Dander', as in 'get your dander up', means feathers 'ruffled in anger, warning or fear'. It is connected to the word 'dandruff' but generally used for animals; the scaly, scurfy skin caught in fur and hair. Horses produce a lot of it apparently.

And then there are expressions that you only *ever* come across in descriptions of birds in field guides. 'Rufous trousers' is a beauty; sounding vaguely like a thirties' jazz saxophonist, it is the reddish plumage near the rump and legs of some birds. The hobby will do nicely for this. And another great phrase, sounding like someone you might like to welcome to the stage to join Rufous Trousers and his band: Buffy Underparts. I won't detain you with the birds whose underparts could be said to be buffy; the list is long.

'Frantling' is the mating call of a peacock. It is a word I've somehow managed to do without for most of my life, but now I use it as often as I can.

'Was that a frantling, darling?'

'No, it was the phone.'

'Oh, I thought the peacocks were at it again!'

But one of my favourite words, which is not from the world of birds but is one I will always associate with birds, is a word I'm afraid I cannot remember.

I've got a feeling it ends with something like '–asthaenia' or '–esthenia'. Anyway, it's one of those Greek medical words you only ever hear on *University Challenge* and which no one knows. Paxman reads the definition out with a sneering 'tut' as if it's a word he's known since he was three. It means, roughly, a psychological dysfunction that causes the sufferer to confuse the senses. So, basically, you hear things you should see and see things you should hear. You taste or smell sound or colour. Any reader who's got very stoned, lain in the back garden on a sunny day with headphones on and listened to Tangerine Dream will know what I mean.

I always remember that word, which, as I say, I can't actually remember, when I see or hear a skylark. Especially somewhere in the flatlands of the Cambridgeshire–Norfolk border. It's a favourite place of mine. The first time I was there is unforgettable. I still find the memory unsettling.

It was a soaking day in February. The dark-white light of rainy sky and black earth made it hard to look out of the train window. I went back to the crossword. I was travelling from Peterborough to Cambridge, via Ely. The railway line arcs to the east then to the south and then to the west, bisecting the flattest land in Britain with a sodden semi-circle. This is a drowning land, a sinking land. The landscape is scarred with the history of man's efforts to keep it from the sea. The twenty-foot drain. A disturbingly dead-straight channel nearly twenty feet wide and nearly twenty miles long. Ditches and canals intersect at unnatural right angles, glaring perpendiculars in the dark peaty soil. At the beginning of the journey the twelfth-century Norman bulk of Peterborough Cathedral recedes into the drizzle; at the end of the journey the ghostly galleon of Ely Cathedral looms towards you *out* of the drizzle. In between, an impossibly low horizon makes it a land of sky. It feels like a journey through the Dark Ages, a journey on the edge of the known world.

Somewhere in the middle, I looked up from the paper and out of the window. It was a shock. I held my breath. The train was out at sea. Water joined the white sky in a continuous sheet of glass.

I looked again. For a second I was frightened.

No, wait.

There's a tree out there in the ocean.

Another one.

A hedge. The land had drowned. These are the Ouse Washes. The Great Ouse river regularly floods the surrounding land, which is so flat it disappears. To the uninitiated, it is a profoundly disturbing landscape. But it makes a great piece of natural wetland which brings in the birds and the watchers all year round.

The next time was a hot summer's day. I was on same meadow. The heat and the light made me feel as if there was nothing between me and the sun. Not even Mercury and Venus.

The scorched earth gave no shelter. There was just the sweltering sky. I lay down on the grass. The intensity of blue weighing down on me.

I was alone with the heavens. Alone but for a bird. A very special bird. A bird that is not of this world. It descends from heaven to nest and then disappears again into the void. A skylark. A skylark singing without pause for what seemed like hours. A small, nondescript brown bird had flown high enough to be invisible to the naked eye and poured out its music. Oh, yes, and that word. That's when I thought of that word I couldn't remember. Something-esthaenia. Mixing up the senses.

I imagined each note of the skylark's song was a droplet of sunlight, and the music was sprinkling down on me in a glittering shower from the bird's tower of song. Each trill and phrase of the melody was a handful of gleaming rose-petals, tossed out in the upper atmosphere by the hands of a beautiful angel; they fluttered down leaving a misty trail of perfume, drenching me in scented light and music.

And the collective noun for skylarks?

An exultation.

Perfect.

Peerless king of the summer sky.

What a bird!

What a day. What a memory. Oh, yes ... and I suppose I should say...

What a joint!

THE NAME OF THE WAITRESS

My studies, if that is not too august or misleading a term for my university days, were increasingly following JJ's timetable. At 10.15 a.m. I'd stop what I was doing, usually sleeping, down tools, so to speak, and go round to Blackwaters and join JJ for her coffee-break. Same for the 4 p.m. break, though I was generally out of bed by this time. One o'clock meant meeting for a pub lunch. Back in those blissful, carefree, pre-health-and-safety days, lunchtime drinking was quite normal. People were eyed with suspicion if they didn't return to their desks with the faint volatile whiff of a swift pint, at least.

One such lunchtime, the weather was still mild enough to find me and JJ outside at the back of the pub. The beer garden, I believe, is the correct term for the expanse of concrete between the bins and the karzies. From the kitchen the obscenities of the cooks wafted over to us on a wave of chip-fumes. This pub garden at least had a plant. A straggly creeper was unconvincingly climbing up a trellis in an attempt to get over the wall into the street and leg it.

'Let's sit here under the honeysuckle,' I said. I'd learned this much in my few short years: girls seemed to be impressed by blokes who know about flowers.

'It's a wisteria,' said JJ.

'Oh, don't tell me you know all the names of plants as well?'

'No, just a few. But if I see something I like, a bird or plant or tree, I like to know what it is.'

'I always thought that a plant was a plant, a flower was a flower and a tree was tree.'

'You can recognize birds and know their names.'

'Yeah, but that's accidental. I drew them – I copied them out of a book.'

'But you enjoy knowing their names, don't you?'

I wasn't sure I understood this question.

'Well, if I didn't know their names and I saw a nicely coloured bird, a great tit, say, I'd probably say, "Hey, that's a nicely coloured bird. How pretty!"'

'What about that girl serving in the café yesterday?'

I vaguely remembered the pretty, dark-haired girl who struggled engagingly with her English as she took our order.

'Yeah, what about her?'

'What was her name?'

'I've no idea. What a strange question.'

'Giancarla. She was called Giancarla.'

'How the hell do you know that?'

'She was wearing a badge with *Giancarla* on it.'

Mmm. Giancarla. That's a nice name. As I thought about it, the image of the girl in my mind became clearer. Yes, it suits her, I thought. Slinky, slim, sexy Giancarla. Yes, that's nice.

'You see, until now she was just the waitress. Now you know her name. It changes things, doesn't it? It changes your relationship with her. If we saw lots of birds on a bird table feeding and I said, "Look at that pretty bird," what would you say?'

'Is it Giancarla?'

'Come on!'

'Er … I'd probably say, "Which pretty bird?"'

'Exactly. But if I said, "Look at that greenfinch," you'd look at the greenfinch.'

'S'pose. But surely that's because it's the name for that bird and if we both know it we can use it to communicate. To be precise.'

'Yes, but the big point is that we both know it. We share a word. We have a shared experience of the greenfinch.'

I would rather have talked about potential shared experiences that didn't involve greenfinches but I admired her wisdom. And the more I thought about it, the more important it seemed. We share our planet with all sorts of animals, some of them human, and plants, some of *them* human, and up till that moment I hadn't really looked at any of them. The world is a big place, and the more you know about it, the smaller it gets.

'But people know more birds than they realize,' she went on. 'Ask anybody how many birds they can name and you'll be surprised. *They* will be surprised.'

I couldn't resist putting this to the test.

'Excuse me, do you know the names of any birds?' I asked a man in paint-spattered overalls who was caressing a pint on the next table. After his initial wariness and the obvious pun, he said, 'Pigeon; that's it. Oh, and seagull.' After a little thought he came up with sparrow, robin, cuckoo, eagle, blackbird, goose, duck, swan, swallow, vulture, starling, wren, blue tit, chicken and ostrich. Not a bad list. Seventeen. And he did surprise himself. In fact, his turned out to be the best list of five customers till a middle-aged lady with half-moon spectacles sat near by.

'As a matter of interest, can you tell us what bird names you can think of?'

After a smile and a 'What a very bizarre question!' she said, 'A warbler? Does that count?'

'Of course,' said JJ. 'Warbler's good. There are quite a few of them actually.'

'Yes, let's think,' said the lady. 'There's sedge warbler, reed, Arctic, barred, Orphean, Sardinian, Dartford, Cetti's, olive-tree, olivaceous, icterine, melodious, great reed, river, grasshopper, aquatic ...'

Eighty-three birds later we let the visiting professor of ornithology get on with her small sherry in peace.

ICE BIRD

From the edges of Hertfordshire and Essex, two insignificant streams, the Rhee and the Granta respectively, join together just to the south-west of the city of Cambridge to form the Cam. The river then runs in a north-easterly direction through the city centre out into the fens joining the Great Ouse south of Ely.

Now, that last sentence doesn't feel quite right. Ah yes, it's the word 'runs'. By no stretch of the imagination does the Cam 'run'. It's as near to stagnant as a moving piece of water can be. The Cam sleepwalks. It snakes lethargically through the village of Grantchester, it idles through a meandering green corridor of willows, it gently laps the edges of a few verses of a Rupert Brooke poem, it glides haughtily past the backs of the colleges and the perpendicular Gothic magnificence of King's Chapel, it ambles glassily on, under the railway arch, under the strident A14 viaduct and wearily lets the Great Ouse carry it off to the North Sea.

That's the Cam.

No white-water rafting here, lads.

But along its length you can occasionally see something extraordinary. Sometimes you see it and shake your head and say, with a sigh, 'Wow!' Sometimes you just have to tap the glass with the back of a knife and say, 'Ladies and gentlemen, please be upstanding and give a big, warm round of applause for … *Alcedo atthis*!'

I can vividly recall the first time I saw it. *Everybody* can vividly recall the first time they see it. I was walking JJ to work along a short stretch of the frosty banks of the Cam one November morning and we saw a darkish bird flying close to the water. Not very special-looking. It was starling-sized. I thought perhaps it was a starling.

'I think it's a starling,' said JJ.

'Mmm, it was darkish. And it was starling-sized. So you never know!' A moment later: 'There it is again.'

It flew back in the other direction and perched downstream, somewhere round a bend in the river. As we rounded this bend it meant that the slanting early sun was now behind us. The bird was perched close by. Our approach frightened it and made it fly away from us. An electric-blue flash darted low above the surface of the brown water. An unreal turquoise brilliance. Unmistakable. Spectacular. Unique ... I had seen my first kingfisher!

JJ's first kingfisher, too.

A special moment shared.

As a child I had drawn a kingfisher many times with coloured pencils. It was a delight to draw. Blue, green, turquoise above, bright orange below. A clear white patch on the side of the neck. Its head tightly barred blue and green. And a long stabby bill. It was almost too exotic to be an English bird. And yet until the sun catches it, you may not even notice it's there. I've heard that some idiots have mistaken it for a starling.

It perches near the water, or hovers above it, before its stiletto dive into the water to catch small fish, amphibians and insects.

Slowed-down film reveals that just before it hits the water, it moves its head from side to side to allow each of its eyes a view of the prey so it can work out how much the refraction of the water has apparently altered the position of its target.

And you can't say it's not well named. 'Kingfisher'. Though the name would not be my automatic choice for an Indian lager, you have to say that any association with this creature adds class.

The Germans call it *Eisvogel*, the 'ice bird', which I love.

The Greeks call it *Alkyona*. Now, you must have heard of *Halcyon Days*. It is a play by Steven Dietz or an album by pianist Bruce Hornsby or a song by the band Whisky Priests. And, of course, a composition by the Baroque composer Henry Purcell. So what are these halcyon days, then, that have so inspired writers, composers and artists? What are these days of the kingfisher? Days of joy, prosperity and tranquillity. Usually calm before a storm. And, of course, being a Greek name means *halcyon* has an ancient and weird story attached to it.

And it goes like this. Once upon a time there was a magic bird that could calm the seas and allay tempests. This bird carried the soul of a beautiful girl called Alcyone. Alcyone was the daughter of Aeolus, ruler of the wind. She was married to Ceyx, the King of Thessaly. One day, Ceyx was shipwrecked in a storm and drowned. In her grief Alcyone threw herself into the ocean. But she didn't drown – instead she was carried to her husband by her father, the wind-king, who calmed the waters so his grandchildren could be born free from danger.

And if that's not a true story, I don't know what is!

So this bird, the halcyon, legendarily lays its eggs directly on to the sea and charms the winds and waves to be calm during its nesting season, the fourteen days before the winter solstice.

Halcyon ultimately derives from the Greek word *hals*, which means 'salt', or by extension 'sea' – remember in chemistry 'the halogens', the salt-makers? Alcyone herself probably was not a kingfisher, though. She was clearly an ocean-going bird: maybe an 'auk'; ah yes, 'auk' (Latin *alca*) from the word *alcyone*.

Wonderful stuff!

Thank you very much, ladies and gentlemen, let's hear it for the kingfisher!

(HUGE APPLAUSE)

… And an old boatman, on the river Test in Hampshire, once told me this: 'If you see a kingfisher, you know it's going to be a special day … but if you've seen a kingfisher, it already is a special day.'

And I was with JJ, so it was already a special day for me anyway.

THE HOLY DOVE

'The dove is a symbol of the soul and the Holy Spirit. It signifies purity, constancy and peace. Doves mate for life. They are devoted. Why else would the turtle dove become a symbol of eternal love?' I paused nervously. Dr Fletcher was glaring at me, unimpressed. As Senior Tutor of the college he represented considerable authority. My Catholic schooling had left me unfashionably deferential to, and frightened of, authority figures. Third-years and graduates were sneering about any authority within the college. My friend Mick, a graduate physiology student, was deeply scathing about the dons.

'They're big fish in microscopic ponds, Rory, they can't harm you. This isn't the real world. Academics live in an unreal, cloistered world. They're living out a perpetual adolescence, obsessed with in-fighting and petty rivalries. Undergraduates larking about don't interest them in the slightest. They're more concerned with who gets to sit next to the master at High Table. You should spit on that pillock Fletcher.'

He was probably right, but that pillock Fletcher was making me decidedly uncomfortable as I rambled on about doves. '"So turtles pair that never mean to part." Florizel to Perdita. *The Winter's Tale*, sir.'

No reaction.

'You know. Shakespeare, sir.'

'I know who wrote *The Winter's Tale*, McGrath.'

'Sorry, sir, with you being an engineer and all that, I—'

'We're not all illiterate morons in the Faculty of Engineering, you know,' he snapped, adding, with a private sneer, 'Though there are a quite a few, it has to be said.'

I went on. 'In heraldry, the dove, interestingly enough—'

Fletcher cut in. 'No, not interestingly enough. Quite dull, in fact. Now, listen, the Christian Union in the college—'

Kramer interrupted. 'Before you go any further, Mr Fletcher—'

'It's doctor.'

'Sorry, Mr Doctor,' Kramer replied, obviously thinking that chutzpah might be the best weapon against the academic. 'The dove is deeply relevant in any matter of Christianity. The dove is the Holy Ghost. Do you know how many times the dove is mentioned in the Bible?'

'No, Kramer.'

'Tell him, Rory.'

'Er ... loads,' I stammered, then I remembered a quote. '"And Noah sent forth a dove from him to see if the waters were abated." That's Genesis.'

'Side one, track four,' added Kramer.

Dr Fletcher stood up and stared out of the window for a few moments, then suddenly spun round and barked, 'Kramer and McGrath!' This theatrical gesture was clearly calculated to make us jump. And, sadly, we both did.

'Last Sunday, the Christian Union were preparing for a prayer breakfast and when they opened the fridge, a pigeon flew out.'

'A miracle!' Kramer exclaimed.

'How do you explain this?' asked Dr Fletcher.

'We couldn't get a live lamb into the fridge, sir,' Kramer replied, persisting with his cheek even though it was falling on very stony ground.

'This is a serious matter for a great number of reasons, and for a great number of reasons, punishment will ensue. Did neither of you dwell on the possible cruelty of enclosing a wild bird in a refrigerator?'

'It wasn't wild,' I said quickly.

'It wasn't over the moon, though, was it?' Kramer added.

'It was only in there for a couple of minutes. Max. And the door was left slightly open.'

'A pigeon is a pigeon,' said Fletcher.

'Very good, sir. You're obviously a bit of an ornithologist, then, Dr Fletcher,' Kramer smirked.

'It was a feral pigeon,' I continued. 'That is, it was once domesticated but has become wild.'

'I think Dr Fletcher knows what "feral" means,' said Kramer. 'He does eat in the Engineering Department canteen.'

Dr Fletcher rounded on Kramer. 'Please do spare us the sub-Marx Brothers wisecracks, Kramer. Now, listen, it is within my gift to punish you severely for this. In one of several ways. You could be banned, for example, from the college bar.'

Mmm, yes, that would be a punishment, but one we'd get over, I thought.

'Or possibly, McGrath, I should ban *you* from Blackwaters bookshop.'

This was a stab wound. The wily old don had rattled me. I wondered how much he actually knew.

'Blackwaters?' I asked, trying to sound baffled. 'I hardly ever go there.'

'Three times a day, every weekday?' he smiled menacingly in my direction. This was deeply disturbing.

'Otherwise, how could you have run up such a debt and be so over your account limit that they've written to me to see to it that you repay the debt immediately, and that you do not enter the shop until you have?'

I wasn't prepared for a blow like this. In my mind I was hastily putting together a defence when Kramer thankfully jerked the conversation off on a different tack.

'They put swastikas on their milk bottles, you know!'

'What are you talking about, Kramer?'

Kramer was centre stage now and was going to make a meal of it.

'Let's not beat about the bush, Dr Fletcher. I am Jewish. McGrath here is a devout Roman Catholic.'

I nodded with hypocritical enthusiasm. Kramer warmed to his theme.

'For some reason, we've ended up on the Christian Union staircase. They clearly don't want "our sort" as their neighbours. They want their own kind: Spotty Miller, the King of Zit. Or Halo Neville. Or any of those Bible-and-bishop bashers, but not us. That's why they put swastikas on their milk. It's persecution. McGrath hasn't forgotten Cromwell and the Pale, have you, Rory?'

'Er … I can't remember.'

'Suffice it to say,' Kramer concluded, 'they won't be happy until we're off that staircase.'

Fletcher maintained a steely composure throughout this.

'Mmm. This all sounds like so much flim-flam-flummery to me. I shall spend twenty-four hours considering my next step. In the meantime, you two can get out of my sight. Good day, gentlemen.'

The stairs leading down from Fletcher's chambers were gloomy with pessimism. I felt something unpleasant was about to happen. After a minute or so of his customary tutting, headshaking and shrugging, Kramer said, 'Well, look on the bright side.'

'And what is that, exactly?'

'I never thought I'd hear anyone say "flim-flam-flummery".'

DUCKS

A duck is a bird. This is less obvious that it seems. To birdwatchers, new and old, it's very easy to discount a duck. They are so familiar. We know about ducks from a very early age. Unless you were actually delivered to your parents by a stork, or were unfortunate enough to have your eyes pecked out by an arctic skua when you were in the cot, it's most probable that your first experience of 'a bird' will have been of a duck.

'Let's put the baby in the buggy and go and feed the ducks.' Ah yes, an appealingly low-maintenance way of spending time with your child.

And what's the first bird children encounter in picture books? It's going to be a duck, isn't it? Not a black-bellied sand grouse. *Down on the Farm*, where dogs go 'woof', cats 'miaow', cows 'moo', sheep go 'baa' and ducks go 'quack, quack'. And it'll no doubt be a cuddly, plump white duck with an orange bill. Not that there's anything to recommend cuddling a duck.

And, to my ear, 'quack, quack' is not a great approximation. I think 'wank, wank' is closer but I've never seen that in any children's book.

Now, Emmanuel College was one of the few Oxbridge colleges with a duck pond, and very pretty it was too. It achieved its duck-pond status by having all the absolute essentials of a duck pond. Water and ducks. It also had a large number of huge carp and, at certain times of the year, waterlilies. But these were fancy extras. Its duckiness came from its ducks, and its pondiness from its water.

As a nineteen-year-old modern languages student, I didn't realize ducks were birds. Obviously I knew the mallard. The ordinary wild duck that everybody knows. But even when I was a child drawing birds, copying or tracing them out of books, I might do the mallard but skip the other twenty or so British ducks.

One lunch-break I suggested to JJ that she come and look at the college gardens and the unique duck pond.

'What's unique about it?'

'It's the only one of its kind in the college.'

'What sort of birds does it have?'

'Well, ducks, funnily enough.'

'I presumed the duck pond had ducks, otherwise it would just be a pond.'

'Well, you know, the usual. Mallards.'

'What else?' Her question made me realize I didn't know any other ducks. I'd heard of Aylesbury duck but I thought you only got those in supermarkets. Or in Aylesbury, if there was such a place. Oh yes, and Bombay duck, which I'd had once in an Indian restaurant and was never one hundred per cent sure of its provenance and was too scared to ask in case it turned out to be smoked baboon scrotum.

'It's beautiful.' JJ loved the college gardens and the duck pond. It was all I could do to stop myself being proud of the place. And it was a delight to have her there, not least because my room was about forty-seven yards from the duck pond. If there was a sudden downpour, which would not be untypical of the time of year, I could legitimately invite her back.

'Wow, you've got loads of different ducks! That's a shelduck.'

She was pointing at what I thought was a goose: a large white and orangey-brown bird with a black head and a bright red bill with what I now know is called a knob on the forehead. Three prettily marked birds, which she told me were a teal, a wigeon and a pochard, also seemed to excite JJ. Then I remembered something – I did know another type of duck after all.

'We used to have a Jamaican whistling duck!'

'Very exotic! What happened to it?'

'Fox got it.'

'Ah well, natural, I suppose.'

I hadn't the heart to tell her that the demise of the Jamaican whistling duck was not as natural as she supposed. The duck had been a gift to the college from an ex-fellow who had gone on to make billions in the pharmaceutical industry. (Drug dealing, of course, was the *de rigueur* rumour we undergraduates circulated.) As a token of gratitude, this multi-millionaire alumnus had decided to reward the college with a duck. There was a low-key ceremony when the bizarre creature was released from its pen and made some unpleasant high-pitched hissing sounds and a few of the fellows applauded and the dean made a speech of thanks about how we would enjoy the bird and remember our benefactor fondly. That very night the bird was, I believe, enjoyed by a few of the undergraduates after it had been 'bagged' by the captain of the rowing club, who, for the record, was called Julian Fox.

The previous spring, the college catering manager had come in for some rough treatment courtesy of the Emmanuel ducks. It was that time of year when the gardens were overrun with duckling. In this 'protected' environment all the ducks bred well. Our catering manager was called Steve Chilton, an obsequious but two-faced toerag. This was Kramer's description of him. 'It's true,' he maintained. 'That's what it says on his CV.' But he did try to improve the standard and variety of college meals. One night in hall he was proud to offer the undergraduates a couple of roast quail each. Luxury. But someone had Tippexed out 'roast quails' from the menu sheets and substituted 'Emmanuel's own baby ducklings'. There was a riot when the animal-rights society found out. The hall was invaded, meals were thrown, plates smashed; Rex the Chaplain's sherry was knocked over and he fainted as a result.

'And a tufted duck,' exclaimed JJ. 'They're fantastic.' Now tufted ducks certainly are value for money. They're like playing-in-the-bath-ducks but black and white with a bright yellow eye and a long, wispy tuft or crest hanging down the back of their head. They are 'diving ducks' and disappear underwater for ages and then reappear somewhere completely different. You can spend many a pleasurable hour watching this duck. Well, you can if you're supposed to be doing something else like working or study-ing; or if you're not in bed with the girl of your dreams. So, yes, I have spent a great deal of time watching the tufted duck.

But there is a drawback to having a duck pond in a college. Put mathematically: duck pond plus student plus alcohol equals student being slung into duck pond late at night in underpants.

But this was Cambridge University so obviously it was a bit more sophisticated than that. The college had a club known as the Ponding Club.

This was basically a drinking club, which, as is often the way with drinking clubs, consisted mainly of rowers and rugby players. It wasn't enough just to go out and get drunk. There had to be rituals, formalities, rules to be obeyed, a hierarchy of officers, a specially designed tie and a song. And like all such clubs there was a Masonic secrecy to it all. Only the committee members knew who the committee members were.

The other-than-alcoholic purpose of the club was to project into the pond, naked or clad only in underwear, certain students who, in the opinion of the committee, deserved it. Needless to say, the usual victims were not rugger hearties or boaties, but long-haired, slightly arty types, or perhaps Marxists, or eccentrics, the odd individual who maybe smoked cannabis, and on one occasion it was the college orchestra's euphonium player. No surprise to anyone then that I should be on the list. Well, a surprise to me, when Lazy Lobby and Degsy from the first XV accosted me one night as I left the bar and dragged me off towards the pond.

'You're making a big mistake,' I told them.

'There has been one mistake, McGrath, you little sewer rat, and you've made it,' said Lobby, tightening his grasp on the lapels of my jacket. I tried again.

'You sure you're not confusing me with the other Rory McGrath?'

They stopped and let me drop to the ground.

'Which other Rory McGrath?' spat Lobby.

I hadn't expected them to take this question seriously so I had no answer prepared. I played for time. 'Er ... that twat!'

'That's you,' Degsy cut in.

Lobby grabbed me again. 'He's stalling.'

'Quit stalling, McGrath!' Degsy's peculiarly Hollywood command sounded more than faintly ludicrous coming from this Old Harrovian with a cut-glass English accent. I declined to mention this.

'Just tell me this, lads: you clearly think I've done something wrong and I clearly think I haven't, so maybe you could just let me know what it is and then you … er, well, can go ahead and throw me in the pond!'

I got to my feet and brushed myself down.

Degsy paused. 'Well, we've heard that you—'

Lobby stopped him. 'Wait, Degsy. You can't tell him why he's being ponded. That's against the rules of the club. The pondees are chosen after solemn deliberation by the committee and when a decision is made, action must be taken.'

'I was only—'

'Degs, listen. The victim knows that the committee wouldn't choose him lightly. This isn't some frivolous piss-head club that chucks wankers in the pond. To explain to the pondee why he is chosen makes it sound like we're in some way unsure, as though we feel we have to justify the sacred and binding judgement of the committee.'

Both the public-school oafs had let go of me in order to discuss the Holy Writ of the Ponders Club elite members. As a non-member, there was little I could contribute to this discussion so I thought it might be a good time to find somewhere else on the planet to stand. I legged it into the cloisters and did a sharp left and into the street. Neither of them seemed to be in pursuit but I did hear Lobby shout, 'We'll get you next time! You call me a poof again and you're dead!'

I didn't think it was worth returning to college too soon so I sought refuge in St John's where the bar manager was a fellow Spanish student of mine.

'Call Lobby a poof? I've never ever done that,' I mused with

Kramer later on in the safety and exceedingly cheap vodka of the Polish Club on Chesterton Road, which Kramer had blagged membership of through a refugee great-aunt of his from Gdansk.

'I know where this is coming from,' said the wise elder. 'The Christians. Branfield! Think about it. We tell Fletcher they put swastikas on our milk and Fletcher bans them from having prayer breakfasts. Branfield plays rugby. He's mates with Degsy and Lobby. It's going to be easy for him to slip in the odd rumour about you or me.' Kramer looked determined. '"We must do something; and i'the heat!" *King Lear*.'

'Don't call me King Lear.'

Kramer, as far as we knew, had not crossed Degsy or Lobby's path and would probably not be known to be one of my 'gang', so he went to work over a chance meeting by the pinball machine. Lobby held the record for the highest score, needless to say.

'That's a hell of a score to beat,' Kramer said.

'I know. It's mine!' Lobby sneered.

'Wow, well done!'

Kramer glossed over the details of the whole conversation but somehow he manoeuvred it to this conclusion:

'And Branfield told me you always wanted to be in that position in the scrum because you liked his arse.'

Lobby was dumbstruck with rage. Kramer rubbed salt into the cliché. 'And apparently you sometimes stroked his bottom and once tried to insert your finger! Well, this is just what Branfield says; I don't believe it for a moment, Lobby, I know you. A man like that doesn't get the record highest score on the college pinball machine!'

Lobby shook with rage and stormed off to convene an emergency committee meeting of the Ponding Club.

*

'Oh no, it's raining,' said JJ.

'Good weather for ducks, as they say,' I said, adding casually, 'Hey, why don't we wait in my room; it's only just up there. Till the rain stops.'

She looked into my eyes, thoughtfully for a moment, then smiled.

'Not today.' She looked sad. I looked sad and she added, 'One day though. Soon.'

And with that we started walking back to the bookshop via a café, leaving the huge raindrops to bounce off the indifferent backs of the college ducks.

Duck. 'Duck' is one of the one of the first words people ever say.

It was the first proper word I ever spoke.

After 'Dada', of course.

Interesting that most babies can articulate 'Dada' as a word earlier than 'Mama'. Clearly, despite the tenderness of maternal love, babies are keener to talk about avant-garde art movements of the early twentieth century.

But for me after 'Dada' came 'duck'.

I don't remember it but my parents still talk fondly about an early visit to a park near Newquay, where we fed the ducks in a pond by the playing fields.

I apparently turned to my father and pointed saying, 'Duck, Dada!' And they all laughed. 'Duck, Dada!' I said again and they all clapped. 'Dada, duck!' I said again. Too late, as my father was hit on the back of the head by a cricket ball.

RAIN

'Damn,' said JJ, 'I'm going to get soaked.' She only had a T-shirt on.

'Here,' I said handing her my jacket and putting it round her shoulders. 'Oh, and what about your hair?' I took off my shirt and put it over her head.

'You're mad! Ooh, it's nice and warm.' It was a cold autumn afternoon and my toplessness drew some baffled and disapproving looks from passers-by. We laughed. I thought I was being well gallant and I didn't mind the rain even though it was colder than I'd anticipated. Looking back, of course, I realize that this larking about was really some sort of courtship behaviour. It was the extravagant male, singing, dancing and flashing for the female.

We arrived at the café and the waitress said, 'Please sit anywhere you like.'

'Great,' I said. 'We'll sit at Roxy's cocktail bar on Bondi beach, thanks.' JJ giggled even though I'd said this in various forms on quite a few of our dates. But there you are, you see: amusing the female can be such a useful, if obvious, way of attracting a human mate.

'If you can make a girl laugh, you're in,' a girl once told me.

'That's easy, I'll drop my trousers,' I'd said. She'd laughed a lot.

'You see, you're putting yourself down, but it's still funny!' She laughed again and, you know what, within days she was going out with my best friend.

Birds have a comparatively simple time. The male frigate bird, after twenty hard minutes of gulping air, can transform his saggy, wrinkled throat pouch into a huge, bright red balloon that attracts females from miles around. And apparently the size of the balloon is important. The Bulwer's pheasant can pull a mate just by expanding and waggling its spectacular wattles. I couldn't compete with that, not with the size of my red throat balloon and the length of my wattles; I was going to have to stick to small talk, and hope that the size of my small talk didn't matter.

I put my wet shirt back on as the waitress guided us to a table in the window. We sat down and watched the busy street trickle in a blur down the glass. I like rain. I do. I really love it. It cheers me up. I love waking up in the morning and hearing rain on the windows. I love returning from a hot, sunny, foreign holiday to a rainy Heathrow, to the comforting blandness of drizzle and grey. There is probably some deep psychological reason for this hidden away in the murkiness of my childhood. I've no idea but I do know that sunshine makes me feel uncomfortable. Bright light means no hiding place. It means exposure and vulnerability. Perhaps there's a shadow of my Catholic guilt being cast over my life by the sun. Is it God's searchlight poking into holes, under rocks and into corners looking for me? The sun makes me feel like I'm under a microscope being examined, assessed and evaluated. What shall we do with this specimen, then? Throw it away; it's useless. Rain is my friend: stroking my forehead, caressing my troubled brow and rhythmically rocking me to sleep.

'Isn't this weather awful,' said JJ, peering out of the café window into the torrential gloom of a November afternoon.

'Dreadful,' I concurred.

In fact, I thought the weather was being rather kind to us. Our time together was so limited that the rain meant we couldn't wander down by the river or over the meadows, looking at birds. We had to sit together in cafés or pubs; we had to sit close together in dark, cosy corners. It also meant that I stood a better chance of being seen by fellow students who would undoubtedly be stopped dead in their tracks at seeing me 'canoodling' with such a gorgeous girl. Not that we were quite on 'canoodling' terms just yet.

'You've got a bit of coffee froth on the side of your mouth,' I told JJ.

I leant over and wiped it off as gently as I could. An electric moment. Tingle, sparkle, crackle and pop.

More animal behaviour. Classic courtship. Mutual grooming and preening. Even the mighty albatross with its huge, deadly bill can delicately caress his female, stroking the feathers and removing the odd bit of dirt or a parasite or, quite possibly, coffee froth.

'It's nice to be all snuggled up inside on a day like this,' I suggested.

'Yes, it would be nice to be in bed, wouldn't it?' she said.

'Extremely.'

We looked at each other and there was an unspoken struggle to change the subject but leave the subject the same.

We laughed. She squeezed my hand. Things were getting more intense. Something would happen soon. It was clear to both of us that we felt the same way and that things would inevitably develop in their own time. These thoughts and feelings were, of course, unspoken. Most of our relationship was unspoken. We spoke of birds and made jokes about friends, colleagues, strangers in bars but the real stuff was never mentioned. Except in eye contact. We'd hardly touched each other literally, but our eye contact must have been X-rated. JJ and I were one of those couples who now get on my nerves. Young lovers staring wordlessly into each other's faces and sighing occasionally over an undrunk beer or a now stone-cold cup of coffee.

'The lapwing,' she said, and suddenly we were back in the bustle of the steamy café.

'The lapwing?'

'Yes, I've just remembered,' she explained. 'The lapwing is sometimes called the rain bird.'

Now the lapwing is an amazing suitor to the ladies. The courtship flight is quite a piece of work; lapwings go for it and just don't care. They climb, they dive, they swoop, they flutter, they zigzag, they swerve, they change speed recklessly. They are that bloke on the disco floor who is on his own but who knows he is the best mover in the place and goes through his entire box of dancing tricks and doesn't give a damn who sees him or what they think.

'I thought the lapwing had enough names already: lapwing, green plover, peewit. So why rain bird?'

'No idea. It's a plover. And "plover" must come from *pluvium*, the Latin for rain.'

'Does it portend rain, then? Does it like the rain? Does it breed in the rain? Does it eat rain? Do lapwings fall from the sky in little drops? I mean, why "rain bird"?'

I was only joking but it came out quite angry-sounding. She smiled at me. I was probably annoyed that the spell had been broken and I think she knew. She lifted my hand to her mouth and kissed it. This was the first uninvited and positively physical thing she'd done to me and it was wonderful. The broken spell was mended and we resumed staring vacantly into each other's eyes.

'Well, look who it is!' said Kramer with unwelcome *bonhomie*. The spell was broken again. Any more breakages and we'd end up having to get a new spell altogether.

'Miserable day,' he went on.

'It is now,' I said.

'Oh, am I disturbing you?'

'Of course not,' said JJ, just getting in ahead of my 'yes, can you go away'. JJ seemed to like Kramer and they got on very well. But she got on well with everybody. She was attractive.

'Do sit down, Mr K,' I said, offering him the seat that was closest to me and furthest from JJ. Ah yes, the male starts behaving differently in the presence of a rival. Kramer wasn't a rival as such but as any male bird will tell you, another male in your territory, however innocent, must be dealt with instantly and aggressively. The capercaillie, a ferocious black grouse from Scotland, will fight to the death to protect what is his. I found myself frowning in Kramer's direction.

'What's wrong with you?' he asked.

'I was thinking about a ferocious black cock.'

'Blimey, I *have* come at the wrong moment. I'll get my buttered teacake and go.'

LOVEBIRDS AND SORROW

The lovebird. From the genus Agapornis. Aha, from the Greek for 'love' and the Greek for 'bird'. Brilliant bit of scientific naming, there.

A small stocky parrot with a short, blunt tail. Their beak is rather large for their overall size. That'll be from all that snogging, I suppose.

They mate for life and are observed to be very affectionate to each other. In German, they're called 'Die Unzertrennlichen', *which means 'the inseparable ones', and in French they're known as* 'Les Inseparables'.

Typical of the French not to have their own word for 'inseparable'.

The lovebird's general over-all colour is green. The Fischer's, the black-cheeked and the collared lovebirds have a white ring round the eye.

They eat mainly fruit, vegetables, grasses and seeds. Black-winged lovebirds enjoy the occasional fig. There are nine separate species, eight come from mainland Africa and one, the Madagascar lovebird, doesn't come from mainland Africa.

What am I doing?

I'm reading about birds from Africa and Madagascar! These aren't British birds. I'm getting obsessed. I AM obsessed. I'm obsessed with birds. No, I'm obsessed with JJ. And she's obsessed with birds. No, she's not. She's not at all obsessed with birds. She's not obsessed with anything. Not even me. She just knows a bit about most British birds. We talk about birds all the time though. No, we don't. We hardly ever talk about birds any more. We see them occasionally, we look out for them and name them if we spot them, but that's it. We talk about everything else.

Everything.

Everything except the future.

This is how it is. I'm either with JJ or I'm reading about birds. Learning about birds is a substitute for being with her. That's what it is. At weekends when I don't see her, I go out for walks in the country and look at birds. I was even getting to like the country-side around Cambridge.

Coming from Cornwall, the countryside here was a shock to me. Cornwall is high moors with spectacular granite outcrops, rolling wooded valleys and steep heather-topped cliffs butting up against Atlantic breakers. Cambridgeshire seems crushed under the weight of the sky. Huge, flat, peaty landscape, intersected with long, dead-straight strips of water, like ribbons of glass against the black soil.

There is no horizon.

Or maybe there is *only* horizon.

But the sun actually rises here. And it sets. It doesn't just prematurely disappear behind a hill. This is a good place for sunrises and sunsets.

And different birds in the drowning fields. One weekend I saw lapwings, curlews and snipe. A snipe in a field. That's not very Cornish. I couldn't wait to tell JJ. Well, I couldn't wait to get back to my room and try to find out what this mottled brown bird with an extremely long bill was, and then learn its Latin name (*Gallinago gallinago*), and then tell JJ.

Kramer swept into my room without knocking.

'How are the lovebirds today?'

I hate that. What a stupid question. Patronizing and euphemistic, with perhaps a hint of envy. It's a demeaning question, equating the people asked with rather feeble-minded, gormless-looking parrots. Or was I reading too much into it?

'Can't you knock?'

'Yes, I can knock, but not today; it's Geknoches, a Jewish festival when it's forbidden to bang on wood with your hands. You weren't doing anything embarrassing, were you?'

'I was reading about parrots.'

'Oh, you were doing something embarrassing, then? So how *are* the lovebirds?'

I ignored him.

'Oh, I see. You don't want to talk about it. I was wondering if you and JJ had got married, had children and emigrated to New Zealand yet?'

'Yes, we have.'

'Or even finally got round to holding hands?'

'Things are progressing nicely.'

'So you haven't touched her yet then?'

I ignored this question.

'Is it love?'

'What is love?' I asked him in return.

'Why are you answering questions with questions?'

'Who wants to know?'

'There's nothing shameful about being in love, you know.'

'I don't think I know the meaning of the word "love".'

'It means nothing.'

'What?'

'In tennis, "love" means "zero".' Kramer was the sort of lippy student who gave students a bad name. Clever and smirking. And eminently punchable.

'That "love" has nothing to do with "love". It's a corruption of the French *oeuf* or "egg".'

Kramer tutted. 'You're the sort of lippy student who gives students a bad name.'

'I haven't seen JJ today. It's her day off.'

'Why don't you see her on her day off?'

'She lives about twenty-five miles away!'

'So?'

'And she lives with her parents; it'd all be a bit difficult.'

'Why doesn't she come and spend the day here in Cambridge with you? It might move things on a bit.'

That was a very good question and one I had asked JJ, only to be told it was awkward; she had arrangements already, family things.

'She's doing family things.'

'Isn't that roughly what you want to do with her?' He smirked and I ignored him.

'I'm in no rush,' I lied to Kramer.

'I've got a bad feeling,' Kramer said, walking over to the window and looking out at the gloomy remains of the November afternoon.

'You always have a bad feeling! You are gloomy. You are pessimistic. You are lugubrious. We've been through this: you're a miserable cunt!'

He seemed pleased by this description of himself. 'Mmm, maybe.'

'It's the time of year.' I joined him at the window and looked out into the college gardens.

He turned balefully to me. 'Look, a magpie.'

'So it is!'

The unmistakably handsome crow. A beautiful bird. Stridently black and white, but with bright blue iridescence and a long glossy greeny-purple tail. It gets a bad press. It steals other birds' eggs and eats other birds' chicks. But, hey, who doesn't? And if you feel like learning the scientific names for all British birds, why not start with the magpie?

Pica pica.

Kramer looked at the bird and looked back at me shaking his head. 'One for sorrow.'

'Oh dear, there you go again. I don't believe you have a superstitious bone in your body.'

'Well, you never know. My uncle Harry walked under a ladder once and was dead within forty-eight years.'

I tutted.

'Take care, my friend!' was Kramer's portentous exit. I watched the magpie for a while. Mmm, I too was beginning to get a bad feeling. I cast an anxious glance across the lawns in the hope of seeing another magpie.

JJ SO FAR

After seeing one magpie, is there a time limit before you see the next one? If I see one at nine in the morning and the next one at five in the afternoon, is that two sorrows or one joy?

As soon as Kramer had gone, I left my room and went for a walk in search of *Pica pica secunda*. It was gone five now and my chances for getting any joy were fading with the light. Not that I was superstitious or anything, or that Kramer had infected me with his pessimism, but I felt perhaps I should assess the JJ situation.

Where were we up to?

I was in love with JJ. I sensed she felt the same way but there was something holding her back from full expression of her desire. Maybe, at some level, she wasn't ready for the intensity of relationship I seemed to be offering. Maybe she had just come out of a difficult and painful relationship and was nervous about getting involved in something 'serious'.

JJ and I had never discussed her previous relationships on the grounds that I didn't really want to hear about them.

Perhaps she just wanted to 'play around' for a few years before getting involved in the 'relationship of a lifetime'. If this were the case, perhaps I should make it clear that if she wanted to play the field I could easily do a convincing impression of a field. Perhaps she was just being nice to me and really thought I was a bit of a twat; pleasant enough company to liven up her boring days in the bookshop, but not worth getting too involved with.

No, come on, Rory, you're letting your self-loathing get in the way here. There is definitely a tingle when you're together.

And a sparkle.

How many tingles to the sparkle, I wondered

And there had been moments of electricity. There were times when our faces had come so close together we could feel each other's breath, eyes fixed on eyes and words pointless; moments when there had been a crackle and the smell of something smouldering. Yes, several moments of crackle.

How many sparkles to the crackle?

Right, let's go over what we've done so far: first of all there was the time we were sitting next to each other and my knee touched hers. This was a pure accident but it sent a glorious shudder through me even though she moved her knee away quite quickly. I mused for a while on the possibility that this wasn't an accident; that she'd deliberately brushed her knee against mine to take, as it were, the temperature of the situation. We had crossed a busy street and I'd taken her by the hand and led her across to the other side and I'd tried to hold on to it a bit longer than was necessary. She let go of my hand quite soon after, overtly to point out a collared dove flying by.

Apparently these birds were almost unknown in Britain and now were on a huge increase. I didn't really care. Since then the number of casual hand-holdings and inadvertent knee-rubbings had increased to the point where I was no longer keeping count. But if you must know, I stopped at twenty-seven casual hand-holdings and nineteen inadvertent knee-rubbings.

Then there were the 'goodbyes' at the bus stop when she went home to her parents each night. I didn't know what status to give the goodbye pecks on the cheek. It was physical contact but there was too much that was everyday about it. Even people who just met for the first time seemed to depart with a peck on the cheek. Or one on each cheek. That was becoming quite widespread, more often than not provoking a shriek of, 'Oooh, going continental, are we?'

Obviously, with JJ, I went continental to double the contact and the time spent kissing her. I was also trying to move mouth-wards with the cheek-pecks.

At first JJ compensated for this by turning her head to the right if I was kissing her left cheek and vice versa, meaning that her mouth was well out of my reach. But as the weeks passed, I noticed that our cheek-pecks were becoming very nearly lip-pecks as JJ did less head-turning to avoid my mouth.

After about a month, the arm round the shoulder had been accepted. As always this starts with a yawn and a stretch of both arms and the one behind the shoulders of the girl you're with stays there, eventually flopping innocently on her shoulder.

The 'arms round JJ's waist' were also accepted as being normal and non-threatening. Clearly the issue now was how firmly I squeezed her. Pressure was being subtly increased on every occasion until one day in a lunchtime pub I squeezed a bit too hard while she was drinking a Coke, which she had to spit out along with some partially digested cheese sandwich.

'Oh, I'm so sorry!'

'It's alright; you just took me a bit by surprise.'

'I just felt like squeezing you.'

'Ah, that's nice. I wasn't expecting it. No harm done,' she said kindly, as she wiped the lump of regurgitate off her blouse.

The resting-of-hand-on-knee had pleasingly moved on as far as squeezing-inner-thigh. I'd worked my way up from resting-hand-on-knee to resting-hand-on-just-above-knee to resting-hand-on-top-of-thigh to dangling-hand-on-inner-thigh and one day, in the basement gloom of the Henecky Tavern, I made my move and put my hand on her upper inner thigh and squeezed it.

'I'll get another round in,' I said straight away and got up and went to the bar; part of my plan was not to hang around for an embarrassing rebuttal or awkward silence. This seemed to work; when I got back with the drinks she did the same to me and I was in heaven.

Our physical intimacy lurched suddenly forward one pre-bus-stop evening drink when we were talking about physical peculiarities.

You know the sort of thing: the sinister implications of being left-handed; curly hair versus straight hair and the shape of follicles; does the size of the gap between your two front teeth mean anything; does not being able to whistle mean you're homosexual; does not being able to whistle while holding up a chair by one leg mean you're homosexual; is it possible to touch your left elbow with your left hand; is the length of your forearm between wrist and elbow exactly the same as your shoe size?

I suddenly had an idea.

'What about tongue length, then?' I asked her.

'What about tongue length?'

'Can you touch the end of your nose with your tongue?'

'Let's see,' she said, and closing her eyes tight she stuck her tongue out as far as it would go and curled it back and upwards towards her nose. She couldn't touch the end of her nose with her tongue but it was the sexiest thing I'd ever seen.

'Oh shame; very close, though.'

She pulled a joke sad face. 'Can you do it?'

'Easily,' I said, and leant over and touched the end of her nose with my tongue.

She laughed a lot.

And I did.

My day was made.

But the silver lining had a black cloud around it in the shape of Carl Kramer.

'You're in a ludicrously good mood for someone in a doomed love affair,' he grumbled later over a pint.

'Yes, I touched the end of JJ's nose with my tongue today!'

'Jesus Christ,' Kramer said, shaking his head in despair. 'Are you taking part in the foreplay marathon or something?'

'A little often, my friend.'

Yet, despite Kramer, it had been a good day. They all had been. Why had a note of doubt crept into my mind? I was walking back to my room down the path by the duck pond and something flew over, a dark, silent shadow flapping slowly.

Amazing.

A tawny owl.

Always a delight to see.

Or was it another magpie, I thought to myself. Yes, you know what: I think that was a magpie.

MR CRITCHLEY

'Hello. Is JJ around?'

'Oh dear.'

It was not the answer I expected. The grey-haired man with thick-lensed glasses precariously close to the end of his pointy nose smiled with a mixture of kindness and pity. 'It's her day off.'

I knew it was her day off. She told me that the last time I saw her. Then why was I here in the natural history department of Blackwaters? Was I turning up to see her in some sort of subconscious reflex action? JJ's immediate boss, Mr Critchley, tilted his head back to line up his eyes with his glasses and looked at me appraisingly.

'You seem like a nice boy,' he said and shook his head. World-weariness weighed down on him like a block of concrete but he gave off no bitterness. Perhaps the blocks of concrete had squeezed it out of him. Bitterness uses up more energy than kindness; perhaps he was too tired to be anything other than benign. 'She's a nice girl.'

'She is,' I agreed enthusiastically.

'You would have made a lovely couple.' He shook his head again. 'Another lifetime, maybe.'

I was unsure what to make of this and was wondering if I should go through the motions of pretending to buy a book when Critchley suddenly became business-like and said, 'Are you going to buy a book or did you only come in to see JJ? Please don't say you want to buy a book because you know you're over your limit on your account card. Don't make me have to refuse you.' The likeable old man seemed genuinely distraught and I started to assure him that I was only there to browse: books and shop-girls.

'Well, obviously I did want to see JJ, but as I'm here—'

I was interrupted by the arrival of a handsome young man in a suit. He was self-assured and immaculate. A lady-killer. A screen idol. Drop-dead gorgeous, if the phrase had been invented in 1975.

'Mr Critchley!' He nodded in Critchley's direction.

'Oh hi, Neil!' said Critchley, and turned to me to introduce the suave devil. 'This is Neil Curtis from social science. He helps me and JJ out from time to time.' He pointed in my general direction and said, 'And, Neil, this is … er … a customer. I'm sorry, I can't remember your name.'

'Rory.'

'Oh yes, of course. Rory's another one who's in love with JJ!'

Neil frowned in my direction. 'Oh, another one I've got to fight off?' He winked at me and patted Critchley on the arm. 'I'll see you later. Call me if you need me!'

The cool Mr Curtis glided effortlessly away, leaving behind a pleasant hint of expensive aftershave and an unpleasant feeling in the pit of my stomach. I felt distinctly uncomfortable about such an obviously good-looking charmer 'helping out' JJ from time to time. My discomfort was increased by his cheeky 'another one I've got to fight off' comment and its attendant wink. Whatever that meant, I did not like it.

I took a quick look through my faces to see if there was a brave one I could put on, and said, 'He seems like a nice bloke.'

Critchley slumped back into his chair, swivelled 360 degrees and grabbed the desk to halt himself abruptly.

'Listen, there's something I should tell you—'

I was distracted from Critchley's revelation by the sound of a familiar boisterous cackling coming from somewhere around organic chemistry. I peeped round the corner and saw Degsy and Lobby, the ponding kings, coming up the stairs towards me. I wasn't in the mood for any interaction with these two. I felt my absence was urgently required.

'Er, listen, I've got to go.' I left Critchley and headed down the back stairs to the basement, to modern languages, where I belonged. I picked up the biggest book I could find, opened it in front of my face and scrutinized it. As the maps showing the migration of Latin began to blur, I sensed that the danger had passed. I put the book back on the shelf and I became aware of the smell of gentleman's cologne. The tap on my shoulder made me jump.

'You get around, don't you? Modern languages now!' Neil winked again and left with a cocky, 'I'll give JJ your love.'

CHICKEN

Kramer burst anxiously into the bar. He paced up and down, glancing around nervously.

He looked troubled. Twitchy and uncertain. Nothing out of the ordinary there, then, I thought. He came up to me at the pinball machine and interrupted a classic studenty discussion about rock music.

Adrian 'Headbanger' Brown was putting forward the theory that the Moody Blues song 'Nights in White Satin' was, in fact, 'Knights in White Satin', on the flimsy argument that 'Nights in white satin never reaching an end' didn't mean anything.

'What sort of knights would wear white satin, then?' I asked. 'I mean, you couldn't go into battle wearing white satin, could you?'

There was a murmur of agreement from my fellow drinkers.

'I mean, what would the king say if you turned up to fight for him in a bloody war against the Saxons wearing white satin?'

A few sniggering nods.

'Sire, here I am, Sir Nigel de Lingerie, come to give myself for your cause, o my liege.'

'No suit of armour then, Sir Nigel?'

'I find it makes me perspire so, your highness, and restricts my use of the sword and lance. Besides, chain-mail is just so passé!'

'It's metaphorical, you twat.' Headbanger was unshaken in his opinion.

Kramer tapped me on the shoulder.

'Bad news,' he said.

'Yes, you are,' I replied.

He took a swig of my lager.

'I need to talk to you urgently in my room.'

'Can it wait?'

'No, and I need some chicken soup. Urgently.'

Kramer sounded serious and I quite fancied some chicken soup.

'So what's the bad news?' I asked as Kramer passed me a bowl of soup and a lump of bread that was well past its incinerate-by date.

'Eat your soup, I'll tell you.'

It was midnight by now, and eating late-night chicken soup in Kramer's room had become quite a common occurrence. His aunt Sadie was visiting at the end of term and all four gallons had to be finished.

'Just throw it away,' I had recommended. 'Chuck it down the toilet.'

'She'd have a heart attack. You don't know my aunt Sadie.'

'She'd never guess.'

'You're kidding; as I said, you *don't* know my aunt Sadie.'

'Answer me this,' I asked. 'Which is the commonest bird in the world?'

'Do I get a mark for "don't give a shit"?'

'No'.

'It must be a pigeon.'

'No, closer to home.'

'A homing pigeon?'

'No. A chicken. The domesticated hen. There are about twenty-four billion of them worldwide.'

Kramer shook his head. 'There wouldn't be if my aunt Sadie had anything to do with it.'

'They're descended from the red-jungle fowl, *Gallus gallus*,' I said, proud of some new titbits of bird information; chicken nuggets, we'd probably call them now.

'I can't believe the domesticated hen is of any interest to ornithologists.'

'Well, in fact, ornithology was originally the study of chickens.'

'Now you *are* talking cock,' said Kramer. 'The trouble with chickens,' he went on portentously, 'is you never know what they're thinking. Whenever I've looked a chicken in the eye I've always thought: what the hell is that bird thinking? It never looks at you back, for a start. Especially if you're about to wring its neck till it dies.'

'Oh yeah, and you've done that a lot, I suppose,' I sneered.

'I spent three months on a kibbutz killing chickens. I know what I'm talking about. That's when I realized you never know what a chicken is thinking.'

'They were probably thinking: "Watch it, chaps, here comes that bastard Kramer and look, he's got that neck-wringing glint in his eye!"'

Kramer ignored this. 'You can't trust a bird called a "chicken" that isn't troubled by chicken pox. When have you heard of a chicken getting chicken pox? Never. Mind you, they used to be very valuable. Roosters particularly. In fact, when Socrates was dying of hemlock poisoning, his last words were, "I owe Asclepius a cock."'

'I didn't even know Socrates was dead. Interestingly, Brazil never won the World Cup when he was captain, you know!'

I thought this fatuous comment would bring Kramer back to his apparently urgent 'bad news'.

'Bad news,' he said.

'What's wrong? Are you dying of cancer?'

Kramer laughed. 'Ha, no, I'm not. Well, I probably am, actually; one day certainly, a long lingering death knowing my luck, but that's not what I wanted to tell you.' He took a deep breath. 'JJ has a boyfriend.'

I said nothing. 'Well, I *think* JJ has a boyfriend.'

But JJ is the love of my life and I think I'm the love of hers. What was Kramer on about?

I finally said, 'My JJ?'

'Well, how many JJ's do you know?'

'What do you mean, she's got a boyfriend?' I was really struggling to take in the meaning of this statement. A statement of unfortunately simple, unambiguous plain English.

'I saw her leaving the bookshop today. Arm in arm with a bloke. They seemed quite giggly and together.'

I misgulped some soup and coughed painfully.

Kramer shrugged helplessly. 'I'm sorry.'

'What did he look like? It's probably one of her friends from the shop that I know and have met before and there's nothing in it really,' I said, trying to convince myself, rather unconvincingly.

Kramer closed his eyes and thought. 'Tall, blond, athletic, well dressed, very good-looking. Not a bit like you.'

It was Neil Curtis.

'When did you see them?'

'As the shop was shutting.'

Normally the time I would be meeting her before she caught

her bus home but tonight I hadn't. She'd said she'd got a prior engagement she couldn't get out of.

'What sort of prior engagement?' I had asked.

'Oh, a really dull one I'd do anything to get out of!' she said, pulling an upside-down smiley face.

'Why don't you just not turn up?'

'I wish it were that easy,' she said, and I loved her more for using the subjunctive. Then I said something which surprised us both.

'Are you seeing your other boyfriend?' How dangerous! How daring! Suppose she'd said 'yes'! 'Yes' would mean she had another boyfriend but that, implicitly, I was her boyfriend as well. If she said 'no' that could mean she did have another boyfriend but she wasn't seeing him tonight. But that I was still therefore the other boyfriend! Or worse: 'yes' or 'no' could still mean she had two boyfriends, neither of which were me. She answered neither 'yes' nor 'no'. She just spluttered out a giggle and said, 'You are *funny*!' then she leaned over and gave me a small but perfectly formed kiss on the cheek.

And now later I hear from Kramer that there is another boyfriend. If not the only one.

'Neil,' I said.

'Are we going to pray?'

'That's his name. He works with JJ. I've met him. Critchley introduced me to him.'

A deeply unpleasant feeling unconnected to Aunt Sadie stabbed me in the guts. 'Critchley was about to tell me something. Something serious, but I didn't stay to find out what it was. I had to go because Degsy and Lobby were hanging around.'

Kramer sounded sympathetic. 'I'm sorry to be the bearer of bad news. It may be nothing.'

I was feeling suddenly empty and alone. Kramer walked over and put his hand on my shoulder.

'You know what you need, my friend. Some soup.'

BUDGIE

I put down my pint on the corner table of the empty pub. I sat down. I stood up again and started pacing up and down. It was hard to relax. I was thinking about Neil and JJ. I was trying not to think about Neil and JJ. That was why I couldn't sit down. I sat down. I sipped the lager and shuddered. It was ten to twelve and it didn't seem to be lager time but I'd asked JJ if we could meet early as I had something important to tell her. Ask her. I bit my nails for a few moments then I stood up and started pacing again.

'You alright, mate?' asked the barman. 'You're like a caged animal.'

I sat down again.

'Hello, Charlie!' said a piercing voice from the other side of the room.

I looked up. A caged animal. A mynah bird, in fact.

'Hello, Charlie!' it said again. And again. The accuracy of the diction was amazing, but I soon gathered that I had heard the full extent of its conversation. I did not like caged birds, but I was glad of the distraction and I walked over to it.

'Hello, Charlie,' I said. Mynah birds can only repeat what they hear, so I assumed this one had heard the phrase 'Hello, Charlie' more than any other and therefore it was called Charlie.

'Hello, Charlie!' it said back to me.

'Sorry to butt in, chaps!' It was JJ. She looked more stunning than I remembered her. I sensed that part of me wanted her to look less than perfect now. Now that she was going out with Neil. Possibly.

'You look great,' I said

'Ah, thanks. Hey, amazing speech that bird's got.'

It was a beautiful bird: glossy black, with stunning yellow flashes on its wings. It hopped neurotically from perch to perch in its cage

'Fantastic to teach a bird to speak so accurately.'

I disagreed. 'I think it's terrible. And anyway it's not speaking, it's imitating. The mynah bird is in the starling family and they're all good mimics; but it's not speaking.'

'It sounds like pretty good English to me.'

'It has no capacity for language like humans have. You can teach a bird to say "cat eats bird" or "bird eats worm" but it will never be able to say, like a human could, "bird eats cat" or "cat eats worm". It can't produce language. It can't make up things that it's never heard before. That's why it only says "Hello, Charlie". Eventually someone called Charlie is going to walk in and that bird is going to make his day. Otherwise it's pretty dull. It hasn't got language pre-wired in its brain like we have.'

'Blimey,' said JJ. 'You did go to a lecture once!'

I realized that I was sounding heavy and stressed. I needed to get this over with quickly. I needed to get out of this cage.

'What would you like to drink?'

'Just an orange juice, thanks.' She was radiant this morning; her brilliance made me feel increasingly like a shadow.

'My parents always had a budgerigar when we were young,' she was saying.

That reminded me. It's true. When we were young and we

would visit neighbours or friends of my parents, I was always intrigued by the number of houses that had a pet budgie. What was it about the budgie? They are brightly coloured. They sing. It seemed quite innocent then. But birds sing to attract a mate. They sing for love; for sex. And then they sing to defend everything that goes with that: the mate, the nest, the eggs, the chicks, the territory; the future of their genes. They do not sing for fun. They do not sing for our enjoyment. And they fly. They fly long distances. They cross continents, they cross oceans. They are creatures of the sky. They are not creatures of the cage. I find it hard to think of anything that symbolizes 'wrong' as neatly as a caged bird. A small, brightly coloured creature flitting helplessly back and forth on an endless two-foot-long journey. A creature that could fly thousands of miles.

The energy of a bird, its colour, its sound and its movement confined behind metals bars is such a potent image of repression it's not hard to see why art and literature have used it so much. Flight is escape; flight is liberty. How often when I've felt imprisoned have I looked upwards, scanning the sky for a bird, a symbol of freedom? Invariably, of course, it's a pigeon. In towns, a feral pigeon; anywhere else, a wood pigeon. Boring for the birdwatcher: it's the bird you can't fail to see, the bird that is so common you can hardly count it as a wild animal. And yet so many times I have felt miserable and confined but been suddenly heartened to see a pigeon flying over with its strong, fast, direct flight, exuberant with a sense of freedom and space. A symbol of hope.

Robert Franklin Stroud was not a nice man. Disruptive, apparently, and divisive. And very violent. How else would you end up in solitary confinement in the island prison of Alcatraz?

Tantalizingly close to San Francisco, the 'Rock' is cut off by fierce sea currents of freezing water. Stroud is immortalized in film as the *Birdman of Alcatraz*. A sanitized and sentimentalized story of his life tells of how he kept insanity at bay by looking after birds, curing injured and sick ones and selling them to fellow inmates or letting them fly off to freedom. The idea of a caged man freeing birds is compelling, and despite its distance from the truth the film became very popular. Stroud himself was never allowed to see it.

There is a strange irony that the 'Birdman' should be the most famous inmate of this hellish prison. *Alcatraz* is the Spanish for pelican. The island is named after the enormous flocks of the bird that early explorers observed there. And it is no longer a prison. It's actually, listen to *this*, a bird sanctuary; home to many rare species.

The aborigines of Australia are closer to nature than we are. For thousands of years they have lived off whatever has been provided by the land. Or the sky. A brightly coloured parrot, small but super-abundant, is a protein-rich meal. Undeniably 'good food'; or, in their own language: *betchyerrigyar*. They would be surprised to see the *betchyerrigyar* (or 'budgerigar') pointlessly caged in so many urban locations. Do the keepers of caged birds perhaps think this is a link to the wilderness, a little piece of wild nature in the city?

Does it make them feel less caged in their human habitation? Surely, a bird flying wild and free is more uplifting? A caged bird in the city to me is a symbol of misery.

'You look miserable,' said JJ, putting her hand on mine. 'Is something the matter?'

Here we go.

'Yes ... er, I wanted to ask you something.' My insides were knotting up nicely. 'Well, the thing is—'

She cut me off instantly. 'Ooh, hang on. I must tell you something first. Sorry to butt in but this is really exciting.'

'Oh, yeah?'

'It's about Neil who works with me. You've met him, haven't you?'

I was beginning to feel sick.

'Er ... I think so. Good-looking bloke?'

'Yeah, really dishy,' she said, a bit too enthusiastically.

I took a deep breath. 'What about him?'

'Well, I went out with him the other night.'

'Really?'

'To the theatre. It was brilliant. He is amazing.'

I took a swig of lager and swallowed hard.

'In what way is he amazing?'

'Well, him and his boyfriend do this brilliant stand-up act. In drag, of course, and camp as you like! But it is funny. You should see it!'

I was dumbstruck.

'Are you alright?'

'Yes.' I was beginning to chuckle. 'Yes, I was just thinking that I should see it. It sounds fantastic. I haven't been to the theatre for ages.'

We hugged and I felt deliriously happy as I left the pub. A bit of a prat, deep down, perhaps; a right idiot, in fact.

The bird looked straight at me. 'Hello, Charlie!'

LONG-TAILED TIT

'Hey, I can't believe it!' I said to the girl in the toyshop. 'You have a long-tailed tit.'

She looked confused rather than offended.

'There, on the shelf behind you. That cuddly toy.'

She looked relieved.

'Well, yes, that's part of our cuddly toy bird range, sir. We have a selection of different birds: common, like the robin, that's this one here, or rare like … er … whatever this one is,' she said waving a fluffy toy in the air.

'That's a hammerhead shark. No, this is the one I want. A long-tailed tit. Amazing!'

The long-tailed tit (*Aegithalos caudatus*) was JJ's favourite bird.

'If you squeeze its tummy it makes the right noise as well.'

Get away, no? Yes! How about that? Squeeze it in the right place and it makes a bird noise. Not every time. Back then I had no idea what a long-tailed tit sounded like, but the noise coming from the toy's tummy was a shrill, tinny chirrup that could easily have been a bird. This was the nineteen-seventies, remember, and a toy like this was pretty damned sensational. If I could have my time on this earth over again, I might have a squeeze on the hammerhead shark's tummy to see what noise that made.

It was four forty-five. I was meeting JJ at five thirty to have a quick drink before she caught her bus at six thirty. I would have time to take it back to college and wrap it. The ideal present.

The long-tailed tit. A fluffy pink ball on a string. A cat's toy. A charming sight, they are, as they move daintily through foliage in social groups. Their thin, needle-like song tinkles down from the treetops. A girly bird to have as a favourite, maybe. But undeniably sweet. And the nest, a masterpiece! A globular, domed, rounded or bottle-shaped ball of soft, springy, elastic moss, lichen and cobweb, that actually expands as the chicks grow.

My short cut back to college would take me through Debenhams department store. In the main doors and through make-up (war-painted hags perched like vultures on stools), then into soft furnishings and haberdashery (prim, trim men giggling and nudging through the curtain material samples), up a couple of steps though the 'cafeteria' (and the unconvincing stench of freshly ground instant coffee), into sport and leisure (shaven-headed muscle-bound youths, inarticulately embarrassed by all but the most basic human conversation), turn left into kitchen appliances (men with suits and glasses proudly demonstrating food-mixer speeds), down a few steps and out though the back doors into the bus station and twenty yards from my room. But things didn't turn out that way.

It was the dash through the cafeteria that was to change the course of this day. My eyes were fixed on the floor ahead as I wove in between tables, chairs and unattended toddlers when, on the outskirts of my visual field, there was a large, ginger blur. Something strong and warm overpowered me.

'Rooooorrrrrry! I don't believe it! The devil himself. Talk of the devil, hey? That's neat!'

Brigid the South African waitress from my first year. If I had a list of names of the people I did not want to meet at that moment, hers would have been on it. Possibly the only one on it. 'How are you?' she effused, treating me to a pre-Christmas boozy waft of warm breath and spittle. 'Let me hug you.'

There was no option. She clasped me and squeezed me hard and in my mind there appeared the worrying image of an alligator wounding its prey so it could be dragged underwater and moved somewhere else to be destroyed later. Firm against my chest I felt her bosom, which was still amazing, but amazingly unappealing. I remembered vividly why she had attracted me and why she had frightened me. She suddenly started kissing me hard, or possibly she was just using odd bits of my face to wipe her lipstick off. After a frenzy of girly gushing and vice-like requests to join her, I found myself sitting opposite the Amazonian Boer with a pre-cappuccino cappuccino in a very seventies glass cup, as if the coffee were showing no shame at its undrinkability.

All I wanted to do in the world at that moment was to go back to my room to wrap the long-tailed tit and meet for a cosy drink with the love of my life. I felt kidnapped. The rasping voice and the overexcited, inconsequential drivel became familiar again. She was so, so different from JJ.

'I really can't stay that long,' I began feebly.

'Don't be daft. I owe you an apology. And,' she added disconcertingly, 'a lot more besides.'

'I must be going; I've got to meet a friend.'

'I'll come with you. Any friend of yours ...'

'Er ...'

'Is it a girl? Even better. Like to see what the competition is!'

'No, it's not girl.'

Now, why did I say that?

'Hey, listen, Rors, remember that night last year? You didn't fuck up; I did. I was stupid and hysterical. We could have had a great night. We could be going out now. We still could. I mean, I was ready for you. I mean … hell, yeah. I was there, man. There wasn't a problem. I dug you fine. And I know you dug me. And I know why!'

She thrust her breasts out towards me and then bit her lip coyly; though her 'coy' lessons had clearly been a waste of money. And where did 'Rors' come from?

I tried to stay focused. It was a quarter past five. I didn't have time to wrap the bird now and I had to start walking to the bookshop at once.

'Hey, I've got to get to Blackwaters before it shuts.' I stood up decisively. She stood up too and grabbed my arm. 'Me too. I'll come with you and then we can go out for a drink. Or three! Ha ha ha!'

'But …'

'And we'll see if our evening can have a different ending this time.'

'I'm sure it will.' My pessimism was undisguised.

I walked slowly back towards the bookshop to give her time to change her mind and disappear. Or just change her mind. Or, even better, just disappear. She showed no inclination to do any of these things.

'Hey, listen, why don't I do what I have to in the bookshop, and maybe we could meet later. After six thirty, maybe? Er … six thirty-one, perhaps?'

'I don't want to let you out of my sight, young man! Hey, we better stop dawdling; that shop's going to be shut!'

It was five twenty-five and the bookshop was in view. I had no idea what to do. I was slowing down, Brigid was speeding up. And pulling me by the arm. Just at that moment, JJ appeared at the main door of the shop. She was looking at her watch and turned away from us to look up the street, then started turning in our direction. I grabbed Brigid and dragged her into an alleyway about three shops away from Blackwaters.

'Let's not bother with the bookshop,' I said. The narrowness of the alleyway crammed us up against each other. She needed no further invitation.

'Oh, Rory.'

We kissed rather incontinently for five twenty-five on an autumn evening. 'I love your impetuousness … your spur-of-the-momentness – maybe you are the devil! I love it.'

I was overwhelmed again by the giant freckled sucker, and coming up briefly for air, I suggested we moved further down the alleyway from the street.

Oh JJ, I'm so, so sorry. What could I do? I couldn't go and meet her like this. I was covered in lipstick. Worse than that, I was covered in a large, ginger South African girl. I had to get this girl away from Trinity Street.

'Let's go for a drink.'

'OK, where?'

'The Moon and Sixpence.'

'That sounds nice; where's that?'

'Newmarket Road. It's a bit of a walk but worth it.'

'Have they got nooky holes?'

What an alarming question. Nooky holes? I hoped that was some sort of South African pub game.

'They've got bar billiards.'

'You're funny. No, I mean cosy little recesses where two people can get to know each other a little bit better.'

'Oh yes, that's why I'm suggesting it.' That, and because it's miles from the centre of town and no self-respecting person, least of all JJ, would turn up there. 'It's where the dead drink,' I'd heard it described. When I first went there I discovered the dead actually served there as well. Spit and sawdust would have been most welcome in this place. They would have been luxurious extras; as would beer, hygiene and a complete roof.

But by the time we got there JJ would be on her bus home. Thinking what? What would she make of my non-appearance? That perhaps I had some important work to finish? That perhaps a lecture or supervision had overrun? No, I'd given her no reason to suppose my studies would ever prevent me seeing her.

That perhaps I'd found someone else? No, she wouldn't think that, would she? That's out of the question. There is no one else. How could she possibly think that?

That maybe I got drunk at some college society drinks do and crashed out in my room? Yes, I don't mind you thinking that, JJ, my lovely. What if she thought that and came to my room to check? Oh no, what if she came to my room and I wasn't there? Well, it would be the first time she's ever come as far as my room. That would be a plus. Or would it? Perhaps I crashed out in somebody else's room. Yes, that's more like it. What if she thought I was dead? What if she really thought I had died, that death would be the only thing to make me miss my appointment with her?

But that's true, JJ. Death is the only thing that would keep me from you. Death or a buxom, overbearing South African girl. In fact, what *was* keeping me from seeing JJ? It wasn't death or Brigid. It was fear and guilt. It never crossed my mind to say, 'I can't see you now, Brigid, because I'm meeting my new girlfriend.

Or the girl who soon will be my new girlfriend when we get to know each other better.' Why didn't I say that? Why didn't I turn up to meet JJ and say, with total innocence, 'Hey, JJ, this is Brigid, an old mate of mine from my first year. She just wanted to say hello to my special new friend. Right, let's go, JJ. See you around, Brigid.' Now it all seems so very easy. Back then, there was fear and guilt. Guilt about the desires I once had for Brigid, and fear of offending JJ, of hurting JJ, of losing her.

'Hey, this pub's closed down,' said Brigid as we arrived at the Moon and Sixpence. 'Look, it's all boarded up and there's a hole in the roof.'

'No, it's always like that,' I assured her. 'Let's go in. You'll like the landlady. She's a lovely person. A great sense of humour for someone who's decomposing.'

We went in and Brigid sniffed the dank air.

'I'm not drinking here; let's go somewhere decent like the Elm Tree or the Blue or the Free Press.'

I looked at my watch. It was six forty-five. It didn't matter any more where we drank. JJ wouldn't be walking in on us. She'd be on her bus home having serious doubts about our relationship. If we still had one. I'm so sorry to have hurt you, JJ. You were my whole life and now you're gone. Thank you for caring about me. But wait, what if she didn't care? A new fear flooded my soul. What if she didn't care that I didn't turn up? What if she found it a bit of a relief that I stood her up. What if she thought, thank God he's not here, I can catch an earlier bus home. Or go out for a drink with a mate from work. Or, it gets worse. Supposing she thought, I can use his not turning up as an excuse to finish this silly non-event of a relationship, which, let's face it, is only based on our common interest in birds. And I'm not convinced he actually cares much about birds anyway; he was probably just infatuated with me in that embarrassing, virginal student way. He was probably just pretending to be interested in birds so he could hang around the shop all day and chat me up like that sad loser he is. I was mortified by this thought.

A searing pain seemed to dart out all over my body starting with my crotch.

'Hello, are you there?'

Brigid had grabbed my balls really tight and was squeezing them in what she claimed was an affectionate manner.

'Where are you? What do I have to do to get your attention, handsome?'

'Oh, sorry, I was miles away.'

'Why don't we just get a bottle of wine and go back to your room?' she asked insistently.

Because I don't like you, I don't want you, I'm madly in love with a special girl whom I'm letting down badly by being with you and I certainly don't want to be alone in the confines of my room with you!

Was the correct answer, but somehow I came out with a rather pompous, and bizarre, alternative.

'Because this country has the most outmoded and repressive licensing laws of anywhere in the world, based on First World War legislation and wholly inappropriate to the nineteen-seventies, so I don't intend to waste any second that a pub is actually open and serving alcohol by not being in a pub!'

'Well said!' She gave me an undeserved hug. 'We'll go back to yours after the pubs shut.'

I resigned myself to the fact that I'd have to 'explain' everything to JJ when I saw her, in whatever way I could find most acceptable, and hope that it hadn't spoiled what we had.

'So, what is it that you have?' I could imagine Kramer saying. 'You have nothing to spoil.'

We had a lot to spoil.

I knew it.

JJ knew it.

… Didn't she?

I wasn't going to shake Brigid off easily and I was really anxious about ending up in bed with her so I thought I'd cut my losses and just try to have a convivial night's drinking. We could do several pubs, then the college bar; she would be ill and have to go home. We'd certainly be too drunk to even attempt anything vaguely carnal – well, maybe a doner kebab from Dodgy Ahmed's later on. The plan, of course, would only work if I could stay one step ahead of (that is, a few drinks behind) Brigid. She was a formidable drinker, but as she would almost certainly insist that I buy the drinks all night, I would retain some control.

The Free Press, Elm Tree, the Cricketers, the Clarendon, the Fountain, the Castle; things were going according to plan. Brigid was significantly tipsier than I. Then we went to the Maypole, where hunchback Harry refused to serve us, and then barred us after some South African expletives. Next on the itinerary was the Bun Shop. Then the Cambridge Arms and then the Maypole, from where, hunchback Harry reminded us, we'd been barred half an hour earlier. Next was the … er … then the … oh, dear I can't seem to remember where we went after that.

Oh dear. At some point in the evening things must have stopped going according to plan.

ALARM

Birds get up early. Birds react to light. The slightest glimmer of dawn rouses them. In the summer, this can be as early as three thirty in the morning. On a cold, cloudy winter's day it can be as late as seven thirty. I record, not with a great sense of pride, that I have observed this mainly by having hangovers. A hangover is a great way to learn how early birds sing. And how loud. Before I got into birdwatching and caught them off guard by actually being up before they started singing, the birds whose songs I knew best were those early morning ones: the song thrush (*Turdus deafeningus*), the blackbird (*Turdus headacheus*), the wren (*Troglodytes shutthefuckuppus*), and, when I was back in Cornwall, the herring gull (*Larus die-for-god's-sakeus*) and the droning out-of-tune cuckooing of the collared dove (*Streptopelia tedius*).

I didn't know what birds they were then; I just knew their singing. Staggering home a couple of times I remember looking behind me just in case they were there, following me. Or maybe just peeping out from their roosts at me and thinking, 'Aha, look at the state of him; early chorus tomorrow, everyone!' And they'd stalk me all the way home to find out which window ledge was my bedroom so they'd know where to perch at 5 a.m.

For years I couldn't have identified the alarm call of the blackbird, so strident and insistent. But once it was pointed out to me, I realized the sound had been with me all my life. Late in the evening, early in the morning, it's the bird sound I've heard most. You will have heard it a thousand times. Since everything in the world seems to alarm the blackbird, its call is extremely easy to hear. The morning after my pub crawl with Brigid I heard a blackbird (unseen and, then, unnamed) loud and clear. It is a beautiful, fruity, flutey song, with trills and warbles. It's peaceful, but melancholy. That's what I think now. Back then it was invasive and mocking. It was one of God's creatures wagging a finger in my hungover Catholic direction. I turned over and felt my brains sloshing around and banging against the sides of my skull.

My room backed on to the bus station. I had eventually got used to the grinding, grunting, shuddering and spluttering of diesel engines. It had taken a while. In the first few weeks I could work out the time of day (or night) from the buses. The night bus to Bedford. The first of the city centre buses at 5 a.m. The six o'clock to Royston, the six thirty to Haverhill via Hospital.

Over the years, different things take over your early morning. Milk floats. Do they still exist? The faint hum of their battery-powered electric motors. The chirpy whistle of the milkman which, he thinks, says, 'God, what a lovely time of day this is to be up and about. It makes me so happy I want to whistle a happy tune.' But we know it really means: 'I'm up at this time while you lucky lot sleep so I'll whistle an annoyingly chirpy tune. Not only that, but I'll whistle it slightly incorrectly so it'll get on your nerves even more.'

And bin men who have to shout to each other, 'Oi, Dave, move the fuckin' thing over here,' and clang as many bin lids as they can to remind people what a dirty yet vital job they perform in the early morning as we sleep.

But that night I was lying in bed with a headache, feeling guilty that I'd let down JJ and probably ruined the best relationship I'd ever had (if I actually had it), and there was that insistent alarm. And a drumming on wood. A woodpecker? Not here surely. The park is close; there are woodpeckers there. No, this is a tapping. Is it a thrush banging a snail shell against a rock? That's what they do, isn't it, thrushes? Everybody knows that. It's one of the primary-school facts about birds: thrushes eat snails and using a rock as an anvil they smash the shells to free the juicy snail inside. Magpies steal shiny things; that's another nursery myth about birds. The thieving magpie. Robins have red breasts and appear on Christmas cards because that's the only time you see robins, isn't it? Blue tits steal cream from the tops of the milk. They peck open the silver tops of milk bottles that have been left in the very early morning by the chirpy, whistling, angry milkman and suck all the cream out. What do blue tits do now that milk comes in cartons, I wonder. What do milkmen do now that everyone buys milk from petrol stations?

And come to think of it, I was lying earlier about collared doves waking me up in Cornwall. There were no collared doves in Cornwall when I was a boy. Now, you can't move for them, but back then, there were none.

How strange memory is: what spoils it most is not the things you forget but the things you keep adding to it, the things you keep rewriting, embellishing and streamlining.

But one thing I'm sure of from that morning, I was lying in a fug of night-before beer and guilt, woken by the alarm call of a blackbird, when I heard a faint tapping on wood.

VISITING THE SICK

I opened my eyes. JJ was standing over my bed.

'The door was open ... I hope you didn't mind. I did knock.'

Panic. Sheer panic. Why was JJ was in my room? I was in bed feeling terrible and a skull-splitting alarm was going off in my head. My brain had to go from zero to 120 miles an hour on a freezing morning in less than one second. A tough call. Working backwards: drinking with Brigid, the South African waitress; miss meeting with JJ; bumped into Brigid on way to meet JJ; just bought a cuddly, singing long-tailed tit for JJ.

'I was just wondering what happened last night?' she asked gently and, I think, with genuine concern.

My reply was instant and delivered with all the insouciance I could manage, 'Er ... I ... Er ...'

It was not one of my smoothest lines. I sat up in bed gripped with fear. I looked round the room, clammy with apprehension. Was Brigid still here? No, there was no sign of her. That was a start.

'I'm really sorry,' I said, 'but the thing is ...'

JJ waited benignly. She was clearly keen to hear my explanation. So was I.

I got out of bed and sat next to JJ. I realized I was fully clothed.

'You've still got your clothes on.'

That was a good sign. That seemed to indicate that if Brigid had come back to my room last night, nothing sexual had taken place. I looked at the clock. 08.30. My memory hadn't reported in for work yet.

'I was worried when you didn't turn up last night.'

She seemed so genuinely upset that my self-hatred quickly went up a notch to self-loathing. Why couldn't I just have told Brigid the truth? And JJ? Why had I been so cowardly? Now I had jeopardized everything we had. I didn't know what it was exactly that we had but I knew it was precious and I knew it was fragile and I knew that I was close to blowing it all – if I hadn't already.

'I was torturing myself with all sorts of fantasies,' she said, putting her hand on my thigh and stroking it. That was the most actively physical thing she'd ever done. I put my hand on hers expecting her to pull it away. She didn't.

'I assumed,' she said, 'that you'd got fed up with me, you know, stringing you along, keeping you at arm's length. Not spending more time with you. I presumed you'd found another girl and decided to have a proper relationship.'

'Not at all!'

'I wouldn't have blamed you.'

'No, there's no other girl!'

'I thought I'd blown everything we've got.' It was heavenly to hear her say the words that made me realize she felt the same as I did. 'I don't know what it is exactly that we've got,' she continued, 'but I know it's very precious to me and I know it's very fragile and I don't want to lose it.'

We hugged.

'I'm so sorry about last night. Nothing's changed between us,' I said.

She clearly felt the same way about our relationship as I did so

I felt confident enough to tell her what exactly happened. 'There was this drinks do at Rex the Chaplain's and I—'

'Look, there's no need to explain. I'm not asking for an excuse or an explanation, let's just leave it.'

Did she know I was telling her a lie and was giving me the opportunity not to? She was sensitive enough to know that genuinely nothing had changed between us whatever happened last night, so why discuss it. Having nothing to feel guilty about didn't stop me feeling guilty and I was desperate to explain.

'Yes, there was a party at Rex the Chaplain's and I think I must have had a few too many glasses of the college sherry, or Wrecks the Chaplain, as it's known, ha, and lost track of the time. When I looked at the time I realized that you would already have got your bus and gone home and I had no way of contacting you.'

'I waited a bit longer for you. I missed my usual bus just in case.'

In my mind the swamp of guilt gurgled louder. Bubbles of poison gas came to the surface and popped. The stench was unbearable.

'Are you alright?'

'Oh yes, I'm just really sorry I didn't come over to the shop in case you were still there.'

'It doesn't matter. It really doesn't matter.'

What a superb girl she was. She was bright, fragrant and sunny sitting next to me on my bed. And I, sweating in my clothes and a cloud of alcoholic vapours, was dark, dank and sleazy, crippled with fear and shame.

Then, on my desk, I saw it. The fluffy, twittering long-tailed-tit. This could be a great help.

'Hey, wait. I've got something for you. Close your eyes.' I

went over to the desk and picked up the bird. As I did so I noticed that on its fluffy white breast was an imprint in blaring pink lipstick of Brigid's outrageously plump lips. I couldn't give this to JJ.

'Can I open my eyes yet?'

'Er ... hang on!' I thrust it into the wastepaper basket. 'Oh damn, I must have left it in Rex the Chaplain's room!'

She opened her eyes.

'I'm really sorry. I'll get it later.'

As I said this a lively, bell-like twittering came from the bin.

'What was that?' she asked.

'I didn't hear anything. Can I make you a coffee?'

'I don't think so.'

'Correct, I've got no coffee.'

'I'm on my way to work so I'd better get going.'

We stood facing each other, holding both hands.

'Thanks for coming over.'

'My pleasure; I'm glad everything's alright.'

'Everything's fine. It's nice to have you in my bedroom. Sure you don't want to stay? Have the day off.' I was straying into unknown territory here. It was exciting. And scary.

Her smile was tender and calm.

'One day. One day soon.'

She leaned towards me.

I leaned towards her.

I could feel the warmth of her breath.

She closed her eyes.

I closed mine.

She kissed me softly, and briefly, on the lips.

We opened our eyes and looked deep into each other's and

knew that the next kiss would be more than a kiss. It would be the crackling, sparkling flame snaking along the fusewire to a bomb. Closer still.

'I was worried there was someone else,' she whispered.

'No,' I breathed. 'No one else.'

We closed our eyes, put our arms round each other and BANG!

'Bloody hell, you've got to walk miles to take a shit in this place!' said a rasping South African voice as the door was flung open and hit the bedside table.

Brigid appeared in the doorway.

Semi-naked and scratching her wispy, ginger pubes.

FEAST

So much pale pink, tasty flesh. Where do you begin? Feel how firm that breast is. Imagine how much one of them weighs. Look at the legs. Dark, muscly and mouth-watering. A carnal feast. A meat treat.

'I think it's disgusting,' Kramer said grabbing a plate and standing in the queue.

I didn't think it was disgusting but I had felt better in my life and the sight of so much food laid out was a tiny bit off-putting, but, then, it was only once a year.

'It's better than the usual shite they serve us.'

'That's not true. There's just more of it and you get a paper cup of watered-down wine,' mumbled the gloom-meister.

'Oh, come on,' I said. 'You can't beat Christmas dinner.'

'Why turkey, though? Why does it have to be turkey?' he grumbled, and I remembered he was Jewish.

'Hey, it's not even your festival, so shut up moaning!'

'It's not *your* festival either. It's a mish-mash. It's mostly pagan. It's the Roman saturnalia.'

The queue had moved slowly as far as the carved turkey. Kramer went on, 'And since when has turkey been traditional in Britain? It's American.'

I ignored him. 'You a leg man or a breast man?'

'I go for the personality, actually.' Kramer was interrupted by Lazy Lobby, the non-homosexual rugby club stalwart and ponding enthusiast, who quipped, 'I think the important thing is how they gobble.'

Kramer suddenly turned to me and caught me off guard with his question. 'Talking of which, there was a lot of laughing and shouting coming from your room last night. Monocellular Mike said he saw you staggering back into college quite late with a girl who definitely did not fit the description of a certain pretty and gamine bookseller.'

'Oh yeah, I was out with a load of the Modern Languages lot. Sort of end-of-term thing.'

He didn't seem convinced. 'Not Brigid that South African girl who worked in the canteen last year?'

'Oh her, I remember her. She was a real ... er ...' I stumbled.

'Turkey?' Kramer helped out.

The turkey is originally Mexican rather than North American, and the Incas were big fans. This unsightly and gormless bird provided everything that was precious to the Incas: meat, eggs and ludicrous headgear. It has almost nothing to do with the country of the same name. Turkey, Greece and those parts of the world provided us with the similarly plumptious guinea fowl which was often called, wait for it, the turkey-cock.

My childhood Christmases would not have been the same without a turkey, and the invariably gigantic bird would do our family of six for several days: roast turkey on Christmas Day; cold turkey on Christmas Night; turkey in white sauce with rice on Boxing Day lunchtime; curried turkey on the 27th; turkey sandwiches on the 28th, and on the next day a broth based on the boiled-down turkey carcass with barley, carrots, onions and, indeed, whatever bits and pieces were left over from the festivities chucked in for luck. This last dish, the 'turkey soup', was in many ways my favourite meal of the whole holiday, even though one year I found a party-popper in it.

Turkey was clearly the Christmas-dinner choice in Dickens' time. Who can forget that charming scene from *A Christmas Carol* when Scrooge, a new man after his ghostly visitors, wakes up bursting with good humour on Christmas morning, opens his bedroom window and shouts down to an urchin in the street, 'What's today, my fine fellow?'

'Why it's Christmas Day, Mr Scrooge!' replies the startled boy.

'I shall give you some money for you to purchase a prize turkey.'

And the chirpy cockney sparrow of a lad replies, 'Where the fuck am I going to get a prize turkey on Christmas Day, you senile old git?'

Or something like that. It's a long time since I read it.

And the actual word 'turkey' has clearly not had great semantic PR over the years. Turkey:

1) An unsuccessful theatrical production, a flop, an embarrassment.
2) A person or thing of little appeal, a dud, a loser.
3) A large ugly, unattractive woman.
4) A naïve, stupid or inept person.
5) Cold turkey; the sickness, nausea and mania of drug withdrawal.

Definitions 2) and 4) just about covered me and how I had felt this morning. The more I thought about it, the worse I felt. Surveying the mounds of limp turkey, greyish sausages, whiffy sprouts, frazzled bacon, charred roast potatoes, sloppy carrots and turnips, mould-speckled cranberry sauce, rubbery trifle, senile mince pies and flaccid whipped cream, I decided that I wasn't that hungry after all. I turned to Kramer.

'Why don't we just nip across the road to the Maypole and have a cheese sandwich?'

'Good idea,' he said.

'Oh, er, hang on ... not the Maypole.'

REED BUNTING

The sombre cubicles of the basement bar of the Turk's Head reminded me too much of the church confessional. I never liked confession. Penance was my least favourite of the seven sacraments.

The seven sacraments: Baptism, Penance, Holy Eucharist, Confirmation, Matrimony, Ordination and Extreme Unction.

Baptism was easy because, as a babe in arms, you didn't have to do much except scream the church down as the priest poured water over you.

Eucharist was great fun. It was your first Holy Communion and in our church you got a huge cooked breakfast afterwards.

Confirmation meant pledging yourself to be a soldier of Christ. This didn't seem too scary even to a thirteen-year-old. The odds, one guessed, of being called up to fight for Christ against the battalions of Satan must have been pretty long. And a perk of confirmation was that you got an extra name. My confirmation name is Peter. (The famous biblical pun on the Greek *petros*, meaning 'rock': 'Thou art Peter and upon this rock I shall build my church.' Of course I didn't know that at the time.)

Then comes the sacrament of Matrimony. Ah, yes, the joys of marriage. Right, moving quickly on, ordination. This is the sacrament of taking Holy Orders: becoming a priest. I didn't think this one would ever be relevant in my particular life, though there have been many times when I thought entering the priesthood looked like a cushy option.

Extreme Unction is the last sacrament: the anointing of the

sick. The most interesting thing about this one is that when, as a Catholic schoolchild, you learn your catechism off by heart, you never really know what any of it means and you're seldom completely sure what the actual words are that you're parroting. The seven sacraments would go: 'baptism, penance, holy eucharist, confirmation, ordination and extree munction.' For years I didn't know what extree munction was. I didn't know if there were any other sorts of 'munction' other than the 'extree' one.

But Penance. You have sinned. You must confess your sins. You must be punished for your sins. When you were very young you had to ask your parents what sins you had committed before you went for your weekly visit to confession. Lying, being rude to your parents and horrible to your brothers and sisters were their usual suggestions. So you'd happily confess to those sins, whether you'd committed them or not. As you got older you could work out the sins for yourself, perhaps throwing in 'using bad language and thinking rude thoughts'. I remember confessing to having rude thoughts long before I knew what a rude thought was. As you get even older, things that you thought were sins before don't seem like sins any more, but part and parcel of being a human being: lying is surely too everyday still to be counted as something worth confessing. Using bad language is almost compulsory nowadays, and having rude thoughts is surely the only way to stay remotely sane in the modern world.

The punishment was invariably having to say a number of prayers. Our local parish priest would listen to your sins and after some deliberation tell you to say three 'Hail Marys'.

It was perfectly clear that he didn't really pay that much attention to what you said your sins were, and I once flirted with the idea of confessing to having stabbed the Pope to death just to see if I still got three 'Hail Marys' as my penance.

It was the day after the apparition of Brigid in my bedroom. JJ had fled without a word. This was the first opportunity I had had to speak to her since. We sat down next to each other in the solemnity of our booth and I prepared to make my confession. Up till then the conversation had been curt and functional.

'Hello, how are you?'

'Fine. You?'

'Fine. White wine?'

'Please.'

At the table we slowly and silently sipped our drinks. Before the pregnant pause gave birth to something unsightly, I produced a carrier bag and offered its contents to JJ.

'This is for you. I meant to give it to you a couple of days ago,' I began nervously, 'but I—'

'—left it at Rex the Chaplain's drinks party,' she helped out.

'It's a reed bunting.'

I gave her the fluffy toy bird and she smiled sweetly and squeezed it and it made a noise like a bird. If not a reed bunting.

'Oh, it's lovely. Thank you so much! I like reed buntings. You don't see them very often.'

'I don't see them at all; I'm reed bunting blind!'

She smiled weakly and I abandoned that line of evasive humour and tried a half-truth instead. Or was it a half-lie?

'I wanted to get you a long-tailed tit coz I know that's your favourite but the shop had sold out.'

'Ah never mind. This is lovely.'

The reed bunting (*Emberiza schoeniclus*) is a striking bird, easy to see and identify, especially in summer. The male sings openly from low perches in wetlands and water's edges. Streaky brown back separated from the black head by a white neck ring. It looks like a sort of elite sparrow. The repeated jangly song is unmistakable; it sounds identical to the thirteenth bar of the intro to 'Martha My Dear' by the Beatles. You know: 'doo doo doodoo doo'. There, I hope that's cleared that up.

She squeezed it again and its tinny unconvincing chirrup was a welcome distraction. And again. And again. The amusing novelty value of this did not last long.

JJ took my hand and clasped it between both of hers. She fixed me with her eyes and spoke softly. 'I've got something to say—'

I didn't let her get any further. 'That girl used to work in the canteen, as a waitress, she's mad! South African, in fact. We had a sort of thing in my first year and I hadn't seen her for ages but I bumped into her on the way to see you and I couldn't shake her off and I thought I'd go for a drink with her because I didn't want to turn up to meet you with her and I lost track of the time and we got drunk and she must have spent the night with me but I know nothing happened even though she had no clothes on and I couldn't get in touch with you and I'm sorry but there's only you and I'm sorry I lied to you and didn't give you a long-tailed tit.'

JJ was looking at me with a look so warm it was melting me. I wonder if I'd get away with something as light as three 'Hail Marys'.

She put one arm round my neck and pulled my face to hers. She kissed me deeply and roughly and desperately. It was the

loveliest kiss in the world ever. I know. I was there. When we separated we were both panting. My heart was pounding on my
ribcage, screaming to be let out.

'Is that all you've got to say?' I asked in between breaths.

'Yes, I've got to go back to work!'

She kissed me again. A peck on the cheek. A microscopic
version of the previous kiss. She shuffled along the bench seat and
sat on something and we heard the unconvincing made-in-Taiwan
squeak of a reed bunting.

ACT ONE

'I won't be catching the bus home straight after work tonight. I'm going to the theatre and my dad's going to pick me up later.' JJ seemed very excited by the prospect of a theatre visit. She seemed nervous, agitated even, but at the same time bright-eyed and eager. I was annoyed; it was close to the end of term and I didn't know how long it would be before I saw her again. I thought it surely must be 'special occasion' time.

'What's on?'

'I don't know.'

'I mean what are you going to see at the theatre? What play?'

'I'm not really going to the theatre. That's just what I've told everyone. And I finish work at five o'clock and then I'm completely yours.' Adding coyly, 'So to speak.'

I was disappointed; mainly because I had not been listening. She seemed so happy but I didn't seem to feature in her excitement.

'I thought you'd be pleased!'

'I just thought that perhaps you and I could spend some time together before the end of term, that's all.'

'That's what I mean, you idiot!'

Then it dawned on me. This was it. She was offering me herself. Our relationship was going to move on in one ecstatic leap. 'One day things will be very different.' She'd said it so many times. 'One day.' 'One day soon.' 'It will happen.' 'We can't stop it happening'. All these things I thought were turning into an empty promise. Now today was going to be the 'one day'. I smiled.

My whole body smiled.

The future was about to begin.

'I'll meet you at five, then!'

'You bet!'

'And we'll go straight back to my room!'

JJ laughed a deep, rich, beautiful laugh full of tenderness. 'You're so gallant. We could go straight back to your room or we could have a nice romantic meal, or a bottle of wine; we could see a film; or, hey, we could go to the theatre!'

'No, I hate the theatre. No close-ups in theatre. Everyone overacts and you can never tell who's talking.'

'Oh right, that's "theatre" dismissed in a few short, sharp sentences.'

I began to retract. 'Oh, sorry, are you a theatre fan?'

'No, I hate it. In fact, I don't know why we've arranged to go to the theatre tonight.'

I put my arm around her. 'Well, let's not go then.'

'Good idea,' she agreed.

'What shall we do then?'

'I know,' she smiled knowingly. 'We could go straight back to your room.'

'Excellent.'

We laughed and kissed and she went off to work leaving me eight painful hours to fill.

What was I going to do?

I sat in my room at my desk.

I looked at the clock. 09.25.

I got up and paced up and down.

I sat down again and looked at the clock. 09.27.

I got up and paced up and down again. A bit longer this time. I sat down and looked at the clock. 09.31.

Mmm. I picked up the clock and examined it. There was clearly something wrong with it. How could six minutes take as long as six minutes to go by?

I shook it. 09.32.

Right; I'll pace up and down for a bit. I paced up and down the length of the room for as long as I could. Must have been at least quarter of an hour.

I looked at the clock. 09.32.

Shit, I've broken it. This is ridiculous, what could I possibly do to take my mind off tonight, to calm down, to relax?

I could do some work. I could start the essay on 'distinctive features in phonology'. It had to be in a month ago, so the sooner I started it the better. I opened the relevant book. My eyes darted around the page, alighting on random words: 'allophonic', 'syntagmatic combination', 'archiphoneme' and 'Grimm's Law'. I slammed the book shut. That's enough phonology for a Friday. I looked at the clock. 09.32.

Aha, of course. 09.32. Time to get a new clock! I'll go into town and do a bit of shopping. I picked my jacket up off the bed. I looked back at the bed fondly. That was to be my portal to heaven a little later on. Just an ordinary, inconsequential bed. Oh no! My bed! Christ, look at it! It's disgusting. I pulled back the bedclothes. Jees! I can't take her to this bed. I looked round the room. I can't bring her back to this shithole. An urgent list of unpleasant jobs appeared in my head from nowhere. Eight hours may not be long enough.

*

'How much did you want to spend?' said the florist.

'I didn't want to spend anything,' I replied.

'Is it for a special occasion?' she went on patiently.

'Yes, a very special occasion. A very, very, very special occasion!' I smiled knowingly, hoping in some vain way I might communicate to the florist just what I'd be doing later.

'Twenty-five pounds?' she suggested.

'Not *that* special,' I said quickly.

'Well, a single red rose can be as special as a huge and pricey bouquet,' she offered, sensing that flowers were not a regular budget item for a student with a tiny overdraft facility and a massive overdraft.

'You took the words out of my mouth,' I said, settling for the simple romantic minimalism of the single red rose. She picked one out to show me.

'Perfect!'

'Right you are,' she said. 'That'll be nine pounds ninety-nine, please.'

'Fuck me!'

'Ah, that's sweet. A single red rose. That's a lovely touch.' JJ was looking exactly as she had at nine o'clock that morning and yet lovelier than I had ever seen her.

She was looking around the room. 'Blimey, it's very clean and tidy. Undergraduate rooms are usually pigsties.'

Please God, don't let her look under the bed. Amen.

'So how many undergraduate rooms have you been in?'

She smiled. 'This is my first.'

Then she kissed me so passionately it was bordering on the obscene.

'Glass of wine?' I said politely when we stopped.

She fell back on to the bed and pulled me on top her.

'We haven't got time for wine!'

There then followed a few minutes of excitingly hurried unbuttoning.

'Clean sheets, look!' I said.

She grinned earthily. 'Not for long!'

NO FOOT

Decaffeinated coffee. Ha ha ha! How that would have made us laugh back in the seventies. So you get some coffee and take out of it the thing that most makes it coffee. That's mad enough, but then you drink it.

Half-fat butter. But butter is all fat, isn't it? So half-fat butter must just be half as much butter, surely?

Low-alcohol lager. Now you *are* messing with things that are no business of us lowly mortals. Tampering with lager. That is surely a job for God and God alone. What's the point of drinking low-alcohol lager? Most lager doesn't taste that good any way, so why take away its spirit, its one *raison d'être*?

What next? Salt-free salt? Unleaded pencils?

But what about this one: flightless bird.

Flightless bird?

Is there not in the word 'bird' a semantic entailment which has to include 'flight'?

This has always troubled me. As a little boy, I was constantly drawing birds. Perching, gliding, hovering, soaring and occasionally swimming. But I don't recall ever drawing a flightless bird.

Yes, penguins are birds, I suppose. Well, there's no 'suppose' about it, I suppose. Penguins are birds. Yes, flightless birds, but not just birds that don't fly; birds that don't even look like birds.

Kiwis are flightless birds but they do look as if they could, if shot at with an air-rifle, suddenly flap briefly into the sky and then disappear into the undergrowth. I mean, a kiwi looks like a bird. It looks like a game bird and we know that they will do anything to avoid flying, and when they do fly it's not that convincing. I presume that's why man shoots game birds and not house martins.

Penguins are odd. But then they're very good in water. Water is a fluid, you might argue, as is air, therefore penguins 'fly' underwater. I'm not convinced. An ostrich is built for speed. But for land speed. Huge, long, tautly muscled legs for high-speed escape. As a birdwatcher I would not be overexcited by seeing a penguin, an ostrich or a kiwi. Well, perhaps in North Norfolk there might be a little excitement in spotting those three. And obviously, if you did see them, you'd have to tick them off the list and add them to your new sightings of the year, but I'd rather see a rufous bush robin.

For me, a bird should be built not for the ground or the sea, but for the sky, and there is perhaps just one such bird. This bird belongs to the sky. Or perhaps the sky belongs to this bird. I'm sure that God, having gone to all that trouble creating the sky, realized he needed at least one of his creatures to be at home there. Or perhaps, after creating this bird, God realized that he would have to create the sky specially for it. A bird that comes to earth so rarely that it finds it nearly impossible to take off from the land, a bird whose scientific name means 'no foot'.

The swift.

'Swift': what a great name for the world's fastest-flying bird too. Superb to watch in sociable groups on a summer's evening, whistling and screaming over the rooftops in death-defying acrobatics: black sickles of lightning.

They eat on the wing, they drink on the wing and they sleep on the wing. But there is more.

They make love on the wing. They mate in flight. Can you think of anything in the natural world that we could envy more?

They fly as high as they can into the air and then they drop down in their lovemaking with a dizzy, exhilarating, spiralling fairground ride, tearing themselves away from gravity at the last minute and back up again to repeat the breath-taking plunge of ecstasy.

Can we compete with that? Does anything come near that liberation from the pull of planet and humanity as an infinite downward carefree tumble locked in the embrace of pleasure?

I thought we came close that night. My first time, my first time with JJ, our first time together. My small, sweaty bedroom flickered with candle gloom. The elderly creaking bed was a pathetic stage for this act. It was no match for the vastness of the swifts' heaven. But our two desires rubbed against each other frictionlessly and were single-mindedly united in a determined struggle, a desperate dance, a blazing arrow's flight towards one urgent goal. Our love and hunger for each other had obligingly unplugged our brains from our bodies, so all fear, tension, guilt and anxiety disappeared and we functioned as simple organisms: cleanly, effortlessly and perfectly. We were lost for a brief, panting eternity during which we were up there with the swifts in endless space and limitless pleasure.

In the next hour or so only two words were spoken. 'No words,' JJ had whispered to me. So we lay there clasped moistly in each other arms, savouring the heavy aftertaste of joy, waiting with wide-open eyes for our one body to smash into the ground and burst like a firework into a billion tiny sparks. For once, though, the spell felt unbreakable.

We were motionless. The silence was ruined by the vast thumping of lovers' hearts.

'Fancy a beer?' Kramer was banging on my door. 'Are you in there?'

We heard the door handle being turned. It was locked. How did we remember to do that in the frenzy of our arrival?

'If you're not in there just say so,' Kramer said kramerishly, hoping, no doubt, to tempt me into saying, 'I'm not in here!'

I resisted.

We listened and waited for the neurotic pacing up and down to stop and Kramer's clumsy footsteps to fade in the direction of the bar.

Then, once again, two swifts took off and headed for the stars.

And they landed again; as much as these two swifts could ever have landed.

And flew again.

'This is so lovely,' she said and I felt compelled to agree. 'It feels as if time has stood still.'

I looked at the clock.

09.32.

But then, unfortunately, it stopped standing still.

Time was up.

We dressed hurriedly in breathless silence, and then dashed through the sodden city streets so JJ could meet up with her lift home from the theatre.

The shady doorway of David's second-hand bookshop next to the graveyard of St Edward's church did no justice to our goodbye.

Why was she crying so much?

'Why are you crying so much?' she asked me.

'I'm happy,' I said weakly.

'Things will be different now,' she said.

'I love you.'

'I know. And I love you.'

After more tears she ran off and the night took her little hand, put its arms around her and swept her away.

THE LONGEST WEEKEND

I hurried back to the college bar, walking on air. Was 'walking on air' already a lazy cliché by the mid-seventies? I can't remember but 'walking on air' was definitely what I was doing after JJ went home that night. That's what it felt like, and those are the only words I can come up with to describe it, so we can safely say that, for all its faults, the phrase is well worthy of its cliché status.

I wouldn't be seeing JJ till Monday morning so this promised to be a very long weekend. But it was my first weekend in my 'new home'. I was a different person now. Notwithstanding the fact that I wasn't the only person in the world ever to have made love, I felt, that night, that I was the newest member of a select club. I was a cut above ordinary humans now. I had touched the hem of God's robe. I was a conquering hero. I had returned from a gruelling and bloody nineteen-year-long war and was now back triumphant among the people of my village. I could see it in people's eyes, the way they glanced at me, the way they stopped and stepped back a pace to look me up and down admiringly. Did I notice a subtle deference that wasn't there before? A slight tilt of the head as they spoke to me, perhaps, the hint of a genuflection? I was a different person. I had grown in stature; metaphorically, perhaps, but others would surely see it physically. I felt so different that I wondered briefly if my friends would recognize me at all. Who is this noble stranger swaggering down the steps towards us? He looks familiar but there is something kingly about him, something majestic and magical, something that is special, beyond the reach of us poor humans. I opened the doors to the college bar and went in. I can't recall my entrance exactly but I feel sure the packed room fell silent, that there were fireworks, brass fanfares and resounding cannonades.

'Eh, McGrath, your flies are undone!' sneered Headbanger.

'You're all red-faced and sweaty,' said one of the pair known as the Twat-twins. 'You look as if you're having a heart attack.'

I brushed away these lesser mortals and found Kramer at the bar.

'Where have you been?' he asked, handing me a pint. 'I came to your room.'

'I was out,' I said failing to keep the beaming from my face.

'Sure you weren't pretending to be out? I thought I heard heavy breathing coming from your room. And I smelled candles.'

I winked at him and said, 'Poltergeist!'

'Bless you!'

'I was in a special place,' I said, trying to sound mystical.

'A special place? The clinic? Have you caught something?' Very down to earth, Kramer, and never missing an opportunity to talk 'medically' if he could.

'I've been in the sky actually.'

'Cloud cuckoo land?'

'Flying.'

Kramer shook his head. I felt a wave of pessimism approaching. 'Trouble with flying is crash landing. Have you noticed how only planes that are flying crash? Planes don't crash when they are on the ground.'

'Haven't you ever heard the expression: "Look on the bright side"?'

Kramer raised his eyebrows dismissively. 'OK, find me the bright side and I'll look on it.'

'I've had the best night of my life tonight.'

'Do I infer from that that you and JJ have finally gone beyond the "holding hands, swapping scientific bird names and giggling in the corner of pubs" stage?'

'I think it's safe to say that things will be different now.'

I was feeling almost delirious and it was wonderful to be immune at last to Kramer's unremitting defeatism.

'You mean things can only go downhill from here,' he grumbled.

I laughed, put my arms around him and kissed him.

He recoiled. 'I'll put that down to alcohol,' he said. 'You clearly haven't had enough.'

I didn't sleep that night. When I wasn't hovering a few feet above the mattress, I was sniffing the pillowcase and sheets for any trace of JJ's perfume, any trace of her body, any trace of two hours ago. I tried to relive every moment. I worked backwards from the hurried and tearful goodbye. I thought about every moment of our love-making. Strenuous but effortless. Fragile but indestructible. Momentary and eternal. Our early nerves and self-consciousness had been quickly overwhelmed and vaporized by the flames.

'It's my first time,' I had whispered to her.

'Try to make it your first time every time,' she'd replied, and I was free.

I couldn't wait for the next day, and the next, but mainly the next. The following daybreak was exceptional. Saturday morning must have been up all night preparing such a resplendent treat for me: a huge spread of tangerine sun and icy blue sky.

I was up so early I even bumped into a sanctimonious clutch of Christians on their way to breakfast in Hall.

'Morning, chaps!' I chirped at them. 'Great to be alive!'

They rounded on me as a unit and stared defensively as if waiting for the booby trap to go off. I wonder if they had an inkling that my ponding had been averted and that Degsy and Lobby had *them* in the cross-hairs.

'Praise the Lord who has given us this beautiful day!' I added, as the chapel doors shut behind them with a hollow echo.

I realized the rest of the day was going to be a struggle. I urgently needed to do something to take my mind off JJ and love and sex. Of course! Why didn't I think of this earlier? I could do some work. I could read the relevant books and write one of the essays I was supposed to write. It had worked briefly on Friday morning. Work, the last resort. If you cannot do something that is useful, constructive or fun, you might as well work. If anything was going to neutralize my newly awakened libido it would be some transformational generative grammar.

I returned to my room, took the appropriate books from my shelf, found an unstarted exercise book and began making notes. Without any hesitation, I waded into the semantic quagmire of deep structure, presuppositions, factuality and sentences like 'the horse miaowed'.

This was just the therapy I needed. The time seemed to flash by. Just as my brain was beginning to rebel, I looked up at the clock. 09.32.

'OK, who are you?' Kramer was standing in the doorway. 'Tell me now or I'll call the police!' Kramer reached over and picked up an empty wine bottle and waved it threateningly in my direction. 'Reading Chomsky? Making notes for an essay? What the hell is going on? Just tell me who you are and what you've done with Rory!'

'Do you want a coffee?'

'This is outrageous! Is this what love does to you? Thanks for the warning!'

I got up to fill the kettle. 'I thought I'd do something constructive to take my mind off JJ.'

'Have you no consideration for your Director of Studies? How's he going to feel, what's he going to think if he finds out that not only have you done an essay but you've handed it in on time?' Kramer picked up my notebook. 'So that's the sum total of your morning's work?'

'Mind your own business.'

'Is this part of your essay then? "I love JJ".'

'Piss off.'

'How long did that take you?'

Then I remembered I was Kramer-proof.

'About twenty minutes. But I did several drafts.'

'It's a highly commendable piece of work.'

'Ah, I know what you're thinking: you're thinking it's just a formal sentence along the basic lines of subject-verb-object, but that's just the surface, Carl, old friend. I'm looking for something deeper. I want to know what is pre-wired deep in our grey cells that allows both of us to understand that apparently simple utterance, "I love JJ".'

He put the notebook down. 'Let's have a beer. Your brain obviously needs sedation.'

'No, I must get on with this. I'm doing a bit of course work precisely because I know if I don't I'll spend the entire day on the piss and wake up tomorrow with a stinking hangover.'

'Suit yourself!'

What a stinking hangover I had the next day! Kramer and I had been up till four o'clock eating chicken soup laced with vodka despite Kramer's periodic prayers: 'Oh God, please don't let Aunt Sadie find out.' We'd managed to upset the Christians with our noise. At about 11 p.m. they'd sent word to the college authorities and Rex the Chaplain had come round to admonish and counsel us.

He'd staggered off about half three singing 'Nights in White Satin'. (Or possibly 'Knights in White Satin'.)

Kramer and I had planned to get up early the next day and make it up to the Christians by attending the morning service. This we didn't manage, which was a shame. It would have been nice to see what they made of Kramer singing 'Hava Nagila' and me doing 'Hail Glorious Saint Patrick'. Another time perhaps.

I emerged fully clothed from my bed about noon still snuffling into my pillow for the last lingering traces of Friday. Any effect was spoiled by the presence of neat alcohol and a large crusty stain of what I hoped was dried chicken soup.

I spent most of Sunday washing and debating whether or not to take JJ a present on the following morning. To take a gift would indicate that what had happened on Friday was a special occasion to be marked in some way. Not to take anything would suggest that Friday night, though special, was just something ordinary and normal which should become a luscious but everyday part of our lives together.

I'd ask Kramer.

He'd be full of objective advice and good sense.

What am I saying? No, I wouldn't ask Kramer.

He'd be full of dismal foreboding. I didn't want him spreading his diseased karma over my relationship with JJ. He'd probably advise me never to see her again.

'My advice ...' Kramer shut his eyes in what I assumed he thought was the manner of a sage and put his joined hands to his mouth. 'My advice is that you should never see her again.'

'Don't be daft.'

'Be strong, move on. That was an episode of your life that's past. Be grateful for the experience, seek out pastures new.'

'You sound like a horoscope.'

'What star sign are you?'

'Pisces.'

'Ooh dear. It's a very bad week for Pisces. Be prepared for a nasty shock. Your life is about to change.'

'My life *is* about to change. I know that. Things will be different now. Anyway, you don't believe in all that bollocks, do you?'

Kramer grinned. 'No, of course I don't. I'm too realistic. Pragmatic. I'm too scientific and rational in my approach to things. Too cynical really.'

'I see.'

'Typical Aries, in fact.'

I held up a small, fluffy toy bird. 'Look. I managed to get a long-tailed tit. JJ's favourite!'

'You've already given her a reed warbler. Don't spoil her!'

I laughed. 'It was a reed bunting. Reed warbler's a very different bird. Looks different, sounds different.'

'Do I look like I care about the difference between a reed bunting and a reed warbler?'

'Ah, well, that's because you're too egocentric. You don't know the names of things. You don't engage with the beauty of the living world.'

'I bet they're both small brown birds.'

'Well, yes, they are sort of, but—'

'There you are, you see. That's plenty of ornithology for a Sunday.'

I was tiring of Kramer and I had calculated that by now my bath would be ready.

'I've got to go and have a bath.'

'When did you start the taps running?' he asked.

'Twenty-five minutes ago.'

'Give it another ten minutes.'

'No, too long. The hot tap will be running cold then or some bastard will have gone in and nabbed it.'

I got up and Kramer left, stopping to ask, 'Are you going to Rex the Chaplain's Christmas drinks tonight?'

'Er ... I could do. I don't want to be hungover tomorrow. A big day.'

He nodded. 'Oh yes, you've got a Spanish supervision, haven't you?'

'Oh yes, but also, it's probably the last day I'll see JJ before the holidays.'

A big tut from Kramer, a dramatic headshake and exit with door-slam.

I took my towel and toiletries down to the basement where the baths were kept. My bath should be just right by now.

The cubicle door was locked.

I don't believe this.

I heard singing.

Bugger. Someone had sneaked in and stolen my bath.

I banged on the door. 'Oi, that's my bathwater, you know!'

'Oh, terribly sorry, I'll leave it in for you!' The voice was distinctive and instantly recognizable. A third-year English student who was a big noise in the university theatre and in Footlights.

'Clean the bath after you and fill it up again,' I shouted at the door. 'Tosser,' I added quietly.

'It's still warm.'

'I don't want your filthy water, Griff. Get a move on!'

'I'm not all that dirty,' he said.

'No, but I'm *very* dirty,' said a mischievous girl's voice after some playful splashing.

'So am I,' giggled another.

By Monday morning I was sufficiently clean to go and meet JJ for her 10.30 a.m. coffee-break. Unfortunately this coincided with the last fifteen minutes of a supervision on 'Symbolism in Lorca'. Having postponed this session every week for nine weeks, this was my last chance of the term and I had to attend. I'd even done the essay. My first of the term. It wasn't a great piece of work: too short and lacking things like insight, facts, comment, thought, originality and decent punctuation, but it was *finished and handed in on time*.

Eventually.

The supervisor for twentieth-century Spanish literature was Dr Clarkson, who was known to be 'fond of a small sherry'. I had my fingers crossed for a 'no-show'. He'd been at Rex the Chaplain's drinks do the night before and had looked destined for a sick-note.

The door to his rooms rather disappointingly did not have a note pinned to it saying, 'Dr Clarkson apologizes, but due to illness he is unable to supervise today.'

'Ah good morning, McGrath.' He swept up the stairs behind and into his rooms, beckoning me to follow.

Damn. Now I'd have to think of some ruse to get out of there early.

'Nice to see you bang on time, Mr McGrath. No ill effects from Rex's sherry, I hope.'

Bingo.

'Er ... actually, Dr Clarkson, funny you should say that but I do feel distinctly queasy. Obviously I couldn't miss the supervision but I hope you'll forgive me if I make an unseemly dash for the lavatory at any moment.'

'Of course.'

'Say about ten-twentyish,' I said under my breath.

He looked at me, frowned then laughed. 'Come to think of it, you do look pretty damned awful, if I may say so!'

Cheeky bastard. I felt great. And I *looked* great. Well, as great as I could. I certainly looked better than he did. He began pouring himself a coffee and took a nibble of biscuit.

'I'm afraid I felt your essay lacked a certain something, Mr McGrath,' he said, spitting crumbs in my direction.

'What, sir?'

'Well: ideas, thought, originality. That sort of thing. In fact—' He stopped suddenly and went disturbingly pale. 'Oh my God!' He put hand to his mouth. 'I think I'm ...' He stood up gingerly.

'Look, I'm sorry, can we call it a day, I'm … oh no!' His dash from the study was as welcome as it was unseemly and within a minute I was walking out of college towards Blackwaters.

My main worry as I approached the shop, giddy with nerves, was how, after the tender heights and erotic depths of Friday night, JJ and I were going to manage to slip back into polite tea-shop normality, sipping our drinks, holding hands, talking inconsequentially of humdrum things, chaperoned by a workaday, drizzly, city-centre Monday morning.

Well, we had the rest of our lives together to solve that problem, I suppose.

Critchley aimed a nervous nod in my direction from the front desk of the natural history department.

'Morning,' he said through a weak smile.

'Morning. Is JJ around?'

He took his glasses off, rubbed his eyes and squinted at me.

'Oh come on, you know where JJ is today. She's away. On her honeymoon. She got married on Saturday.'

DEATH IN THE SKY

A punch in the back of the neck. No karate chop this, but an eternity of pain squeezed tightly into a fist of feathers. Approaching at two hundred miles an hour from nowhere. First there is serenity; there are the everyday things that every day brings in an everyday sort of way; you are going about your humdrum business or, perhaps, you are grasping the day with expectation and joy, perhaps you are even flying, then BANG!

Pain.

And blackness.

Maybe just blackness. Pain would be a luxury. Pain means you still feel. Pain is a message from your brain to say that you are still alive. Yes, pain means life.

The cliff-dwelling pigeon may feel nothing at all. There is wind, there is sea, there is sky, there is a huge expanse of light and sound, then nothing. But you don't feel nothing. You can't feel 'nothing'. You just stop feeling something. But, then, you can't stop feeling something, because that implies you can feel the feeling stopping. Death is not part of your life. There is your life and then there is death. There is no in between.

But let us think about the peregrine falcon. One of the world's fastest birds. But it's only fast with the powerful hand of gravity behind it. It could not catch a spine-tailed swift in level flight. But its deadly mastery of the sky deserves more than a little consideration and respect. Pigeons are very fast fliers, but they don't manoeuvre in a particularly agile way. The peregrine requires much skill and some very specialist equipment to hunt and kill in its unique style.

Altitude. That's its first weapon. It needs to be high enough not only to effect its lightning dive, but to be unseen. You surely do not expect an insignificant dark grey dot in the white sky to blossom within a few seconds into your bright red death.

Its victims cannot easily cover the sky above them. They can't fly upside-down. So the falcon has to gain altitude. For this, of course, the bird uses its wings. But it has virtually two sets of wings. Low-altitude wings and high-altitude wings. It has two broad wings with feathers spread wide, quickly and robustly flapped by its pugnacious breast till it reaches the desired height, and then its wings change. They become narrow and pointed. The commercial cargo plane becomes the jetfighter. It starts its descent, swimming downwards with gravity, gaining speed and then ... No wings at all. It is now plummeting vertically in what is known as a 'stoop' and the wings are tucked back out of the way. It has what it needs now. The required speed and the required target.

This is all very well. But it's easy to overlook a few essentials in this stunning piece of aerobatics. The bird has to see. It has to keep its eyes focused on the target until it strikes and after. It has to breathe. This is a high-fuel operation; the bird can't hold its breath till the deed is done.

We would find it impossible without goggles and visor to travel through the air at that speed. Evolution has provided the peregrine with an 'extra' eyelid bathed with thick, viscous, transparent tears which don't evaporate. At such high speeds it would be impossible for us to breathe: the air trapped in our nostrils would prevent any other air from entering. The peregrine's nostril contains a cone-shaped structure that causes air flowing past it to spin and thus be sucked in.

And one more thing we could not do is to pull out of a dive of two hundred miles an hour and go gently off in another direction. The G-forces would mash our insides. The peregrine is built to withstand these G-forces. Everything about this bird is minutely and perfectly designed for its purpose. And its purpose is to be a peregrine falcon. God would have been very excited about this one. I bet he couldn't wait to show his mates this one.

And what a great case in favour of birdwatching the peregrine falcon is! Why do you go birdwatching, people ask. Isn't it boring? At times it may be, but if once, just once will do, you see a peregrine take a pigeon in mid-air, you'll know it's all been worth it.

In the Middle Ages, such a bird was the glitzy fashion accessory of the rich and the aristocratic. No nobleman could be without his falcon. What a sleek status symbol it is too. A Ferrari perhaps, or something more deadly to show off to your peers: a gun.

Now, the peregrine, and indeed many other falcons, has a habit that is very fortunate for the falconer. When a falcon 'downs' a bird, it tends to stand over it with its wings outspread as if protecting its quarry from others. This is called 'mantling' – which, for you etymology fans, comes from the Latin *mantellum*, meaning a napkin, towel, blanket or cloak. And while the falcon shields its victim in a feathery cloak, it devours its favourite bit: the head, especially the choice titbits of brain and eyes. Precisely the bits of a game bird the falconer, the butchers, and you and me, have no interest in.

And this bird is not just a bird of the wilderness. Its territory is much closer to home than the remote moorland and the lofty clifftops. I have seen one several times – or rather caught out of the corner of my eye the streamlined anchor shape – along the edges of Cornish cliffs. There is a place called Symond's Yat in Herefordshire where the picturesque river Wye makes a voluptuous bend through a limestone gorge and where it is almost impossible *not* to see a peregrine. And I've seen one take a pigeon from its perch on Tyne Bridge in the heart of Newcastle. In fact, in many ways, the heart of the city is *the* habitat. It has two perfect ingredients: lots of high places to nest and keep watch, and lots of pigeons.

The city falcon is such a beautiful example of man and nature side by side. And I mean *nature*, the old 'red-in-tooth-and-claw' nature, raw nature rubbing shoulders with bankers and secretaries eating their lunchtime sandwiches on the roof terrace. You don't have to know anything about birds, but you see this one in the middle of the city and you just know from some distant folk memory, from some dim instinct, that this is more than just a bird.

I remember seeing out of the corner of my eye a bird perched openly on a bare tree in the middle of Cambridge city centre and thinking, wow, this is something. Anyone, just anyone, I'm convinced, would have noticed it and thought the same thing. Not a pigeon, no – a kestrel? No, wait, wait, wait. Stop. It's too chunky. Kestrels have a slim delicacy. A sparrowhawk? No, those markings aren't 'sparrowhawk'.

This is a peregrine. The falconer's falcon. Perhaps, even, the falcon's falcon. I stared at it. Its body was solid with power, its yellow feet squeezing the branch. The whole *bird* looked like a trap, a deadly trap poised and ready to snap. It returned my stare with full raptor intensity. Did it know? Did it know that I knew?

That I knew it was special, not a kestrel or a sparrowhawk? Did it know that I was a worshipper? That I'd stopped at its feet to pay homage. Did it know that for those few moments I was numb with awe?

No, it didn't give a shit. As far as I know, it hadn't even bothered separating me from the gloomy November background. After a few seconds, it flew away. With hardly a flap, it slunk sideways with such indifference to me it seemed like a yawn on wings slanting down into the shrubby shadows.

Was it like that? Whenever I think about it, I feel there was something more. The way it flew away without flying. Perhaps its mastery of the air was such that it didn't fly. It just let go of the branch it was perched on. It unhooked its golden claws and let go. It stayed where it was and everything else moved: the branch, the tree, the garden, the city, the world just rolled away into the void, leaving falcon alone in the universe, the Master of Space.

FLEDGLING

Our children are beautiful. We want to protect them. We want to protect them so that they will grow up to live happy and productive lives. They will have children. Their children will be beautiful and they will want to protect them so that they will live happy and productive lives.

And so on.

That's it.

That's all there is.

Everything else is vanity.

Art, science, music, business, technology, shopping, barbecues, third-division celebrities eating millipedes in the jungle, the Ryder Cup, flying to the moon, robbing a post office at knifepoint and learning the Latin names for birds are just vanity, rococo baubles stuck haphazardly on the urge to have children, to survive, not to die. Now that we have lost God, there is only survival. God could have cured us of our mortality but we spurned Him, we spurned the doctor and he has abandoned us and taken the medicine with him. We are alone in eternity with nothing to do but try to cling desperately on to life with increasingly fragile fingernails. The child is the best way. A child affords you the taste of eternity more than writing a poem, painting a masterpiece or winning a war.

Our children, therefore, will always be beautiful because they are an incarnation of our desire to be immortal; a personification of our eternity; a living symbol of a triumph over death.

And so all children are beautiful. Not just the beautiful ones.

The ugly, the spotty, the gawky, the unlovely, the selfish, the vain, the ginger, the violent, the deformed and the sick. Adored by their parents; they're adorable. Human activities, the invention of the soul, the worship of the mind, the obedience to the heart, have obscured the message from nature to man. Somewhere scribbled in a jumble of mass and energy is the big, inescapable message, scrawled in gigantic letters on sub-microscopic particles, the message of life: your life won't last, pass it on.

Human culture and civilization has smudged this message but for the birds it's much more sharply focused. The breathless fever with which the adult bird attends to its offspring may seem inhumanly mechanical, but the message is the same.

Look at that baby – isn't she cute?

Ah, look, a baby seal – gorgeous eyes!

Look, a newborn calf – sweet!

Mummy, look, kittens – can I have one?

Wow, baby bunnies, where's my camera?

But there aren't many cute baby birds.

Young girls don't flock around the sparrow's nest to see her babies. They don't 'coo' and 'aah' at the youngsters inside.

Look into a bird's nest in the spring and recoil at the abomination inside. A troubling and troubled Jurassic shadow. Baby bird: a saggy-skinned, hairy-feathered, translucent trembling bag of shrieks; a dagger-faced abortion; a body like a severed scrotum with a blank, gawping, bug-eyed head.

But beautiful, of course.

See how the parents labour to feed this gaping mutant. See how they fuss over their mini-dinosaur. See how they want to pass life on!

And in these ugly bundles, the message is written in ruthless capitals. The strongest, largest chick gets another message from deep within its maze of molecules. It learns that it is the strongest, largest chick and it learns what that means. In a contest for food and survival, it has an advantage. It looks around at the competition. Its brother and sisters. Weaker by an hour maybe, lighter by a milligram. That's enough. No longer family, but enemy. A few stabs and the fight is over. And then, no longer dead brother, but food. Free food. More advantage. More chance of passing down my genes to eternity.

And so the surviving chick fledges. To the human eye, a pathetic no-man's land between baby and adult, between dependence and freedom, between nest and sky. Bigger than the adult but still helpless. In human terms, an adolescent. A student. A second-year undergraduate, maybe. Awkward, uncool, knowing everything and nothing at the same time, cocky and prepared to take some risks; prepared to learn to fly by learning to fall. It ruffles its feathers on the rim of the nest, stretches its puny wings, and flaps. This is its life for a few weeks now: stretching and flapping, punctuated with pitiful yelps for food.

Then one day, its flaps, its strength and the wind combine to free it from the nest and it glides a few feet till it reaches another branch – if it's skilful; or lucky. More likely it hits a wall; or the ground, where it will sit motionless and panting till the urge to fly hits again. But this a dangerous time. There is a banner in the sky: a huge advert written in fireworks, brass bands and tickertape, foghorns and mortars, perceptible only to animals, announcing that there is a fledgling on the ground, in the open. Cat, dog, fox, weasel, crow, magpie, kestrel, sparrowhawk, peregrine and gull will be on the scene in seconds. For the baby bird, it is down to luck or skill as somewhere the dice are being shaken for the biggest game of chance available.

So often you see them. March, April and May. In the gutter. Nuzzled by passing dogs and cats to assess their edibility. Pecked half-heartedly by crows. A little feathery pouch that once contained a lifetime's potential and now contains maggots. Ready for the earth; never ready enough for the sky. A long way from home. A sodden bundle that leapt, too soon, off the ledge into the unknown.

Is it a sad truth that for the sake of the species a child has to die?

Is dying all part of growing up?

It seemed to me that I had fledged successfully but that part of me had died leaving the nest.

But it was a long, long time ago ...

And, I think, on a different planet.

FEATHERED MEMENTOES

I somehow dragged my body out of the bookshop and manhandled myself back to college. Oblivious to aggressive words and gestures as I bumped my way through the crowded streets; oblivious, too, to Branfield, soaking wet, wearing just his underpants and some pond-weed, trudging back to his room; oblivious even to Kramer's sympathetic offer of chicken soup.

JJ went on a honeymoon and never returned to the shop. Kramer's lugubrious but vague predictions were right; though he claimed, of course, that it gave him nothing but anguish to be right yet again.

It wouldn't have happened nowadays. Mobile phones would have made this episode in my life, so huge then, so tiny now, an impossibility. But mobile phones had not been invented and neither had 'closure'.

In those days instead of closure I had to make do with confusion and bewilderment. And tears. In a little over three months, I'd discovered what I most wanted in the world: what seemed like the only thing I'd ever wanted and the only thing I would ever want. And not only that, but I had actually attained it. For just a few hours. Then I'd lost it.

I'd also rather oddly attained a deep knowledge, a keen interest and a strange affection for birds. The knowledge seemed bizarre and meaningless now. It was as if I had been burgled. I had been robbed of all my possessions, of everything that was dear to me, but the burglars had left behind the *Bumper Book of*

British Birds, fully illustrated with colour photos and a note saying, 'Enjoy!'

The problem with birds, though, is that they are public. They're there. Visible. In the sky. In your face. Loud. Brightly coloured. Ever-present. In all weathers, all seasons. But that's the joy of birds too! But no good if you don't want reminding of a loss.

Animals are private. Mammals are boring. They are quiet and secretive. If it were not for cars driving too fast late at night down country roads, I do not think anyone would know we had wild animals in Britain. They mainly operate at night and spend all day in burrows, lairs, setts, forms, earths. I mean, what a ludicrously long list of names for the rank holes where animals spend most of their time. Animals are generally brown or browny grey. They lurk, they smell, they snuffle furtively in dank places. Yes, I know, the badger, of course, has a brightly streaked black and white face, but it only comes out at night and you rarely see it except when it's dead on the roads in the morning. For a long time I thought badgers were only dead badgers. Rabbits, hares and hedgehogs are mainly known for their flat, splotchy appearance on our roads. Despite their predilection for playing Russian roulette by the side of our motorways, crows, rooks and jackdaws rarely end up as road-kill.

And, yes, the fox is an impressive animal with its dashing, orangey coat. But the fox would much rather not be seen by humans for all manner of reasons. If you see a mammal by day: a vole, a weasel, a rat etc, it is invariably scuttling away from you at great speed. It's in the nature of these creatures to get away from you as quickly as possible. Except to the viewer with elaborate and expensive infra-red cameras and a flask of strong coffee, these creatures are never the spectacle that birds are.

A visit to the zoo I think will confirm that, apes and monkeys apart, the furry, snuffly, stinking, hairy, browny-grey mammals are the dullest inmates. often indistinguishable from the fetid pile of straw they live in.

Outside the zoo, in day-to-day life, in the city, in the country, in the mountains, by the sea, there are only the birds. You can't avoid birds. And for me now, every one of them was going to be a painful reminder of the one and only girl ever.

A stinging memory of JJ would always be there: in the daily, everyday, inevitable cooing of pigeons; the insistent alarm of the evening blackbird; the unworldly, electric-blue streak of a king-fisher; the cruciform kestrel frozen in mid-air by the motorway's edge; the tinkling bells of long-tailed tits dancing through shrub-bery; the loud and lucid two-tones of a chiffchaff; the exotic yellowy-green bounce of a woodpecker as it cackles off to an invis-ible tree-trunk; the handsome and colourful jay, searching for acorns with its life mate; the drowsy, sweltering, midsummer song of the yellowhammer; the ghostly barn owl quartering the silence of twilight farmland; the plaintive oystercatcher scattering its musi-cal tears over the bleak marshes; the huge, slate-grey grace of a heron taking off from the reeds; the constant flitting, flicking, bouncing yellow of a wagtail down by the monochrome weir; the tame but feisty robin, sometimes posing for a Christmas card on a snow-capped gatepost, sometimes defending its territory right to the red-breasted death; the black and white strobing of a lapwing's acrobatics; the lightning blur of blood and feathers in the jet-stream of a sparrowhawk; the broad, slow-motion majesty of a marsh harrier; extravagantly coloured and sociable goldfinches, tumbling over the wasteland looking for seeds; clouds of starlings above the twilight streets; a skylark singing invisibly from the hidden heights of heaven; the tiny flame-headed goldcrest, tingling from the tall pines; a boldly perched thrush revelling in its rich repertoire of music, repeating its flutey hits over and over; the black and white serenity of an avocet gracefully sweeping through the tidal pools; a microscopic wren shattering the dawn with its gigantic song; the scornful seaside laughter of herring gulls and black-headed gulls; greenfinches, beautifully coloured and wheezing unmistakably; house sparrows chattering energetically along the eaves and gutters; swallows bringing summer from the south on their fragile wings; the snap of a flycatcher darting from its perch to grab a passing insect; jackdaws roosting and shredding the dusk with axe-like calls; the magnificent blue and orange of the upside-down nuthatch, guest of honour at the bird-feeder; a cormorant drying its wings on a dead tree, a disturbing snapshot of prehistory; a buzzard soaring and god-like on its broad feather-fingered wings; the treecreeper, tree-trunk brown and busy as a mouse, flying from tree to tree revealing a breast of snow; moorhens, close up, dark olive velvet, tiptoeing over the lily pads on their pale-green legs; the pink, blue, black, white, brown, olive chaffinch spluttering the arrival of spring; the nagging, non-stop call of the brashly coloured great tit; and, of course, swifts; the birds for whom flight was invented; another of JJ's favourites and the definition of summer: swifts, screaming in a sapphire sky.

Part Two:
Flapping
Around
A Lot

BIRDING FOR ADULTS

Twenty-five years' worth of dark, bright, deep, shallow, murky and quirky water had sloshed under the bridge between the day I first laid eyes on the JJ and the day when I found myself on stage in a civic hall in Cheltenham addressing a room full of 'twitchers' – serious birdwatchers. I was taking part in a 'forum' discussing a recent bird book. I felt that I was out of my depth and that somehow I was an interloper who shouldn't really be involved in matters 'bird'. I think the audience sensed this and more questions than I expected were directed at me. A middle-aged man in the fifth row put his hand up.

'So, can I ask, Rory, when did you first start twitching?'

'Well, it started as a nervous tic when I was at school,' I explained.

Laughter engulfed a twentieth of the auditorium.

Twitchers are serious birdwatchers. They take it seriously. They don't want 'upstarts' from the telly making jokes about twitching; especially a joke they'd heard so many times before; especially the most obvious pun available, a pun that faintly ridicules the whole world of birdwatching.

'Oh, when did I first start birdwatching? Oh that's easy,' I continued with a well-rehearsed lie. 'Well, when I was sixteen I was in this bookshop and I came across a book called *The Easy Bird Guide* and I think I must have misunderstood the title!'

At least double the laughter now. About six people. Yes, that's more like it. That's birdwatchers for you, you see. They're usually

of an age when the word 'bird' still has a dangerous double meaning. Apart from 'feathered flying animal', the word is racy slang
for 'girl'.

'Bird' is good for 'girl' though. I think it would be a shame to
lose it. It's neutral. Not too patronizing or demeaning. It's safe.
Bird. I mean, compare the word 'chick'. A chick: something
lovable, small, sweet, perhaps vulnerable, needs looking after,
nurturing and cherishing. And girls have 'hen nights', do they not?
And the Scotsmen use 'hen' as an endearment without any social
or political repercussions.

My teenage children tell me that 'bird' for 'girl' is not quite as
common amongst their peers, and their friends don't use it at all.
I attempted to verify this as part of my research.

'So when you and your mates go to a party, do you say things
like "Mmm, some nice birds here"?'

'No, Dad,' says my son as if he's talking tactfully to a person
with mental-health problems.

'What about "chick"? You know, "I like the look of that chick
over there".'

'You're a perve,' says my sixteen-year-old daughter.

'Totty?'

'Totty? Ha!' says the boy-child. 'Yes, we use that word if we're
taking the piss out of repressed middle-aged people.'

'What about "babe"? Would you say to a girl, "Hiya, babe"?'

'Babe is a fictional pig, Daddy, I wouldn't advise it,' warns my
daughter, shaking her head.

'When I was a boy growing up in Cornwall, we used to say
"maid". You know, "She's a nice maid" or "Have you got a maid
at the moment?"'

'What did they call *you*?' asks my son.

'Arsehole,' says my daughter.

So here I am, addressing a room full of birdwatchers in Cheltenham and feeling very much like an impostor. Not a bird-watcher, not a twitcher, not an ornithologist, but just someone who loves being outdoors, alone in the country, in the woods, on the moors, in the mountains or by the sea. And someone who happens to know the scientific names for most British birds.

'Is that true, though?' asked a lady in the audience. 'About your interest in ornithology? *The Easy Bird Guide* and all that? Or was it just an easy pun on the word "bird"?'

No, lady in the second row, it's not true.

'No. As a child I used to love drawing birds and colouring them in. And then in the first term of my second year at Cambridge, I met and fell in love with a girl called JJ who was into birds.'

And my interest in the subject became accidentally more public than I had anticipated while taking part in a television panel show called *QI*, on which I stumbled into giving the scientific names for various British birds, and while filming a programme called *Three Men in a Boat*, where I expressed my love for the odd 'twitch'.

'So do you go birdwatching now, then? Proper birdwatching?' asked somebody from the back.

'Well, my girlfriend, Tori, and I took it up properly about six or seven years ago. And we still go when we can; we've even got a 'scope now. But we don't go very far afield to do it. We keep it quite local. And we still haven't seen a golden oriole!'

A sweet, young woman near the front raised a tentative hand and asked with an embarrassed smile, 'What happened to JJ?'

Now, that *was* an interesting question.

NORFOLK RUSSIAN

My hometown of Cambridge is well placed for birdwatching. It's in East Anglia. The wetlands of the fens and the coasts and varied inland habitats of Norfolk, Suffolk and Essex are just a short drive away. Cambridge is but twenty miles from the headquarters of the RSPB at Sandy in Bedfordshire. Cambridgeshire boasts the birding paradises of Wicken Fen and the Ouse Washes; Norfolk has the Breckland, Titchwell and Holme bird reserves and Suffolk has Minsmere, the jewel in the RSPB's crown; which is also very handy for Southwold and the Adnams brewery.

Tori and I had decided to start our birdwatching career in North Norfolk. A love for nature and the outdoors was just one of the many things we had in common. Notable others included the joy of marriage and parenthood and the hell of separation and divorce. We had both emerged at the other end of the latter two and their attendant nightmares, wiser and stronger; and completely knackered. Birding up on the coast was a comforting symptom of a new period of serenity in our lives.

A convenient, straight line north from Cambridge would take us beyond King's Lynn to Hunstanton and then we could take the coast road eastwards. It was going to be a first for me. Being a western man, I knew nothing of the landscape, the people, the towns, the geography or history of North Norfolk. I'd heard of the Norfolk Broads and probably made comments about them being a girl-band from Norwich. I'm sure there probably was one, or has been one since. Norwich, I knew, was famous for Colman's mustard, and the football team was called the Canaries and played in yellow, a source of much amusement to schoolboy football fans. Delia Smith, their celebrity-chef fan, had not been invented back then. I had heard of Cromer crabs, which I am sure we Cornish schoolboys had assumed were something venereal peculiar to East Anglia. And I think Bernard Matthews' turkey farms might have impinged on our remote south-western consciousness with the way he said 'boootiful' in the advert, which also contained the line 'Bernard Matthews' turkeys; they're good and they're from Norfolk', giving rise to the joke slogan: 'Norfolk 'n' good!'

And at university, a fellow language student was a girl who came from a place called Wells.

'That's near Bath, isn't it?' I'd asked her.

'No, not that Wells; Wells-next-the-Sea.'

My, my, how I laughed. A placed called Wells-next-the-Sea. This gave the little-travelled Cornish boy a lot of mirth.

'Is it on the coast, then?' I laughed.

'Of course, it is. Hence the name.'

'Does it change its name when the tide goes out, then? Wells-not-quite-as-next-the-Sea-as-earlier-on-today?'

I was later to learn that Wells is in fact at least a mile from the open sea due to changes in the coastline, but it was until the sixteenth century a bustling seaport.

'You've some need to laugh,' said the Norfolk girl. 'You're from Cornwall; you have the daftest place names in Britain.'

Ridiculous. My home village is called Illogan and we are within easy reach of places called Prospidnick, Warleggan, Gwennap, Ponsanooth and Praze-an-Beeble.

*

The priority was accommodation. After an hour of yellow-paged frenzy, I was armed with a list of hotels, B&Bs and pubs in Norfolk. This was the huge first step. Tori and I were about to become real birdwatchers. We were actually going to go to find the birds, rather than have them find us.

We were about to change from people who liked birds to people who deliberately went out looking for species they had never seen before. We were about to write lists: birds seen that day; birds seen that year; total bird species seen in our life. We were about to cross the line. Move up to the next tier of twitching. We now had binoculars, a Thermos flask and an RSPB sticker on our car windscreen.

OK, some might say we were about to become even sadder, even more middle-aged or that we were taking a big step further along the autistic spectrum, but let them scoff; for us it was an adventure. All things considered it was just me and my beloved, spending time together in the countryside, sharing a new experience.

I was not having much luck. All accommodation in the whole of North Norfolk seemed to be taken.

'Ooh, no, I'm sorry. You did say *this* weekend?' asked one lady with the incredulous outrage of someone who'd been asked if I could take her teenage son away in a sack and tie him up in my basement for a kinky *soirée* I was having with some Middle-Eastern business clients of mine.

'Yes.'

'That's only four days away. I've been fully booked for this weekend since last year!'

'Oh, I thought, as it was only the middle of April—'

Her interruption came snapping down the line.

'Well, exactly. Haven't you heard of "birdwatching"? It's *the* time of year, you know. Some people have rooms booked continuously year after year. You won't find anywhere round here at this late stage!'

'Oh I see,' I said blandly, which for me, in the circumstances, was quite an achievement.

'You're clearly not a birdwatcher,' she added. Well, that almost did it. I just hoped I didn't bump into her one daybreak in the salt marshes. I wouldn't be responsible for the final destination of my spotting-scope.

I explained the situation to Tori.

'Apparently in April and May all accommodation within a hundred yards of a bird is taken. By birdwatchers, of all people.'

Tori tutted. 'Sad bastards. Why don't they get a proper hobby?'

'Well, at least it sounds as if we've hit upon the right time of year to start.'

There was one place left on my list. A pub that had rooms. Very close to Titchwell bird reserve. I called it, ready to adopt a different tone. A booming, cut-glass English voice answered.

'Good morning, Black Swan ...' Must be an aristocrat down on his luck. 'Vladimir Sobolnikovski speaking.'

That threw me off guard.

'Oh hi, Mr Sobolnikovski, my wife and I thought, at the last minute, you realize, that we fancied a bit of twitching this weekend. So just ringing around the usual places seeing if there were any cancellations to be had ... maybe? You know, sort of ... er ... last-minute cancellations ... er, coz obviously we normally book the year before, being twitchers and all that ... in April?'

I could hear pages being turned at the other end.

'No, sorry … no, wait. Yes. You're in luck. Cancelled last night. Best room in the place. Facing the marshes and the coast and what-have-you.'

'Sounds fantastic!'

Sobolnikovski went on, 'And I'll guarantee you see marsh harriers without leaving your bedroom.'

'Why, are they in the wardrobe?' There was a pause, then welcome laughter.

'What? Oh ha ha ha, yes. You silly arse!'

'How serious are you about this lark?' asked Sobolnikovski.

'Which lark? Sky? Crested? Short-toed? Thekla?' I replied.

'Well, you obviously know your stuff.'

'No, we don't. He just know the names of lots of birds. This is really our first "grown-up" expedition,' Tori admitted.

Sobolnikovski eyed me up and down from beneath a furrowed brow on hearing the phrase 'grown-up'.

He was refilling the shot glasses with bison-grass vodka as the clock behind the bar pinged midnight. The three of us were alone. The really grown-up twitchers were well into their serious early nights and probably dreaming of dark-eyed juncos or Corsican nuthatches, eagerly awaiting their five-thirty alarms.

'Where are you from then originally, Mr Sobolnikovski?' I asked our host.

'Oh that's not my real name, that's just a sham. I changed my name years ago. Didn't like the original.'

'What was it?'

'Anatoly Zhukovovitch ...' He paused. 'Too Russian-sounding.' He laughed uproariously. And so did we. I was beginning to like Vlad the Imbiber. This birdwatching business seemed most agreeable. And we hadn't even seen a bird yet.

'What time's breakfast?' asked Tori in a practical, female way.

'Six to nine.'

'That's a bit early, isn't it?' I spluttered through the vodka.

'Some of my residents think it's too *late*! Especially when the mornings get lighter. Every one of my residents this weekend is a serious birder, you realize.' He paused and knocked back the firewater adding, 'Apart from you two phoneys. Of course.'

A few more *za nashe zdorovje*s later and we were tucked up on top of the bed, fully clothed and snoring contentedly.

DANNY

Whisper it softly, but there are more birdwatchers than you think. It could be as many as one in five people. Look around you on a crowded train or at a party, and someone, possibly someone standing near you, is a birdwatcher. Another thing about your birdwatcher is that he is not always prepared to admit it. It's one of those things you do that you think should be kept to yourself. A dodgy secret. It just takes one person in the room to own up and say, 'I go birdwatching occasionally,' to make the other closet twitchers open up.

'Do you? Oh, so do I!'

'Where do you go?'

'Have you seen a purple gallinule?'

'I'm going next week, will you join me?'

'I saw a Montague's harrier last year!'

It's one of those things like voting Conservative, watching porn and liking Leonard Cohen songs: we all deny it, but a lot of us are doing it.

But surely you'd recognize them, wouldn't you?

Birdwatchers are country people, aren't they? Middle-aged anoraks with beards who like to make lists and get up early. Birdwatchers are low-level eco-warriors, aren't they? Into conservation and 'save the planet' and anti-bloodsports and all that.

Well, for a start most real 'country' people seem to be in favour of bloodsports and a large number of the people I go birdwatching with in Norfolk shoot for fun. Birds and animals, that is. But the point is that, in general, people have a fixed idea of what a bird-watcher is like. People like to have fixed ideas. It's easy. It's unchallenging. It's always unsettling when you find out, for example, that someone whose politics you despise likes the same sort of rock music as you. Or that someone you like and admire as a bit of a whacky, slightly louche renegade turns out to be a devoted church-goer; or a golfer; or a newt-keeper.

It's like discovering that your fusty old chemistry teacher likes to smoke the occasional spliff.

People feel easy with 'pigeon-holes'. This was brought home to me by a rude fellow I met one morning at RSPB Titchwell. I was lining up my binoculars on a group of people who had just seen a Montague's harrier – this was the next best thing to seeing the bird itself – when someone pulled my sleeve and said with unbridled surprise, 'Rory, what are you doing here? You're an Arsenal supporter!'

'Er, yes ... but I'm birdwatching.'

'Didn't you go to that game yesterday?'

'Yes, I did. But that was yesterday and today I'm birdwatching.'

'Didn't you have a few beers after the match?'

'Er ... yes. And then I went home. Then I went to bed, then I got up and then I came here. To birdwatch.'

'Yeah, but you're a Gunner and all that. What are you doing birdwatching up here?'

'Unlike you, I'm minding my own business!'

'Alright, alright! That's funny, though. I thought you was a look-alike, like.'

'Unfortunately not; now, perhaps you'd like to piss off?'

'Alright, alright; keep your hair on.' He backed away mumbling, 'Didn't mean to upset you, Mr Bremner.'

And I have a confession to make in this area too. Simon Barnes is the chief sportswriter for *The Times* newspaper. I have been a big fan of his sports writing for years. But there is another Simon Barnes: a birdwatcher, a writer of books about birds and a regular contributor to the RSPB magazine *Birds*. Only he isn't another Simon Barnes. He is the same one. For years I didn't realize this and I was quite shocked. If I'd met him one morning birding on the early morning reed beds I would have probably said, 'What are you doing here? You're the chief sports writer of *The Times*!'

To make it easy for you, I will sum up. There are three types of birdwatchers: 1) twitchers, 2) birders, and 3) my friend Danny.

Twitchers are the real thing. They are experts. Experts by experience, practice or by self-appointment. They know the common names of birds, most of the scientific names, they have always seen more birds than you, if not each other, and they claim to be able to tell apart closely related species like the chiffchaff and the Siberian chiffchaff, which are, in fact, impossible to tell apart.

They carry pagers, so if there is a rare sighting they can be bleeped, drop everything, lie to their boss and hurtle off to Dungeness to see a black-winged pratincole. The point of the whole thing for a real twitcher is to tick things off a list, like a green-wellied trainspotter. They want to see every bird in the world so, at twitching dinner-parties, they never have to begin a sentence with, 'Now, a bird I've never seen is …'

They suffer from a form of *Anoraksia nervosa*. It is predominantly a male thing. Semi-autistic list-learning.

There's a case for saying it's a little sad. But I'm aware I'm on dodgy ground on this one as someone who, for fun, used to spend a lot of school holidays learning lists of things: presidents of the United States; capital cities of the world; prime ministers of Britain; kings and queens of Britain; FA Cup winners since 1945, and the atomic numbers of the elements.

Twitchers have an uncanny way of making *your* birdwatching a little inferior. Here is a typical conversational snippet from the pub, post-twitching.

Me: I saw a marsh harrier today.

Twitcher 1: Oh, that thing's still about, is it?

Twitcher 2: Male, female or juvenile?

Me: Er … the greyish one.

Twitcher 3: Sure it wasn't the hen harrier?

Me: Er … not sure, really.

Twitcher 1: Blimey, that's back, is it? I haven't seen that since yesterday.

Twitcher 2: Sure it wasn't a Montague's?

Me: Er …

Twitcher 3: Well, white rump or no white rump?

Me: I think I'll get another pint.

All: That's very kind of you, don't mind if I do.

Or, conversely, they express their superiority by pleading ignorance and asking you for help. One particular incident springs to mind. I was once stopped at a bird reserve in North Norfolk by a man with a telescope, who laughingly said, 'Well, I really don't know. 'Scuse me, how are your pipits?'

'Not great,' I said, though I'm sure somewhere there was a long list of music-hall answers to this question.

'Look through here and tell me what that is.'

Obligingly I shut one eye and stood on tiptoe and leant over the eyepiece.

'I can't see anything.'

'Use the eye that's open.'

'Oh yes.'

I peered into the viewfinder. All I could see was a circular blur which changed after a few seconds to a circular blur with a black patch round the edge. And then an oval blur with brown spots. Then a grey oval blur with a man in a red baseball cap. And then a bright white circle with a green number at the top.

'Mmm,' I pondered. 'Tough one!'

I'd only heard of a meadow pipit, which is fairly common, so I assumed it wasn't that one that was troubling the expert.

'Not a meadow!' I offered with a laugh. 'I know a meadow pipit when I see one. Had a close encounter once when I was building a bypass in Cornwall. Strafed by one when I was having a shit!' I reminisced.

He did not follow up this piece of information with further questions.

'Yeah, I think we can safely say it's not a meadow.' Then he added with a sage frown: 'Rock.' Then, 'Water!'

I just stopped myself saying, 'Or scissors!'

Twitchers also have tons of elaborate equipment: not just binoculars, but spotting-scopes, telescopes and telephoto jibs with a flat screen to look at. These people are not happy unless they can see a goldcrest on the moon.

*

Birders are a less severe form of twitcher. They know about birds and like watching them. It doesn't matter to a birder that they haven't seen every known species. They won't drop everything to drive to Pembrokeshire to see a pallid swift. If they actually *live* in Pembrokeshire they might drop *some* things to see a pallid swift.

Birders like being outdoors, enjoy the countryside and probably have greenish, conservational leanings. Twitchers and birders dress the same, though. For practical reasons, to do with camouflage I suppose, dull greens, browns, beiges and blacks abound. A smattering of dark blue, and a few matt reds occasionally. Fluorescent yellow is not very common, even in this age of compulsory high-visibility jackets. Pinks are not very birdwatchery. You rarely see fuchsia, carnation or 'deep lipstick' among the reed beds of Minsmere. Very little cerise or 'candyfloss'. Neither would they wear tight, retro, lime-green loons, an orange Motorhead tour T-shirt or a beaten-up leather bomber jacket. These *are*, however, the sort of clothes worn by ...

... My friend Danny.

Now I suppose it's not really fair to group Danny with other birdwatchers. Until I met him, he wouldn't have been on the World's Top Billion Birdwatchers list. He was very much a beginner and he decided he'd give it a go because he thought if I enjoyed it, it can't be as 'twattish' as he thought it was. We'd met a few years earlier in a pub and he seemed to have a higher intelligence, superior social skills and a more advanced sense of humour than most of the regular clientele; though if you knew the Imperial Arms at all, you might think this a rather meagre compliment. It turned out that he was a bit of a computer whiz-kid, and as I have always been the village idiot of the IT community, Danny was forever in my house troubleshooting. I had decided to introduce him to the hobby of birdwatching, partly because I thought it would do him good to do something other than drink, smoke and womanize, and partly because he'd be a good person to have around at the end of a day's birdwatching, when we could sit together in the pub, drinking, smoking and womanizing. Well, that's not strictly true; I was living with Tori so a lot of my womanizing was theoretical, but Danny was single and lived alone but for his vegetarian cat so was relentlessly footloose and fancy-free. And I have never smoked. Danny, however, smoked on the duty-free-carton scale. I'm normally fairly libertarian about vice, and so long as I am not importuned, I encourage others with as much alacrity as possible to practise their vices. I'd even watch, if it were appropriate. But Danny was giving cause for concern. He was an amusing, bright, eager and loyal friend and I didn't want to lose him to something dark and nasty on an X-ray.

'Hello, guv'nor!' he said as I answered the phone.

'Oh, hi, Danny; didn't expect to hear from you on a Sunday morning.'

'Is it Sunday? Shit, I thought it was Tuesday. It's been a heavy week.'

'OK, tell me this, Dan: how many cigarettes have you had today?'

'Six.'

'Sure?'

'Yes.'

'How long have you been up?'

'Half an hour. Here, fancy meeting up for a beer or three?'

'I'm going up to the coast. Birdwatching.'

'Snatch, you mean?'

'No. Bird birds. Tweet tweet.'

'Ha ha ha – seriously?'

'Seriously.'

'Bloody hell, mate. I'm getting worried about you. You'll be turning veggie next.'

The following day in the pub, I tried to explain it to him. 'I suppose you have to do it to like it. Same as golf, I suppose. Thing about golf is, you either play it or hate it.'

'Oh, I hate golf, mate, it's a pillock's game!' he said, drawing in a lungful of death.

'I know; I hate it as well. But that's because I don't play it. There's no "in between". If you don't go birdwatching, you think it's for pillocks. A lot of people think I'm a pillock, coz I go bird-watching.'

'And other reasons,' he said, nodding. 'So what do you do, exactly?'

'Well, it's very simple. You go outside and look at birds.'

'Bloody hell, mate. Is that it?'

'Well, you take your binoculars and go out to the countryside, preferably, but not necessarily. Or the coast or woods or river or wherever, and watch the birds.'

'OK. Right, say I'm in a wood with my bins and I see a bird. What bird would I see in a wood?' he asks.

'Woodpecker, maybe.'

'Alright, I'm watching a woodpecker through my bins, then what do I do?'

This line of questioning was getting tough. He was beginning to sound like one of my children. I answered rather unconvincingly, 'Keep watching it for as long as you can.'

'Why, what's it going to do?'

'Fly away, probably; that's what birds do.'

'OK, I see.' He smiled in a humouring-me sort of way.

'It's hard to explain.'

'I'll tell you what, mate. I'm warming to golf.'

UNCOOL

'You sad bastard,' said my daughter in that no-way-to-speak-to-your-father way that daughters have nowadays when they speak to their fathers.

'It *was* the spoken English prize you got, wasn't it, Louise?'

'I'm sorry; I just can't believe you want to go birdwatching. I mean, what is the point?'

Such a huge question. A huge question to which the answer, if I had one, would seem, at best, microscopic.

'That's a very dangerous question to ask, Loulou.'

'Why?'

'Because any question beginning "what is the point of" is doomed to failure.'

'Why?'

'Because the logic will collapse like a house of cards until only one question remains: "What is the point of anything?"'

'What *is* the point of anything?' my son chipped in unhelpfully.

'What is the point of anything?' I thought for a while. 'Well, it's something to do to fill in time before you die.'

Jon replied, 'But everything is something to do to fill in time before you die, so why birdwatch, why not do something immediately pleasurable and rewarding?'

'OK.' I tried again. 'It's a way of getting out into the countryside.'

'But you can do that without birdwatching.'

'True, but it's a way of reminding yourself that humans, that "you", in fact, are not the only creature in the world; of reminding you that we share our planet with other living things that are just as important as us.'

'Who says they're just as important as us?' My son was beginning to annoy me. I hoped he wasn't going to grow up to be a lawyer. 'And you can know we share our planet with other creatures without going out to look at them.'

'Alright,' I said, determined not to back down. 'If you go out birdwatching with me, it would give me pleasure; it's a way I can do something I like and spend time with my children.'

Louise's turn. 'So you want to spend time with your children when they're being bored? Why not spend time with them doing something they want to do, something that gives them pleasure?'

'Yes,' Jon added. 'Like *not* going out birdwatching.'

Loulou laughed.

They were turning into quite a double act, these two. The only plus for me was that I had never experienced them being so united, so 'on the same side', so 'not scratching each other's eyes out'.

Then Jon asked the predictable question. 'Isn't birdwatching the same as trainspotting?'

I was ready. 'What? I can't believe you said that! Where's the skill in trainspotting? Trains follow timetables. You know exactly where each train is going to be at any time. Even if you're trying to spot an obscure bit of rolling stock you know it's not going to fly off when you approach it. Or go and hide in a bush. Trains behave in a predictable way; there's nothing exciting about their behaviour: they don't fly, they don't sing, they don't think, they don't surprise you!'

I was pleased with this. Jon's face betrayed the formation of a smart-arse comment.

'They sometimes turn up on time. That surprises me!'

'Well, let's put it this way,' I went on, 'what would the world be like if there were no birds?'

'Birdless.' Where *did* he get this irritating habit of fatuous banter?

'Wouldn't you miss the sound of birdsong in the woods?'

'I wouldn't miss it at five on a summer's morning when I've got a hangover and I'm trying to sleep.'

I hadn't realized my son knew what a hangover was. He must have been showing off.

'OK, birds are nice to watch because they're lively and interesting, and they make nice sounds and have pretty colours!' There was no immediate answer coming from my children, though if they'd known more about birds they might have said that some make repulsive sounds: moorhens, magpies, bitterns, corncrakes, pheasants, peacocks; and that a large number of them are not pretty and colourful, in fact, most of them are variations of brown and grey.

'And they can fly; that's impressive – they can fly without an aeroplane, we can't.'

Aha, I had them.

My son was quickly on the attack again. 'OK, but who invented the aeroplane? Man. Not a bird. Not a red-knobbed hornbill!'

Loulou laughed.

'So, Jon, how come you've heard of a red-knobbed hornbill?'

'I was watching a programme about it last night. Very interesting.'

'I see; so you were watching a programme about the natural history of birds?'

'Yeah, well, I was hoping to watch the beach volleyball but I couldn't find the remote.'

'OK. So we invented the aeroplane and loads of other clever, technical things because we are intellectually so far ahead of most other species on our planet; surely that very fact means we are in the unique position of having control over our planet's future. So we can look after it and all the species on it.'

Jon was undeterred in his role as non-twitching *Advocatus diabli*.

'How much control do we really have? Volcanoes, tsunamis, earthquakes, meteors, disease: a lot is out of our control.'

'Well, we can control some of it.'

'Besides, what's birdwatching got to do with saving the planet and safeguarding our species as well as others?' asked Louise.

'It's to raise your awareness. If you start learning about birds, and other creatures, then you will "feel" for them: an affection; a sense that they belong in the world as much as we do. All creatures are equal.'

As soon as I said this I realized I would be hearing some of my own words thrown back at me. I had often argued that as you save badgers you endanger bumble bees. Who chooses? Why badgers over bumble bees? I once worked on a programme about the endangered European eel. This mysterious creature is threatened by a parasitic nematode worm that destroys its swim bladder and causes it to drown. But who decides we save the eel and threaten the nematode worm? The red kite was once a pest but we reintroduced this glorious bird so successfully that it will soon be a pest again, so now we are talking about controlling it. Who is man to play God? I have no answer to this and was glad my children didn't pick me up on it. Nor did they mention the animals and birds we don't manage to work up an affection for as we observe or study them: the repulsive marabou stork or the scary lappet-headed vulture or the irritatingly dim corncrake which evolution seems to be doing its best to eliminate.

'Are you saying, then' – my daughter again – 'that our intelligence gives us the duty to look after all other creatures because they can't do it themselves and we can?'

'No, not at all. We are not looking after other little fluffy and furry things; we're looking after ourselves. We *need* a bit of wild. We need a bit of wilderness. We need to be in touch with wild nature. The countryside is better for us than the city. There is less stress where you can see animals, birds, trees, fields and rivers.'

'Like on the telly!'

'Shut up, Jon. People feel more at ease near nature, they recover from illness quicker and they feel healthier. It's been scientifically proven.'

Thank goodness they didn't ask me for my references and bibliography. I was on shaky ground but I do remember reading somewhere about a strictly scientific study that proved exactly what I was saying.

'The more wilderness there is, the more human we are. Man has, after all, lived almost 99 per cent of his life in the wild. To make the world a better place for all other creatures is to make the world a better place for us. Going out into the countryside and looking at birds raises your awareness of wild things and that is a step, a small step, a microscopic step, maybe, in saving the planet for humans.'

An excited smile lit up my daughter's face. 'Hey, *Friends* is on in a minute!'

'Loulou, it will help you look outside your tiny, private and egocentric world, the world of school, social life, television, Xbox, Facebook and *Friends*. It'll make you open your eyes and see what there is in the world. Can you name all the flowers, trees and birds you see in a day?'

I had lost Louise now, who was sorting through the remote-control handsets.

Jon answered instead. 'Why would I need to?'

'Supposing you're stuck in the middle of a forest and desperate for food: would you know which trees were useful and which were poisonous?'

He hit back straight away. 'Ah, so you are saying that knowledge of the flora and fauna of a place is a purely functional thing, the end of which is helping with, or ensuring, one's personal survival?'

'No, that's just an extra perk, I suppose.' I took a deep breath. 'Alright, alright, I've worked it out. The point of birdwatching is inexplicable. It's pointless except in so far as it's fun for the people who find it fun. Aha, I've got you here! What's the point of cricket? It's dull, boring and repetitive. Oh yes, but some people find it fun. And golf? That seems to be the epitome of pointlessness. Trainspotting, collecting beer mats, yoga, astronomy – in fact, work. What is the point of work? Ah well, you have to work, don't you?'

'Why?' said Jon.

'To get money.'

'Money for what?'

'So you can eat.'

'What's the point of that?'

'You've got to eat to stay alive.'

'Why, what's the point of staying alive?'

As I said, I love arguments that begin with: 'what's the point of … ?' They can only have one end. If one thing is pointless, everything is pointless.

'So let's go birdwatching then.'

A 'tut' from the girl-child.

'After *Friends*, of course.

'Do we have to, Daddy, it's really boring,' she whined.

'How do you know it's boring if you haven't tried it?' I said, sounding distressingly like my parents.

'Er … how do we know it's boring if we haven't tried it? It's not sitting in a nice warm room watching *WWF* on telly. It's standing outside in a field in the cold. It's watching, or trying to watch, small things that are continuously flying off to avoid being watched by you. It's trying to separate one dull brown thing from another. It's looking directly into the sun at a black silhouette which could be—'

'I think you mean "continually" not "continuously",' I interrupted – and, yes, I know it was a pathetic interruption. Even by my lofty standards of pedantry it was unnecessary. But I had to stop him. Not least, because he was beginning to sound like a lawyer again, and no self-respecting parent wants that of their child.

'Neither of you mind exercising; just think of this as a walk in the fresh air.'

A wince from Louise at the mere mention of the dread phrase 'fresh air'.

'How do you know the air is fresh? I mean, who defines or quantifies the "freshness" of "fresh air"?'

Don't you love teenage boys?

'Shut up, you two. *Friends* is starting.'

The eventual deal was four episodes of *Friends* in exchange for a walk in the country with some mild birdwatching.

'And don't interrupt every five minutes asking stupid questions like "Which one is Ross?"' said Louise.

'Or "Why do girls in American sitcoms always look anorexic?"' added Jon.

I promised and we started watching the first one.

'Which one is Buffy?' I asked.

QUITE INTERESTING

A stranger came up to me and said, 'You're full of shit, aren't you?'

Ah, one of the unforeseen perks of being on television is the charm of the passing stranger.

'Sorry?' I ask politely, as always; there's no other way, unfortunately.

'Yeah, I saw you on that B&Q thing.'

'Oh, *QI*, you mean.'

'Yeah, whatever. And you was going on about birds and their scientific names and all that bollocks.'

'Oh, yes, I remember.'

'I mean, fair play, but what's the point of knowing all that toss?'

A very good question, I concede inwardly.

'No offence, like. My gran likes you!'

What *is* the point of knowing all that toss? Well, as you know, I do love questions that begin with 'what is the point of … ?'.

Well, yes, I do know the scientific names for most British birds, and as I have told you about the girl called JJ, you now know why.

There are about a hundred British birds you can regularly see in a year, so it's not a long list to learn, especially if there's love and happiness at the end of it. But knowing the scientific names for birds is not particularly useful. Maybe it is *Quite Interesting* but it doesn't mean you know anything about birds. A lot of serious ornithologists and world-class 'bird people' don't bother that much about it.

I know Bill Oddie is indifferent to it. I once met him socially and the first thing I said to him was, 'Hey, Bill, here's one for you: *Plectrophenax nivalis.*'

And you know what, quick as a flash, he said, 'Oh fuck off, Rory, don't start that crap!'

(He wasn't even close; it was snow bunting.)

The scientific names are a sort of universal language. You may be talking to a Russian and not know the Russian for 'kestrel' and he might not know the English for *poostelygya.* But if one of you says *Falco tinnunculus,* you're laughing. Well, maybe not laughing. I can think of funnier things than talking about kestrels to a Russian twitcher, but you get the idea. And I should point out that *Falco tinnunculus* means 'little-bell-ringing falcon'. (No, I've no idea either.)

But a close examination reveals that neither the English names nor the scientific names are that precise or appropriate anyway.

Take the *Laridae* family.

They're gulls. *Larus* is a seagull.

Yes, seagulls!

Come on, you know: white birds that steal the fish and chips out of your hand in Brighton.

They're the noisy ones that like landfill sites and follow dust-carts about.

They're all fairly big and you'll certainly know if it's a *Larus* that has crapped on your car windscreen.

One of the commonest gulls in Britain is the black-headed gull. Now, careful. Most of the year its head is white with a dark smudge just behind the eye. Even in the summer the adult does not have a black head at all, but a chocolate-brown hood on the face.

The scientific name for the black-headed gull should be

Larus melanocephalus, which means 'black-headed gull', but *Larus melanocephalus* is the scientific name for the Mediterranean gull, which, unlike the black-headed gull, has a black head. The scientific name for the black-headed gull is *Larus ridibundus*, which means 'laughing gull'. From the Latin *ridere*: to laugh, of course. ('Ridiculous', 'risible', you get the idea.) And, you guessed it: the black-headed gull has a call that is very much like a wild, cackling laughter.

But what about the bird that is called the laughing gull? Ah, well, the scientific name for the laughing gull is *Larus cachinnans*, which means 'gull with the wild cackling laughter', not unlike the black-headed gull.

It's dead easy, really, isn't it?

Oh, by the way, most people call the laughing gull the 'yellow-legged gull' nowadays, as it's the only gull with yellow legs. Apart from the other ones.

As you know, most gulls are large, white underneath and grey on the back and some have black heads, though not, as we have seen, the black-headed gull. The commonest gull in Britain with a grey back is the herring gull. Now, before you say anything, this bird does *not* look anything like a herring. However, it may possibly eat herrings. This is not reflected in its scientific name, *Larus argentatus*, which mean 'silver gull', and is because of its grey back. *Argentatus*: silvery, get it? Latin *argentum*: silver. Chemical symbol for silver? Ag. (Atomic no. 47: if you're making notes.) And Argentina, the country famous for its silver mines on the banks of the river Plate (from the Spanish *plata*, meaning silver). Remember the flamenco guitarist, Manitas de Plata, 'little silver hands'? You see it all ties up nicely.

Now, less common than the herring gull is the common gull. This is *Larus canus*, which means 'grey gull', to distinguish it from the more common herring gull, which has a grey back. But just to cheer you up, the little gull is a little gull and its scientific name is *Larus minutus* ... say no more!

And what about *Oenanthe oenanthe*? A lovely bird. A joy to see hopping across farmland. Bouncing from cowpat to clod. Keeping its distance but affording you very good close-ups through your binoculars. Not much in the scientific name, but, in case you're wondering, it has nothing to do with *oenanthe*: the flowering plant that looks superficially like celery but exudes a yellow juice that stains the skin and is highly poisonous.

No: it's the charming wheatear, with the unmissable bright white rump clearly seen when it flies. However, its name has nothing to do with 'wheat', 'ears' or 'ears of wheat'. The name is all to do with its 'white arse'.

No, I kid you not.

White arse > wheet-earse > wheat-ears > wheatear. Love it.

And that's also an example of a repeated Latin (or Greek) word. There are many of these. *Anser anser*, for example. *Anser* is the Latin for a goose. So the *Anser anser* my friend, is (not blowing in the wind wind) but the 'goose goose', or more properly the greylag goose.

This is our commonest goose. It looks like a browny-grey, barred version of a farmyard goose. It is, in fact, the direct ancestor of the domesticated bird. And as its scientific name suggests, it is the goose's goose. The goosiest goose of all. The basic unit of goosedom.

Then there's *Regulus regulus*. Britain's smallest bird. The unfeasibly cute goldcrest. Tiny and olive green with a fiercely yellow and black crown. It deserves its Latin appellation: 'little king little king'. In French *roitelet*, in Spanish *reyezuelo*, in Italian *regolo* and in Greek the same again, *chrysovasilisko*, little gold king.

Another is *Cygnus cygnus*. Those of you with a pub-quiz level of Latin (or astronomy) will know that *cygnus* is the swan. (A baby swan is a cygnet, of course.) In the bird world, *Cygnus cygnus*, the basic unit of swanhood, is, surprisingly, *not* our very own, very common mute swan, but the whooper swan. A little smaller than our swan and less elegant with a yellow, as opposed to orange, bill. Clearly, though, it was considered by whichever nineteenth-century taxonomist named it to be just about as swanny as any swan could be. If you're not a pub-quiz regular and don't know this already, you may be interested to know that the mute swan is Britain's largest and heaviest bird, and the one with the most feathers. And it is a bird to be seriously avoided if it has a nest full of eggs or young.

The mute swan is also officially protected by the Queen. She can quite often been seen at night with her machine-gun, patrolling the perimeter fence of the swan enclosure.

One of my favourites, and very easy to remember, is the wren, one of Europe's smallest birds. The tiny wren moves fast and furtively over short distances. It lives in holes in banks, trees or hedges, under overhangs or deep in low-lying bushes. In German, it's the *Zaunkönig* (king of the fence), in Dutch the *Winterkoning* (winter king), in Greek *trypofrahtis* (hole-in-the-hedge maker); its scientific name is *Troglodytes troglodytes*. A man who lives in a hole in the ground.

Quite interesting.

Well, I think so.

MARSH HARRIER
AND BREAKFAST

A cursory grope around my immediate vicinity (warm woman with all the duvet wrapped round her to my right, bedside table, clock, knocked-over glass of water and soaking watch to my left) revealed that Tori and I were not down in the reed beds looking for warblers. Suddenly the loudest birdsong in the world struck up.

I groaned.

'What are you grunting about?' she asked.

'It was a groan, actually. That bloody bird.'

'Wren,' mumbled the pile of bedclothes.

'No, that's not a wren. Wrens are tiny!'

'Size is not important,' she said laughing in a way I did not find particularly funny. 'It's a wren. It is loud, but it's louder if you've been drinking vodka till two in the morning.'

An important birding lesson there: small, dull bird: big, interesting song. Big, coloured bird: small, dull song.

Our arrival at breakfast was very much at the 'till nine' end of the 'six till nine' range. The clock in the breakfast room said 08.57.02. Made it! We chose a table for four, as it was just me and Tori and the hangovers. Vlad was nowhere to be seen. Typical of these Russians. Can't take it. They talk the talk, but can't walk the walk.

A bustling old lady hurried to our table to take our order. One eye scarcely left the clock. The remaining seconds of her shift were running down. The last thing she wanted was a couple of dilettante birders extending her working day.

'You're cutting things fine. I think the kitchen's still open.'

I looked at the clock. 08.59.31.

'Not nine o'clock yet,' I informed her.

She tutted and her face contorted with disapproval. But that could have been caused by the invisible cloud of bison-grass vapour reaching her nose.

'No sign of Mr Sobolnikovski this morning I see,' I continued, chatty and amiable, pretending I didn't have the mother and father of all headaches. And the children, the grandparents, the grand-children, some distant cousins who'd turned up unexpectedly and the neighbours who'd just dropped in. 'I expect he had a late one!' I chuckled.

'Mr Sobolnikovski was up and out at six this morning, horse-riding down on the beach. Same as every morning.'

These Russians, eh? They know how to drink.

As is customary for English people with stinking hangovers, we just ordered a grapefruit juice and coffee … followed by the full English breakfast with two fried eggs, the optional black pudding, extra sautéed potatoes and fried bread, white toast and marmalade. And excellent it was, too. Tori said she couldn't believe she'd eaten so much considering how awful she felt.

'Well, let's go watch some birdies, then.'

We were happy. Dehydrated but happy. We kissed and left the table to go back to our room to fetch our binoculars, just stopping off briefly while Tori popped into the ladies' to vomit violently for fifteen minutes.

It was a fine day. Perfect birdwatching weather. By precisely 10.30 a.m. we were back in bed.

'It's a lovely day,' I said, snuggling down under the bedclothes.

'Oh yes, that reminds me,' moaned Tori. 'You couldn't shut the curtains, could you? That sun's hellish.'

I got up and glanced casually out of the window as I closed one of the curtains—

Wow! It was incredible. 'Tori, Tori, come here quick! Look at this!' This was urgent. She joined me groggily at the window.

A bird like none I'd seen before, barely twenty yards from the hotel, just over the car-park wall flying low and slow across the edge of the reeds. It seemed huge. Long, broad, silvery-grey black-tipped wings held in a V glide in between lazy flaps. Dark brown shoulders. Underside streaked orange and brown. A pale, creamy head. Big claws and the telltale hooked beak of a raptor. It obligingly swept up and down the waterlogged fields by the marsh. It was almost saying, 'This one's for you. You two beginners. This is a freebie.'

Incredible. We'd seen our first marsh harrier. There are several species of harrier and, yes, they do get their name from the word 'to harry'. To pester or harass. The Old English is *hergian*, to 'torment with hostile attacks'. What a fab verb! This, of course, describes its method of hunting and catching prey. The scientific name for this one, the marsh harrier, is *Circus aeruginosus. Circus*, as you know, is from the Greek for 'circle' or 'something generally ring-shaped', as in the place where children get bored or frightened by clowns, moth-eaten ponies and abused lions. The harriers were observed to search out their feeding ground in wide, circular glides, the circle decreasing until its prey was cornered. *Aeruginosus* refers to the bird's colour. More obvious in the females and juveniles. It means, roughly, 'rust-coloured', from the Latin *aes* meaning 'copper or bronze'.

A marsh harrier. Tori and I smiled at each other. This was first on our list of 'great bird moments', and not a bad start to our first day as real birdwatchers. We hugged. And, without a second to lose, we got back into bed.

BUT THEY CAN FLY

The idea of flight bewitches us. Because we cannot fly, we are enthralled by those who can. Birds. They can leave the ground. They can rise above it all. They can take flight. Think of that: 'take flight'. 'Take flight' means to run away. To escape. They escape.

We may have invented aeroplanes, but anyone who has seen a peregrine falcon take a pigeon at 200 mph and then disappear knows what flying is really all about.

Gravity can do nothing but watch helplessly as a kestrel spins into the wind and glides to an effortless standstill. Any day. Every day. The M25, for example: an obscene circular weal on the landscape, but there, above the daily drudgery of traffic, is the kestrel. Motionless. Whatever the air, the wind, the earth's magnet and the planet's orbit decide to do, the kestrel chooses its perfect spot. It makes its adjustments and freezes in midair. A stark-still, elegant dart, stencilled on the white sky.

Kestrel, a goodie for beginners. Easy to see because they like the fringes of man's infrastructure: roads and railway lines. These form a barrier to small rodents, which therefore tend to be more abundant here. Their movements, as cars or trains go past and frighten them, become more visible in these places. Kestrels also see parts of the spectrum invisible to humans. This means that the rodents' marker of trails of urine seem startlingly bright to the kestrel. And it was precisely a kestrel that did it for Jon and Louise.

'Look at that, Daddy. Is that a bird?'

'Blimey,' said Jon, squinting into the sun at a static silhouette. 'It's not moving!'

'A kestrel. It points itself into the wind and hovers. It's not hovering now, not flapping its wings, well, not noticeably because the wind's obviously blowing just the right speed. Usually they're flapping like mad to stay in one place. It's looking for a vole or mouse or something. Watch, it will drop down on something in a minute. Or it might drop to just a few feet from the ground and pinpoint its victim and then go in for the kill. Watch this!'

The bird had clearly got something in its sights. The children would love this display of cruel and ruthless nature. 'Keep watching!'

All four of us, me, the children and the kestrel, were stock-still, waiting for that critical moment of attack. Then, all of a sudden, the kestrel flew off and disappeared into some trees.

'They sometimes just fly away as well.'

My son followed its departure. 'I think that's cool, the kestrel.'

Ah, yes. Birds of prey are definitely boys' toys.

The kestrel (*Falco tinnunculus*) is a deeply satisfying bird to see. Almost impossible not to see one every day. And certainly impossible not to identify. Fluttering, or motionless, in the sky above a road or railway line, homing in on a vole. In outline, a smooth, chestnut-coloured paper-aeroplane with long tail and narrow, angular wings. And when motionless and against a pale sky, a cross. A crucifix, perhaps. The Christ on the Cross of Gerard Manley Hopkins' kestrel poem 'The Windhover'.

And birds of prey are easy. Not to identify, mind you. Take it from someone who has spent hours underneath a Bonelli's eagle thinking it was a booted eagle. Or was it the other way round? In the end I decided to call it an 'eagle-beginning-with-b'. (The word 'beagle' had already been taken.) No, birds of prey are an easy way in to appreciating birds. Especially for blokes. They are attractive, fast, smart, crafty and, at some stage, they tear other living things to shreds. And men like women, too. And the great thing is, by and large, they glide, soar or hover in the open, clear skies. So easy to see. And they're generally on their own.

I suppose there is some sense in that. Blue tits do not tend to make social groups with sparrowhawks, just as we don't tend to invite psychopathic serial killers round for dinner (oh, and please bring a carving knife!).

But the sparrowhawk does not like to be too conspicuous. It relies on stealth and ambush. It flies low and fast and its short, broad wings make it highly manoeuvrable. It can zigzag between trees, change direction and suddenly appear from behind a hedge to grab a chaffinch that 'will never know what hit it'. I had seen three sparrowhawks before I realized I had seen any at all. In fact, I was beginning to think that 'a sparrowhawk' was not an object at all, but an event. This is how it goes: there is stillness. A polite garden tucked away in a well-behaved suburban street. The clean feeders are well stocked with nuts and seeds. All the regulars are there. Same lot, every day; wonderful to see them all, though. Blue tits, great tits, chaffinches, greenfinches, sparrows and, if you're very lucky, maybe a nuthatch. But the scene is one of serenity. Humanity on the fringes of nature. Nature on the fringes of humanity. Man interfering with nature in a benign way. We love it. The bird table: for birds, children and old people. And then—

What was that? A bolt of feathered lightning. A whoosh. A dark, grey-brown flash. Noise. Alarms. The garden is now empty. Empty but for a few fluffy, blue-ish feathers, floating in the air, a bright red streak on the bird table and the stillness of death. Ladies and gentlemen – the sparrowhawk.

'It's not really birdwatching you do, is it, Dad?' Jon asked. 'It's just walking in the country. Not even in the country, always. I mean, you could walk to a pub three miles away and if you see a bird you can identify you call it birdwatching, when it's really going to the pub!'

'Don't give my secret away, son!'

The mini-idyll was spoiled by the tinny ringtone of a mobile phone.

'Oh, Lou, I can't believe you brought your mobile phone with you.'

'I only brought one of them!' she said, scowling. 'Hey, Rozzie, hi, how are you? … No, I'm out at the moment … no, I'm with Jon and my dad … What are we doing? Oh, we're … um … we're out.' Louise looked at me sheepishly. 'We're shopping in town!'

DANNY SEES A BIRD

It's hard to explain the appeal of watching birds. They are not even fluffy and cuddly. There are some cute little ones and some brightly coloured ones but they are, in the main, spiky and reptilian with blank cold eyes. They don't do anything special when you watch them; just get on with their lives. But maybe that is special. They eat, have sex, have children and die. And they are not that worried by us. Animals avoid us, but birds can always fly away, so they are taking less of a risk in being around. And they've adapted to us fairly well. If you watch crows on the motorway scavenging the dead carcass of a hedgehog, a pheasant or even a crow, they move out of the way when a car comes hurtling towards them. But they've learned to time it very well. You can see a rook stabbing at the dead body, casually stepping aside as a car bombs past, then nonchalantly returning to its food seconds later. And be honest: you don't see many dead crows on the carriageway. Birds are there, doing their thing, right under our very noses.

But it's hard to explain all this, especially to someone like Danny who is, shall we say, rather 'urban' in most ways.

By day he drives around the country, visiting factories, schools, hospitals and offices, servicing computers and secretaries, and by night he's salivating over or dropping ash on some poor girl at a back-of-the-pub rock gig. I was determined to get him out birdwatching. No lifestyle and twitching can be mutually exclusive. Unless your lifestyle is shooting as many birds as you can as they fly over your house. But let's not get sidetracked into talking about the French in these pages.

'I think Danny needs a hobby,' I had said to Tori.

'He's got a several hobbies: smoking, drinking, shagging ...'

'No, that's his work; he needs something to take his mind off those things; something to help him relax.'

'He needs a girlfriend,' said Tori.

'Ah, that's the girl's solution to everything, isn't it?' I teased her. 'You wives don't like the idea of there being single, rogue males wandering around the jungle. Perhaps you're worried he'll lead me astray.'

'He was definitely a different person when he was with Diana. Much nicer.'

'Yes,' I agreed, 'but she broke his heart. That's the trouble. He's frightened of being hurt again, you see. He suspects all girls are like her and will end up dumping him.'

'Mmm,' said a sceptical Tori. 'I think that's his excuse to behave the way he does. He needs company.'

'He's got Danny the cat. The only vegetarian cat on the planet.'

'Yes, but the cat is Diana's, isn't it?'

'Yes, that was a horrible irony.'

Diana was the love of Danny's life. They were together for five years, but you always sensed that her mind and her life were elsewhere. She'd had a couple of flings towards the end and it became obvious the relationship was doomed. About a year before the official split, Danny bought her a cute, fluffy kitten and named it after himself so that if she left him, she'd have to take it with her and always have a reminder of him. When she did leave him, she left the cat as well. But not before she'd trained it to be vegetarian. Something she didn't manage with Danny.

'He's into photography, isn't he? He was good. He was forever taking photos of Diana,' she reminded me.

'Well, he's still got a lot of gear, but I don't think he's done it for ages. It's hard to hold a camera and light a cigarette at the same time.'

I knew, of course, that birdwatching was never going to be 'up Danny's street', nor would it 'save' him from the devil, but it would be a very new and different experience for him.

Oh, and it might stop him telling me I was such a sad anorak if *he* dabbled in it occasionally.

I have always tried to avoid encouraging friends to do things just because I enjoy doing them. I was lobbied for years by people saying things like:

'You should go skiing, Rory, you'd love it!' I loved the scenery but that was about it. I loathed the queuing for hours for a chair-lift to go very slowly up a mountain, only to come down it again in thirty seconds. (Oh, and I liked the mugs of hot wine as well.)

'You should go to a grand prix, Rory, you'd love it!' Boring. Some very attractive women hanging around in tight leather, though, but not enough to endure the smell of rubber and petrol and the sound of the Doppler effect.

'You should go to an opera, Rory, you'd love it!' Er ... no comment.

'What's so great about birdwatching, then, Rory?'

Er, nothing's great about it. I like doing it occasionally; that's all.

To be honest, I had little hope and less expectation of ever getting Danny to the woods, hills, moors or rivers with a pair of binoculars, and that was fine, but something I had said about birds one time had clearly stuck in his mind. The next time I met him he was visibly excited. He could hardly hold his fag still to light it.

'Mate, you won't believe this. I've just seen a bird. It was amazing, mate. I couldn't wait to tell you!'

'What sort of bird?'

'Oh, mate, it was a … er … a bird. A dicky bird!'

'A dicky bird?'

'Yeah, a little … er … tweety-tweet dicky bird!'

'Can you describe it?'

'Well, this is the thing, it was incredible. Such markings and colours. Probably quite rare. I've never seen anything like it before, I know that, hand on heart, mate.'

'Go on.'

'Little. Really small. I mean, mate, it was a fucking cute little tweety thing.'

'Colours?'

'I've written everything down here, look.'

He produced a torn piece of cardboard, which had once housed twenty Silk Cut, and on it was a drawing and some writing. It was actually quite good. Danny had made some detailed and comprehensive notes. More than I'd ever done before or since. I read it.

'Dicky bird. Tiny. In bush by dustbin. Yellow tummy. Blue head. White side of head. Black eye-liner. Blue bonce. Greeny-blue back and wings. Blue tail.'

That was very good. It was a textbook piece of fieldwork, albeit no field was involved as such. Danny had done it all from the comfort of armchair, fag and can of London Pride. But it was well described.

Danny had seen his first blue tit.

'I can't believe I've never seen one before! Are they rare?'

'No, very common. One of our commonest birds, in fact.'

'So why have they been hiding from me?'

Well, Danny, in a way you've been hiding from them. But this one wasn't the first one he'd seen, literally, with his eyes. This one was the first one he'd seen with his brain, his heart. And now he knew it was called a blue tit, and from then on he would see them all the time and become joined to a new bit of the planet. As the lovely JJ had said all those years ago, the name connects you to something, and to others who also know the name. You begin to share the world because of the name. I wouldn't lumber Danny with these musings just yet.

A blue tit is a great start.

Parus caeruleus could wait as well.

LATE SHIFT IN THE REED BEDS

We were up again at the crack of lunchtime and were back in the bar of the Black Swan to have a restorative pint of orange juice and fizzy water. There are many unwritten rules of birdwatching and I think our late night with the Rooski had broken several of them. Certainly our absence from the reserve at six in the morning would have been noted by the Watcher in the sky. But, hey, we were just beginners.

A useful and interesting discovery made that lunchtime was that the gents was a good place to pick up twitching titbits.

I was sitting there in a cubicle eavesdropping on the urinal conversations when I heard one bloke say to another, 'Great morning. I'm going back late afternoon to see if I can see that yellow-browed warbler again.'

'Really?' his co-pisser said non-committally.

'You see it, did you?'

'Er … no. 'Fraid not.'

I was pleased to hear that not only was there a yellow-browed warbler, whatever that was, on the loose, but also that it was quite respectable, in bird circles, to twitch in the late afternoon. Tori was very keen to see some new things, though I didn't think we could top the morning's marsh harrier. I was at the bar when a friendly beard nodded and asked, 'How's it going? Your first time, the Russian tells me.'

'That's right.'

'Have a good morning?'

'Marsh harrier and shag,' I answered.

'Not bad. Plenty more out there today.'

'Yes, I know. Going back later on this afternoon.' I paused; should I or shouldn't I? Oh what the hell, let's give it a go. 'I haven't seen the yellow-browed warbler yet.'

He turned to face me and then let out a disparaging snort.

'Someone in the bog just told me he'd seen a yellow-browed warbler. He's a well-known bullshitter. He's talking bollocks. It was probably a willow warbler.'

'Ha!' I nodded. 'Just what I thought!'

Though I was secretly excited. I had never seen a willow warbler before either.

The Titchwell Marsh reserve is one of the best of its kind. We got there around four o'clock. The car park was packed, which I found rather alarming. In a few of the cars, couples munched sandwiches and drank tea from Thermos flasks. It could have been my guilt, but they seemed to eye us with suspicion, if not scorn. No, there was definitely a hint of 'oh, they've finally made it out of bed, then!' in their perusal of us.

There is a very good shop and visitors' centre before the path on to the marshes.

By the exit of the shop there is a book in which you are invited to list what you've seen. This was going to be a great help. We could make a note of what others had seen and try to fit any unknown bird to the name.

And what a lot of unknowns there were: scaup, scoter, purple sandpiper, whimbrel, glaucous gull, Kentish plover, smew and merganser. I'd never heard of any of these. They must have been on the black-and-white pages of the *Observer's Book of Birds*.

'What's a scoter?' I asked Tori.

'I've no idea. Ask one of this lot.'

I was too worried about being scoffed at to ask a question like that to one of the many experts milling around the shop looking at telescope upgrades.

'A scoter?' I imagined they'd say. 'Don't you know what a scoter is? You ignoramus! What are you doing here if you don't know what a scoter is?' I was in the mood for avoiding humiliation when Tori made a unilateral decision and grabbed a passing twitcher to ask.

'Excuse me, what's a scoter?' The man couldn't have been more charming.

'A scoter. Oh, it's a black sea-duck ... er, that's about it, really. There's the common one, very black, and a dark greyish one called a velvet scoter. There's quite a few out there today actually. Why don't you come up to the beach with me and I'll show you?'

Not so fast, mister! I thought to myself. You're not taking my missus up the shingle to show her a velvet scoter.

'He was quite good looking,' she later informed me. 'And charming!'

'Don't fall for that,' I enlightened her. 'You're a good-looking woman. Just coz he's a birdwatcher doesn't mean he stops being a bloke.' Though, I confess, I hadn't thought that the issue of eye-candy would crop up on a birdwatching trip in the Norfolk marshes.

Behind the visitors' centre at Titchwell is a row of well-stocked bird-feeders. And what a lot of birds. I'd never seen such a collection in so small an area. Sparrow, chaffinch, goldfinch, greenfinch, blue tit, great tit, coal tit, wren, dunnock and, for Tori and me … (drum roll) … two new species!

Now that was gratifying. We hadn't really started our walk and already we could welcome a couple of new boys to the list. It must be admitted, though, that we probably would not have noticed them had it not been for a keen father talking his son through the visitors to the feeder.

'And look, Raymond. You see the chaffinch.'

'I think so,' said Raymond, who was clearly bored rigid and whose binoculars weren't quite in line with his eyes. Or any of his face, for that matter.

'Yes, you do. You know the chaffinch, Raymond, it's the one we call the pink bird. Well, look at that one next to it. The one that looks like an off-coloured chaffinch …'

I was looking at the same bird. I certainly had it down as an off-coloured chaffinch.

'… well, that's a brambling, Raymond.'

Is it? Bugger me, so it is. I've never seen one of those. Tori nudged me and whispered, 'That's a brambling!'

'So I hear. Fab! That's a first for me.'

'Me too.'

Raymond's dad then, in a rather neighbourly way, turned his attention, and his son's, and ours, to the little greeny, black and yellow bird that Tori and I were perfectly prepared to pass over and dismiss as a baby greenfinch, or possibly a mutant adult. 'Look, Raymond, you see that one that looks like a little, streaky greenfinch?'

Yeah, that's not a bad description.

'... well, that's a siskin!'

Tori and I looked at each other with genuine excitement. A siskin. A little, streaky greenfinch. Write that down in the list of firsts.

This was turning out to be *fun*.

But for the headache.

FINCHES

It was the first time I'd seen a brambling. Or a siskin, in fact. Two very different but very lovely types of finch. If you want to see a siskin in a hurry you need to go to the RSPB headquarters at Sandy in Bedfordshire in the winter and look at the feeders there. There are hundreds of them.

I love finches.

They're easy starters for new birdwatchers. All finches are roughly the same size and shape but they are generally very nicely coloured. And they don't mind mixing with each other so you can see goldfinches, greenfinches, chaffinches, bramblings, linnets and siskins all in the same place. This would be an excellent sight for the beginner and an eye-opener for Danny-like people who think that colourful birds in Britain must be escapees from a zoo.

The brambling, an orangey, northern version of the chaffinch, is a charming bird to see. A welcome change from the abundant chaffinch but not too dissimilar to be frightening. It comes with the binomial *Fringilla montifringilla*, meaning 'finch of the hills finch'. Its English name means something like 'little creature from the brambles'.

And what a pretty little bird the siskin is! The sweet name for this canary-like bird is apparently an eastern European word, for a canary-like bird, which has come into English via Dutch and German. Its old name was the 'aberdevine', which sounds suspiciously Scottish to me, or possibly even Welsh, so I'm sticking with 'siskin'. Its 'brainy' name is *Carduelis spinus. Spinus* no doubt refers to the spiky trees of its habitat – conifers and the like – though *spinus* is the Latin for the blackthorn (or sloe), and actually the bird is mainly partial to alders and birch. *Carduelis* comes eventually from the Latin for 'thistle' (*carduus*), which gives us, among other things, *Carduelis carduelis* – the thistle finch, or goldfinch as we call it. Now there's a wonderful bird. If you ever get a close-up look at a goldfinch, I guarantee you will want to take up birdwatching.

Then there is the *Carduelis chloris*, the greenfinch – from the Greek *chloros*, meaning 'light-green', the colour of a certain deadly poisonous gas. (Atomic no. 17, if you're revising GCSE chemistry.) You cannot argue with the word 'greenfinch'. It's a finch and it's green, which I think is all you can reasonably expect from a bird with a name like that. But as a striking extra they have bright yellow flashes on their wings and tails. The beak is noticeably larger and heftier than that of other finches, a perfect tool for this inveterate seed-eater. The greenfinch is a gift for someone like me who is not very good at recognizing the sounds of birds, especially when, in spring and early summer, it utters its unique sound: a sleepy, decaying wheeze. I think the word is 'dzzzweeooo' or possibly 'zweeooooo', but spelling birdsongs has also never been a strong point of mine. But I assure you that it is very rewarding to be able to identify a bird, categorically, from its song, and this one is easy. Once you recognize the descending droning buzz of the greenfinch, you will hear them everywhere. Impress your friends.

Carduelis flavirostris is the amusingly named 'twite'. *Flavirostris* means yellow-faced because the male in summer has a noticeable pink rump. In the winter, however, the twite changes the colour of its bill to pale yellow. Well, there's not much else to do, is there?

The redpoll has a pale pink chest and a reddish patch on its forehead so it gets the hard-sell name *Carduelis flammea* – the 'fiery' or 'blazing' finch.

But what about the bullfinch? Aaah (pulls sad face), the bullfinch. Such a great bird to draw and colour in. A new set of felt-tip pens. Must draw a bullfinch. What a challenge to get that breast right. Such a vivid blaze of pinky, orangey red. In my child-hood Cornwall, where every garden seemed to have a flowering cherry tree, we used to see bullfinches all the time. And they keep very still, so when you know where one is, you can watch it for hours, if you've got nothing better to do.

And there can't be that many better things to do, can there?

Besides, your time may be running out to see the bullfinch. Its taste for the flowering buds of fruit trees means that this plump pink beauty has been and is being persecuted.

Rather excitingly for me, there is a bunch of British finches I've never seen. I am not the sort of person who keeps lists of names and times and places. With birds, you do not forget whether you have seen one or not. And invariably you remember exactly when and where you saw your 'first' something: spotted flycatcher, Bait's Bite Lock on the river Cam; dipper, Middleton-on-Tees; blue rock thrush, El Toro in Menorca; chiffchaff, dog-shit lane (of which, more later); marsh harrier, bedroom in Black Swan; red kite, junction 3, M40; lammergeier, London Zoo, etc.

You definitely know what you have *not* seen and I'm looking forward to my first citril finch, serin, scarlet rosefinch, crossbill and what about *Coccothraustes coccothraustes*, the hawfinch? What can you say about this one? Scary beak, scary eyes, scary scientific name.

Then we have *Carduelis cannabina*, the linnet. 'Cannabis', I believe, is a widespread, straggly weed and has a variety of inter-esting uses, including rope-making and canvas. The linnet, because of its pretty song, was a popular caged bird. You'll recall, no doubt, the music-hall favourite from the 1880s 'Don't Dilly Dally', which contains the line: 'My old man said follow the van, and don't dilly dally on the way; off went the cart with my home packed in it; I walked behind with my old cock linnet ...'

And so it goes on. Incidentally, we Arsenal supporters have a song based on this, which starts: 'My old man said be a Tottenham fan!' The rest of the lyric does not come within the scope of this book, I'm afraid.

A GOOD HIDING

After siskins and bramblings, another first for our first day: going into a hide. A hide, as it says in the dictionary, is 'a place of concealment for the observation or hunting of wildlife'.

Well, let's skip the 'hunting' bit for now; an industrial-sized drum of worms would be opened if we started discussing hunting in a book about birdwatchers. Not that I'm by any means indifferent to an occasional bit of freshly caught, wild bird meat. Pigeon pie ... yummy? And there's no denying the appeal of pheasant or grouse. Partridge and quail cook up nicely, as do wigeon, teal and all manner of brightly coloured waterfowl. Woodcock and snipe are always a bit special on the tea table. The puffin, apparently, made for an agreeable supper for seafaring and coastal folk at one time. The Scandinavians, Faroese, Icelanders and people from eastern Canada were all more than a tad partial to puffin. And I imagine it must have looked damn fetching on the serving platter with its large red, yellow and blue bill. Though someone once told me that those people were, in fact, eating Manx shearwaters, whose scientific name – as, indeed, you know – is *Puffinus puffinus*, hence the confusion. I'm not quite sure of the veracity of the source as the man in question went on to tell me that if you *were* going to cook a puffin, you shouldn't microwave it; apparently, they tend to explode and your kitchen will smell of burnt sardine for months.

Any decent birding site will have strategically placed hides dotted around with good, unobstructed views of various habitats: tidal marshes, reed beds, rivers, woodlands, etc. They're usually wooden cabins with letterbox-like slits round the walls just wide enough to stick a pair of binoculars through.

The hide we were heading for was on a spit of land between two huge tidal pools. More firsts for me and Tori. Our favourite: the avocet. This bird must be on a shortlist for prizes in several categories. Tall, slim, elegant. Pure white with pure black lines and a fine, dark, delicately upturned bill. This it uses for sifting for food through the silt, sweeping its head from side to side.

It is the logo of the Royal Society for the Protection of Birds, and it's hard to imagine a better bird for the purpose. And that is not just because it must be a gift to draw for the logo-artist, even one without coloured pens. Before the forties, this bird had all but disappeared from our shores, and the large numbers of avocet around today are the results of one of the first and most successful conservation and protection schemes ever undertaken in Britain. Among the massed flocks of streaky, brown and grey waders, this graceful bird is a star.

I was excited and nervous as I unlatched the door of the salt-marsh hide. Holding my breath, I went in and Tori followed. It was warm and dark and smelled of that stuff that does what it says on the tin.

I peered through the gloom. There was total silence. I breathed out and said heartily, 'Ah, good, there's no one here!'

Twenty-five people hissed 'Ssshhh!' at us. We jumped.

Ah yes, as my eyes got accustomed to the dark, I realized that quite a few of our fellow birders were in there. Through the narrow letterboxes, they were all peering intently across the wide expanse of water. We joined them. There were mainly ducks and seagulls. But an incontinent number of both. It really was quite special.

And more superb avocets.

'A few ducks out there, I see,' I said amicably to the earnest lady next to me. I wish I hadn't.

I soon realized that we didn't have the vocabulary, let alone the knowledge, to hold a conversation in 'hide-speak'.

'Barwit's off again.'

'That American wigeon's back.'

'Where?'

'Behind that female greenshank.'

'Are they ices out there?'

'Glaucs, I think.'

'No!'

'Yes. I've seen ices today but I reckon at the moment we're talking glauc.'

'Whoa, look at that! That's very acrobatic for a sandwich!'

'No, that's normal.'

My binoculars were jerking left and right, up and down, in an effort to keep up with this outlandish dialogue. And when someone said, 'Look at those juvenile ruffs,' I focused my bins and immediately started scanning the horizon for some hoodies down from Cromer.

All business in the hide is conducted at a whisper. This becomes a slightly louder stage-whisper if you happened to have seen something rare or something that nobody else has seen. It's not considered twitching 'cricket' to emit a skittish yelp of 'Wow, what's this?', as Tori did when she saw something large and dark and quite unlike any bird she'd seen before appear in her object lens. All eyes turned to her, part annoyed, part expectant.

'Oh, it doesn't matter!' she said to a communal 'tsk'. They all went back to their own private twitch.

'What was it?' I asked.

'A spider crawling over the end of my binoculars.'

Yes, this was best hushed up, I thought. It's been quite a few years since we lost our hide-virginity, and I realize now that such is the nature of 'twitchers' that if you did say, 'Oh look, a spider on my binoculars,' they'd probably say:

'That's most likely a diadematus.'

'Could be a dolomedes.'

'No, not big enough; they wouldn't come in here anyway.'

'No, I think we're talking thomisus.'

And so on.

The hide experience is strange. It has the silence of a public library, but one where everyone is reading the same book. Occasionally some good-natured fellow would lean over and point out a word that you may not have read or noticed. Birding in a hide is an odd mix of competition and co-operation. You want to be the first to see something, or the first to identify something, but you also want to help or instruct those not as knowledgeable or experienced as you.

Yes, there's an element of showing off, but it benefits both parties. I often wondered at what level of expertise you have to be to engage a fellow twitcher. If, for example, a blackbird, flew past and you said, 'Wow, what's that? A medium-sized bird. All black with a yellow bill!' would they say with contempt or amusement, 'That's a blackbird!', with perhaps 'you cretin' in brackets.

Or would they, with eager patience, say, 'Well, you've described a blackbird but, obviously, you know what one of those looks like, so I wonder what it could be. A ring ouzel? Did it have a pale bib? Er … was it a blue rock thrush; that would be a great spot for round here!'

I have never had the guts to try this one, but over the years I have fantasized about playing those sorts of games in a hide full of twitchers. Saying things like, 'Do ostriches dive into water and grab eels?'

'No, course they don't.'

'Well, it wasn't an ostrich I just saw then!'

The very fact that I think about arsing around like this reveals something about my levels of commitment to the hobby. Maybe I just do not want to immerse myself totally in birding. Perhaps I need to retain an ironic distance. But I have to admit that that first afternoon in the hide at Titchwell was a special event.

There were a few old friends from the days of JJ and the Emmanuel College ponding committee. The tufted duck, the wigeon, the teal, the shelduck and, of course, mallards. There were a few speciality acts too. The shoveler. What a great name. What a great bird. Boldly marked with a bottle-green head, white breast, black back and an orange-brown belly and flanks. But what is special is its bill, which is huge and wide and, you know what, like a shovel. It sweeps this broadly from side to side through water and wet mud to find food.

'Look, that's a shoveler!' Tori's excitement drew indulgent glances from the twitching brotherhood.

'That's the female next to it,' someone pointed out. This was helpful as the two sexes, like many ducks, were completely different but for one feature.

'The bill is the giveaway,' the twitcher went on. 'In both sexes, it's spatulate.'

Excellent. 'In both sexes, it's spatulate.' Another first for the day. The word *spatulate*. (From the Latin for 'a little shovel'.)

DANNY TWITCHES AT WORK

'No, I can't ... Possibly later ... No, I'm still in Norwich ... The Eastern Evening Press, their whole system's gone down. I could be here for hours ...'

Danny was in the middle of a spiky conversation with his team manager.

'I'll call you back. This could be an all-day job.'

He switched off his mobile. I put the two pints on the table. 'Bloody work hassling me!' We were in the back garden of a pub in Cambridge. He lit up a cigarette.

'How many have you had today, Danny?'

'This is my second ...'

'Good.'

'... packet.'

'I read somewhere that smoking's bad for you.'

'I don't pay any attention to all that scaremongering; they'll be saying drinking's bad for you soon.'

There was little hope.

'And what about those awful things you're stuffing down you?'

I stopped mid-crunch and thought about the Thai prawn-flavoured mini-poppadums that filled my mouth. I was sure they would not give me lung cancer, but Danny's comment made me reflect as an unworldly, spicy, salty slime trickled down my throat.

'Mmm. You're probably right. I'll chuck the rest.'

He grabbed the open bag. 'No, don't. I'll take them home for the cat.'

A sparrow hopped by our feet. 'Er ... don't tell me. Sparrow!' spluttered Danny excitedly.

'Very good.'

Building on the excitement of his first blue tit, he was eager to learn, and had begun to notice that birds were all around him, every day, even when he was at 'work' like today.

'House sparrow,' I explained to him, desperately trying not to sound condescending. 'That's the only one we see regularly. But there's a few others around. There's the tree sparrow.'

'Hangs around trees?'

'Er, sort of. And the Spanish sparrow.'

'Hangs around Spain?'

'Indeed; and the rock sparrow.'

'Likes rock music.'

'Excellent. And this is the house sparrow.'

'Likes house music.'

'Close enough!'

'Pretty thing though, isn't it?'

Danny, who's only known the existence of birds for two weeks, says that the sparrow is a 'pretty thing'. Now, that is really something! The sparrow, especially the house sparrow, is usually considered the dull bird's dull bird. An annoyingly abundant streaky-brown thing. I'd even heard myself say on numerous occasions, 'Oh. It's only a sparrow.'

But listen to Danny; he was blind, but now he sees! He thinks it's pretty. Look closely. It is. Quite a mixture of black, dark brown, reddish-brown, light brown, grey and black. It is sociable and noisy, and do you know something? It sounds like a bird. No, what I mean is that it sounds like you'd expect a bird to sound.

Its song is almost the prototype 'chirrup chirrup'. It always sounds slightly out of tune, though, as if it's struggling to be musical. They're not difficult to see because they're not that shy and they always hang around human habitation. And, of course, they are very common.

But are they?

Their numbers are declining with worrying speed.

'Hey, Danny, look hard and close at this pretty brown bird, because time is running out.'

'OK, I won't smoke any more today!'

'I meant the house sparrow's time is running out.'

'Oh look, there's another one.' He was pointing at a similar-looking bird. 'But that's got slightly different markings. Female?'

I was impressed. He'd looked long enough to notice that the second bird was different, and he'd taken on board the idea that the female is often distinct from the male; usually less well marked. He'd also noticed that the new bird was, to all intents and purposes, sufficiently sparrow-like to be a sparrow.

But it wasn't.

'Not bad. Actually that bird is what used to be commonly called a hedge sparrow. Most people call it a dunnock.'

Judging by Danny's reply I must have been sounding a bit pompous and twitchery. 'Really? I don't call it a dunnock; I'm going to call it Fred the Bird,' said Danny.

Now, dismiss the dunnock as a duller, greyer version of the sparrow, if you dare. This is an intriguing bird. The dunnock, *Prunella modularis*, has a saucy, Sunday tabloid secret. Its mating habits are more than a tad spicy.

It's into the ménage à trois. Well, the lady of the house is; or should that be the lady of the hedge? Its mating sessions often include one female and two males or one male and two females. In fact, so promiscuous is the female that quite often, while husband is away, Mrs Dunnock (whom we have to call Pru, surely) will mate with another male dunnock (whom we'll call, say, Roger). As if that's not 'when-suburban-housewives-get-hot' enough in itself, when the male returns he demands to know what Pru's been up to in his absence. Has she had a man in to repair her nest? Or slip her an earthworm? Why is she looking so red-faced and guilty?

Well, what the male does is even less subtle than the interrogation of a suspicious husband. With his fine spike of a beak, he pecks her repeatedly in the vagina in case there's some 'foreign' seed therein. This will be discharged by the invasion and the husband immediately mates with her again to ensure that his descendants will truly be his.

Ah, what a romantic tale.

'Bloody hell, mate,' said Danny. 'That's a bit full on! I wonder if they know Diana, that cheating cow! She—'

Danny's acidic reminiscence was interrupted by a searing, high-pitched, screaming whistle overhead. Looking up Danny exclaimed confidently, 'Ah easy one; swallow!'

Another scream overhead. And another. And still more.

'One swallow doesn't make a blowjob, as my gran didn't use to say! Ha!'

'They're swifts,' I corrected him.

'You're not even looking at them, mate!'

No, I wasn't looking at them, and a vivid memory returned to me.

Long ago, just before the days of JJ, when I was still blind to the world of nature, I was coming out of a lecture hall with my friend Dave.

Dave had a reputation at college for being 'a bit of a loner'. He was not a 'weirdo', and not 'a bit of a loner' in the way they report serial killers on the news. Just someone who kept himself to himself, who enjoyed his own company. And, yes, he was a birdwatcher.

We were on our way to the next lecture in a different building, and I noticed some birds swooping and diving acrobatically at great speed. Even to a non-birder like me, the arc of the wings and the forked tail suggested these could only be swallows. I looked up and said, 'Ah, the swallows are here!'

'They're swifts,' said Dave instantly, head-down, not looking up from his purposeful walk.

'You're not even looking at them!' I said.

'Don't have to. Listen to that screaming whistle. Unmistakable.'

Weirdo, I thought.

And twenty-five years later, there I am sitting with my mate Danny saying, 'Don't have to. Listen to that screaming whistle. Unmistakable.'

We sat and watched the swifts in silence. You can do that with swifts. To the first-time birdwatcher, swifts are easy money. They put on a show. And what a show!

'They're amazing, mate,' said Danny, who was captivated enough to pause between drags of his cigarette. 'I might even dig out my camera gear. I bet that lot are a challenge to photograph!' He sipped his beer. 'Hey, this is actually a bit of fun.'

'It certainly is.'

'What a shame I'm in Norwich, fixing a computer.'

TEACHER TEACHER TEACHER

Tori has a good ear. Two good ears, in fact. She has two good eyes, as well, and lips and legs and, indeed, a whole host of body parts that are worth some consideration, but in a book about birds, we shall concentrate on her ears, which, as I say, are very good. Not only placed on either side of her head, like the best of good ears, but also highly effective in identifying the slightest differences in sounds, variations of pitch and tone and quality. In short, very sharp at naming the bird, based only on its sound.

This is more difficult for me. I'm not at all tone deaf. I can sing well enough to have earned roughly £7 a day one week busking on the London Underground, till I was moved on by the authorities. I can tell the difference between musical notes, but not with any scientific precision. A great deal of music, therefore, sounds exactly the same to me, but then I do listen to a lot of country and western. The trouble with birdsong, I suppose, is that I have too long associated it with the disruption of sleep after a particularly large night.

Slowly but surely Tori has educated me in this field, which is surprisingly rewarding, not least because a lot of birds can be heard very easily, but seen with great difficulty.

A fine example of this is the Cetti's warbler. It is one of Britain's only two resident warblers, the other being the Dartford warbler. That's got to be British, hasn't it: the Dartford warbler. A lovely, bird too. Dark for a warbler, with a rich reddish-brown breast and a striking red eye-ring. A marked long slender tail, prominent in its short, bouncy flights from bush to bush. The Dartford warbler: take a picture of it with you to have in your car when you're stuck in diabolical traffic crossing the Thames in East London.

Our other local, very British warbler was named, needless to say, after Francisco Cetti, an Italian Jesuit monk born in Germany in 1726. You will probably never see this bird, no matter how close you're standing to it, but you will get no marks for hearing it. It is a small, nondescript bird, brown on top and pale underneath. It sings from deep cover in bushes, ditches, reeds or hedgerows, and it goes like this: doot, doot, doodoodoodoodoodoodoo doo doo.

Or if you prefer: chwee ... chwee, ... chewechewecheweche-wechewechewe.

You get the idea? Two sharp, single, abrupt notes followed by a splurging trill. Tori compares it to the opening phrase of Elgar's 'Pomp and Circumstance' march No 1 in D major; you know, the one that goes 'bom ... bom ... bombombombombombom'.

She started me off with the easy ones. Not just *simple* songs, but the ones you hear all the time because they're either the first in the year, the loudest or the most far-reaching.

Cuckoo? I think you've all got that one. Next!

A great tit? Two notes. The first higher than the other. Is the professor of music around? No? Oh well – the interval, I reckon, is about a fourth. You know the melody of the first line of 'Street Fighting Man' by the Rolling Stones? The Rolling Stones? Well, they were a huge rock and roll band ... oh this is silly!

Just imagine an insistent schoolboy, desperate to answer the question, frantically waving his raised arm and screaming, 'Teacher, teacher, teacher!' That's it. Great tit.

The chiffchaff is another song that's difficult to miss. This tiny bird often delivers its two-note song from high up in the treetops. It carries for miles and seems to cut through all other birdsong, apart from the great tit. It's similar to 'teacher, teacher, teacher' but the other way round. The second note is higher and the song comes out for longer periods than the great tit. It sort of goes: 'doot-dit doot-dit doot-dit doot-dit doot-dit doot-dit', with the 'dit' being higher than the 'doot'. It occasionally slips in a crafty extra 'doot', giving us 'doot doot-dit doot-dit doot doot-dit.' You get the idea. Its name imitates its sound, though I think 'chaff-chiff' would be a more accurate name. For me, it has the quality of a knife being sharpened on a steel, but I could be alone in this.

OK, a quick pub-quiz moment: which common British bird is sometimes called the yaffle? Yes, that's right, the green woodpecker. 'Yaffle' is a supposed imitation of its loud, laugh-like song. Other names for it include eccle, hewhole, highhoe, yaffingale, yappingale or yackel. That should give you a broad feel for what we're talking about. It sounds like laugh of a fictional baddie. It's the cackle that will follow a line like: 'You shall never escape from here and the treasure will be all mine!' Starting high and shrill, then descending in pitch and energy. (And definitely not 'dood a lee dee doo, dood a lee dee doo', the call of the Disney bird Woody Woodpecker.)

The skylark is easy, too. I once fell asleep on a summer meadow listening to a skylark. At least, I think it was me. It was long enough ago to be someone else. But this bird demands special mention. The skylark perhaps offers the best clue to man's affinity with birds. Think of all the art, literature and music inspired by it. I would defy anyone who has heard a skylark to improve on George Meredith's poem which begins:

He rises and begins to round
He drops the silver chain of sound
Of many links without a break
In chirrup, whistle, slur and shake
All intervolved and spreading wide
Like water-dimples down a tide
Where ripple ripple overcurls
And eddy into eddy whirls.

William Blake calls it the 'mighty angel'. Shelley famously calls it 'blithe spirit'. Wordsworth tops them both with 'ethereal minstrel', and Chaucer gives us 'bisy larke, messager of the day'. All inspired and inspiring, and most of them spelled correctly.

Tori has taught me song thrush too. A masterful singer. Loud, bright, short fruity phrases, all different but each sung at least three or four times so you do not miss how good they are. Robert Browning, who was yearning to be in 'England, now that April's there', spoke of the wise thrush that:

… sings each song twice over
Lest you should think he never could recapture
The first fine careless rapture.

In Hardy's 'Darkling Thrush', birdsong is uplifting and positive. He is walking through the countryside one bleak, winter's evening when a thrush starts singing. He wonders what the thrush knows that he doesn't know.

So little cause for carolings
Of such ecstatic sound
Was written on terrestrial things
Afar or nigh around
That I could think there trembled through
His happy good-night air
Some blessed hope whereof he knew
And I was unaware.

Nightingales, blackbirds, swallows, swifts, sparrows and so many others make a near endless list of bird- or birdsong-inspired art. And invariably birdsong is life-affirming, it is about joy, about hope, about freedom. Sebastian Faulks's beautifully grim novel about love in the First World War is entitled simply *Birdsong*.

To most people the sound of birds is their first, sometimes only, contact with nature. It is a powerful and beguiling connection to a non-human world. It is a contact number for the wild.

But Tori, for all her good ears and delight at birdsong, is a wise girl. She knows the true meaning of birdsong.

'Listen to that!' she said. It was one I recognized. We were on a scrubby heath above the town of Sheringham. It was an easy sound to learn. Two pebbles being clacked against each other followed by a short chirrup. The stonechat. So evocative of the high, coastal heath where we were. A beautiful sound.

'Beautiful to us,' Tori reminded me. 'Not to them. We humans plaster all sorts of deep and romantic meanings on to birdsong but to them it's communication. They're only interested in food, sex and territory.'

'Territory's never bothered me that much,' I said as a

whitethroat started its song nearby. 'Now, are you going to say that's not beautiful?'

Tori smiled. 'It is beautiful but it probably means "Get away from my nest".'

We walked back down the footpath towards the sea and took in the beautiful, joyous, romantic sounds of birds, tweeting their beautiful, joyous, romantic birdy messages.

'Look at the colour of my breast!'

'Get off my land!'

'Any chance of a fuck?'

HOBBY

No, not that sort of hobby. Not the bird. The pastime. Oh yes, there is a bird called the 'hobby'. The bloke who invented the flicky table version of football called Subbuteo, wanted to call it 'Hobby', but he couldn't. So he chose the scientific name for the small bird of prey called 'hobby', which is *Falco subbuteo*, and means something like 'falcon lesser than a buzzard'. An odd description of this fascinating raptor. A favourite of mine.

Deadly as a hawk, sleek and elegant as a swift.

The only bird of prey that can take a swift on the wing.

And how else could it do it but by looking like a swift: small, slim, compact body with long, pointed, sickle-like wings. Snatching beetles and dragonflies from just above the water or reeds, this bird has no equal. It is effortless in grace and finesse. It's unusual, too, for a British bird of prey, in that it is a summer visitor to us from Africa. But that's not the hobby I meant.

I suppose drawing was my hobby as I grew up. Cartoons, silly monsters and birds. A lot of birds; cartoon birds and silly monster birds, as well. But it was never a proper hobby; it was something I'd do to while away the time when I should have been doing something else. But there comes a point when a mild interest becomes a hobby, an obsession.

My boyhood home in Cornwall overlooked a football pitch. Illogan British Legion FC. The bedroom I shared with my two brothers had a fantastic view of the pitch. In Highbury speak, we were at the 'Clock End'. Every Saturday afternoon, we'd gather at the window and cheer on 'Luggan'. But unfortunately the goal at our end was obscured by a large hawthorn bush. From the age of seven to the present day, I've wanted to sneak out in the middle of the night with a chainsaw and chop it down. It would not have been difficult to work out who the culprit was, though. And the standard of football in those days probably wouldn't have merited such arboreal vandalism. On the one occasion our father actually took us into the ground to watch the match (and both sets of goalposts), we were shocked to find out they charged an entry fee.

'Four shillings?' scoffed my dad. 'We want to watch the match, not buy the team!'

But football was growing from while-away-the-time to mild interest and beyond.

I was nine in 1965 and bolshy enough to support the opposite team to my parents in the FA Cup final. As my parents were natives of St Helens in Lancashire, they supported Liverpool, of course. So I ended up supporting Leeds. This was sacrilege in our house: not only was Leeds not Liverpool, but it was also in Yorkshire! But Leeds had only just come up from the second division so it was a foregone conclusion that the Reds would stuff them. In the event, Liverpool won two–one in extra time, and this merely cemented my fondness for Leeds, the underdog.

When you live in Cornwall and your nearest league team is Plymouth Argyle, you're allowed to support anyone. My interest in football outlived my interest in Leeds United and for years I was 'unaffiliated', except, of course, for watching Illogan out of the bedroom window whenever possible and keeping an amused eye on Argyle. I watched England matches in the unique way that England fans have: if they lost, it was because of individual players from a club you didn't support, or because of the FA, the despised footballing authorities that managed to cock up every tiny aspect of running the game.

But it was moving to London in the late seventies and living less than a mile from Highbury, the home of Arsenal, that made football for me go from mild interest to obsession.

My parents were dismayed. 'But, Rory, they're southern. How can you support a team from the south? A London team?'

The moment that made me realize Arsenal were going to be big in my life was the day I bought the 'travel club' card. I already had a season ticket for the North Bank for home games; now I was going to be an away supporter. That was the defining Arsenal moment for me.

Of course, things change. You get married, have a mortgage and two children, and no money; Arsenal frustrate and irritate the hell out of you and stop being an obsession, a way of life, and go back to being a mild interest.

Then there was running. One Christmas my younger brother returned from Spain, where he was living, looking fitter than I had ever seen him. He had taken up running.

'Running?' I said disparagingly. 'How can you take up running? Isn't running what you do when you run? You know, when you walk very fast? It's hardly a sport. It's hardly something you can "take up"!'

He'd been running ten miles a day, five days a week for two years, and I foolishly accepted a challenge to race him.

'One mile,' I said confidently, because the last time I'd run I'd been quite fast. That was about ten years earlier, a factor I should probably have taken into consideration.

'No, a mile's too much for you,' my brother disparaged back.

'Bollocks,' I said. 'A mile is nothing.'

And so the race went ahead. We were together at the beginning for a few seconds then he disappeared into the distance. The next time I saw him was about five minutes later. He was leaning over me where I lay in the gutter about seventy-five yards from our house.

'Are you OK?'

'I think I started too quickly,' I eventually uttered in between painful gasps for air.

Within a year, I had entered the London Marathon. Another defining moment. A new hobby. A weekly Sunday morning drive to take part in half marathons all over southern England. (Braintree was my best half-marathon time: ninety-three minutes.)

And as for the London Marathon ... Well, at the risk of sounding vain, I could have won it. I should have won; but unfortunately there were 17,000 other people in front of me. Then getting married, having children, getting divorced, eating and drinking too much came between me and my athletics career, so I eventually moved on to something more sedentary.

Then there was country and western music. I was asked to write a comedy country and western song. This would be great fun, I thought; C&W may be appallingly schmaltzy and embarrassingly self-pitying, but it is 'lyric led' so you can make verbal jokes, and also it only requires minimal guitar playing and compositional skills. (Three chords good ... two chords perfect, as the saying goes.) For a fortnight I immersed myself in country music, listening to hundreds of tracks, traditional and contemporary. At the end of those two weeks, I was hooked; I loved country music and my life was going to be a waste unless I had actually sung on the stage of the Grand Ole Opry in Nashville, Tennessee.

And, dear reader, that I did. I'll explain later in a book that isn't about birdwatching.

Ah yes, birdwatching. The point at which I crossed the line between mild interest and obsession was the day I bought a spotting-scope. That's when you know you're hooked: the day you buy a bit of equipment, a piece of kit, a gadget. It was the day before my birthday, which is in the middle of March and therefore coming up to the best birdwatching time of the year. This was all the excuse I needed to splash out a bit of the overdraft on some pointless self-indulgence. And as any beginner knows, the worst thing about buying a gadget is that you have to go to a shop where everyone's an expert whose principal aim seems to be to make you look stupid and inferior.

'I'd like to buy a telescope, please.' Glances are smirked between the older, balding shop assistant and the spiky gel-headed junior.

'A telescope?' says the baldy.

'Yes, for birdwatching,' I offer helpfully.

A snigger from the youth who says, 'You want a telescope for birdwatching?'

There is palpable mirth in the air. I have definitely made their day.

'So, where are these birds then? On the moon?'

Another snigger.

'Er, I'm not sure I understand what you mean,' I said with as little amusement as possible, and they realized they were close to losing a customer.

'No, sorry, ha, no, we're just messing about. Thing is, erm … a telescope is usually for astronomy and things like that. If you're a twitcher, you want a spotting-scope, which I suppose is like a small telescope …'

Oh I see, of course; we're talking about arcane jargon, of which I'm ignorant and they're not, so they can make themselves feel briefly superior. Well, I wasn't standing for that.

'What about if you want to spy on the woman in the house across the road?'

This shut them up and drew a worried glance from another customer.

'Right, I'll let you deal with this gentleman,' said the bald one to the youngster.

We established that I was a birdwatching beginner who needed a not-too-complex 'spotting-scope'. 'What sort of magnification were you thinking of?' the younger man went on matter-of-factly.

'Mmm, good question. It depends. I don't know how small the bird is yet.' I beamed inanely at him. The gel-head ignored this and proceeded to show me what he had in stock. He had become business-like but was still keen to pull technical rank on me.

'This is the MM2 Travelscope, retractable to 18cm, with wide-band focusing wheel and retractable lens hood, dedicated MM2 25x and 15-40x eyepieces.' He hardly paused for breath.

'Mmm,' I mused expertly. 'Have you got a light blue one?'

'Black only,' he said, with no-nonsense eye contact.

'Shame. What about those three-legged things you stick them on?'

'Tripod?'

'Ah yes, tripod. That's the word I was looking for.'

'The Delta 1V has a fluid head with reversible handle for left and right use and the G-clamp converts to a hide clamp system.' He finished with a small self-satisfied smirk.

'Excellent. Do you have one of *those* in light blue?'

'No.'

'Shame. I'll take them anyway.'

Still just about on the warm side of frosty, but happy to have made such a pricey sale, the young man went about getting all the bits of kit from the stockroom, then unpacking, packing, wrapping and bagging them before writing up the bill of sale and putting it though the till. The whole process took about ten minutes, at the end of which he announced primly, '£335.75, please.'

'Oh, hang on,' I said. 'I've changed my mind. How much is that magnifying glass?'

Pleased with my day's shopping I returned home and showed Tori my exciting new purchase.

'Look at this. Magnifying glass. £2.50. It's not quite what I wanted but it'll be fun. We can go ant-watching. And burn holes in bits of paper in the summer.'

'Right, well, while we're on the subject of buying silly things, I've got you something for your birthday. I know it's not till tomorrow but I'll give it to you now anyway. Close your eyes!'

When I opened my eyes I was thrilled. There before me was an MM2 Travelscope, with wide-band focusing wheel and retractable lens hood and a Delta 1V tripod plus fluid head with reversible handle for left and right use, and with a G-clamp that converts to a hide clamp system.

A SMALL DULL BIRD

There is a narrow tree-lined track that goes from the North Norfolk coast road (the A149) down to the salt marshes. It skirts the graveyard of Titchwell church with its distinctive round flint tower. The lane is memorable to me for two reasons: first, there is a spectacular amount of dog shit there, particularly tricky to avoid when your eyes are on the sky; and, secondly, it was also the venue for a 'first' in my career as a grown-up birdwatcher. A beginner's true 'bird moment'.

One Sunday afternoon we were slaloming down this track in between the unscooped poopers when we were stopped by a loud, clear, quite singular bird call. Though 'singular' may not be the best description. It consisted of two notes, the second slightly higher than the other. The bird producing this unique sound was perching openly high on the bare branches of a dead tree. Through our binoculars we could see a very small, pale brownish bird with a faint pale stripe through its eye.

Its song was unstinting. We were intrigued.

'No idea what that is,' said Tori.

'Me neither.'

Two men were walking down the path towards us. Judging by the amount of optical equipment they had strapped about them, these were hardened twitchers. I suppose we could have asked them if they knew what the bird was. But that might have made us look like foolish neophytes. So we relentlessly peered through our binoculars as they approached.

They might even say something like, 'Oh, I see you're looking at that fine specimen of a [say] dunnock.' Then we could nod knowingly with a, 'Yes, always nice to see a dunnock.'

They didn't say anything. In fact, as they walked past us they peered at us through narrowed eyes, then up to the bird, then back to us with an expression that said, loud and clear, 'What on earth are you looking at that for?' With that hint of displeasure, they went on their way, no doubt to photograph a flock of resplendent quetzals that had been blown off-course from Costa Rica.

At this point I should make it clear that there are thousands of birders out there who would obligingly and without any patronizing whatsoever help out a struggling beginner to find or identify a particular bird. These two men just were not of that clan. Similarly there are probably thousands of beginners who would happily accost a superior with a cheery: 'Do excuse us, but we're new at this birdwatching business and are struggling to identify this particular individual; we were wondering if you might be able to lend us a bit of your undoubtedly huge expertise?' But unfortunately, Tori and I, despite our inexperience and lack of technical knowledge, were blocked by pride and couldn't bring ourselves to ask.

Not only that, Tori and I felt, and still feel, that birding is not a communal thing; it's a personal thing. It's something just for the three of us: me, Tori and the bird, whatever that bird is. We, therefore, are disinclined to invite strangers into our little world. Though it would be nice to know what this tireless chirper was.

We watched and listened and listened and watched but we got no nearer to identifying it. Minute, with a piercing call; that was about it. Nondescript was the only way of describing it. After about forty minutes of scrutiny we, reluctantly, left and started walking back to the car to scrape the bottom of our shoes. On the way we were stopped in our tracks by another bird. We couldn't see this one but its noise was very distinctive. A harsh, explosive 'tchik!' Sometimes a double 'tchik, tchik!'

Tori and I looked blankly at each other.

'Never heard that before,' I shrugged.

'Me neither.'

A man walking a dog was approaching us. I thought I'd try a more cordial approach to birdwatching and ask him if he could help us.

'Do excuse us, but we're new at this birdwatching business and are struggling to identify this particular individual; we were wondering if you might be able to lend us a bit of your undoubtedly huge expertise?'

He gave us a look somewhere between defence and attack.

Another loud 'tchik, tchik!'

'Have you any idea what bird's making that sound?'

'I don't know,' he growled. 'And I don't care. Birds are all the bloody same.' He grumbled off down the track.

I shouted after him, the hand of birding friendship still extended, 'Thanks for your time anyway!' Then, under my breath after a pause, 'Hope you clear up your dog shit, arsehole.'

But, hey, do you know what? Coincidentally, a week later, Tori got a birthday present from one of her children: a DVD of common garden birds. The first bit was devoted to birds that come to your garden to visit nut-feeders. One was the flamboyant great-spotted woodpecker. 'Unmistakable,' said the commentary, 'at your feeder, but hard to see in a deciduous wood. Most easily located by its distinctive call: a harsh, explosive *tchik!*'

Aha. A new chunky piece of bird knowledge.

Also featured on the DVD was a bird singing from the bare branches of a dead tree. It could have been filmed down dog-shit lane in Titchwell, hurling its disproportionately loud, bi-tonic song from the treetops.

As one, Tori and I pointed at the screen and said, 'That's it!'

A chiffchaff.

It was a first for both of us. A special 'bird moment' and a special 'us moment'.

We have since seen many chiffchaffs and they are always a delight. I would never sneer at anyone who had stopped to look at one. In fact, I'd go out of my way to say, 'Ah, yes, a chiffchaff; one of my favourites!'

And hope that they wouldn't say in reply, 'Mind your own fucking business!'

DANNY AND A LATE DRINK

A disdainful snort erupted from behind the newspaper.

'You are joking, aren't you?' Tori said.

'Not at all. He's coming with me. He's going to bring all his camera gear. Turn it into a photographic shoot. In case he gets bored.'

She put down the paper. 'No, the bit that sounds like the joke is that you're going round to his house at four o'clock in the morning and expect him: a) to be there, b) to be in a fit state to drive to Norfolk birdwatching, and c) to remember the arrangement in the first place and not tell you to fuck off. And a *Sunday* morning on top of that.'

'He's promised not to go to the pub on Saturday and to get an early night.'

Tori would take some convincing. And, in truth, so would I.

'I've explained that late-night drinking and birdwatching are not comfortable bed-fellows. Well, unless you stay up all night.'

'I hope you didn't tell him that! He'll stay up all night and end up falling asleep in the reed beds and be eaten by foxes.'

'He's not totally irresponsible, you know.'

'No, just partially.'

'He's managed to keep down a fairly respectable job for three years.'

'Isn't that more to do with the fact that he lets his boss use his house for his extra-marital activities?'

'Anyway, as I've said, *you* are invited as well. Your expertise would be welcome.'

She laughed again. 'No fear; I don't want to be there when he falls asleep in the hide with a fag in his mouth and burns the whole thing down. I can just see it now. *Flash fire destroys acres of reed beds, hundred of breeding birds killed. Police suspect arsehole.*'

I joined in the laughter, acutely aware that the scenario was well within the realm of possibilities.

'I'll make it very clear to him that smoking is a no-no.'

'Will he be able to go for four hours or so without a snout break?'

'I'll tell him to wear his full-body-length Nicorette patch.'

'I foresee disaster. I don't think the birdlife of Britain is ready for Danny Davidson. I predict he'll be on the front cover of the RSPB magazine: *Wanted: have you seen this man?*'

'He's very keen to do some photography. I showed him some pictures in the magazine; he was convinced he could do better.'

'Remind him to take a camera with him then.'

'Ha.'

'It won't happen.' She was adamant. 'You and Danny going on an early morning birdwatching trip on a Sunday will not happen.'

'Don't be daft. Course it will.'

She held out her hand. 'Fifty quid it won't happen.'

I shook her hand.

'You're on! I'll make it happen.'

'You'll have to phone him at home on Saturday evening, once an hour, just to make sure he's there and not out of it.'

'No, I'm not doing that. That's patronizing and controlling. I'd hate it if someone did that to me. He's a grown man, we've made an arrangement and I trust him. I'm not going to check up on him; that's pathetic.'

*

It was six o'clock on Saturday evening.

'Hi, Danny, it's me. What you up to?'

'Just getting ready for my early night. Watching crap telly; fighting the cat off my pizza.'

'Good for you,' I said. 'Quiet one in then?'

'Yeah, I've got some twitcher coming round at four in the morning to take me to Norfolk.'

'You're not going out for a quickie then?'

'I thought about it, mate, but I couldn't trust myself. If I nipped in for one, I'd probably have two then three et fuckin' cetera, pardon my Latin.'

'Good for you, mate. I'll see you bright and early then.'

'OK, see you then. Looking forward.'

'Cheers.'

Seven o'clock.

'Oh hi, Danny; it's only me again. Sorry to pester.'

'No worries, what's up?'

'Nothing. Just to say, don't forget to bring all your camera gear.'

'Are you taking the piss?'

I felt slightly ashamed. 'Ha, no. But you know these early starts. It's dark; we're in a hurry; very easy to forget things!'

'Don't worry,' he assured me. 'It's all packed ready here, mate. I'm looking at it now.'

'OK, see you tomorrow.'

'Cheers.'

Eight o'clock. 'You are through to Danny Davidson. I'm afraid I'm not here at the moment.'

'Answerphone.'

'Oh dear.' Tori was shaking her head.

'I'll try his mobile.'

Voicemail.

'Try the Imperial Arms.' Tori grinned.

'No, he's probably turned his phone off because he's fed up with me pestering him. I'll leave it.'

In an annoying sing-song voice, Tori was saying, 'It's not going to hap-pen. It's not going to hap-pen.'

'Shut up.'

'That's fifty quid you owe me.'

Nine o'clock. I found myself walking past the Imperial Arms. Just as I thought. There in the car park was Danny's car. Oh dear.

Now, the Imperial is not a place I frequent. For a Cambridge city centre pub, it attracted a rough crowd. Loonies, pond-life, mutants, ageing skinheads, ageing hippies, druggies and knife-wielding pikeys. It did do a decent pint of Adnams for £1.90, though, and the jukebox always seemed to be playing 'Echo Beach' by Martha and the Muffins, so it wasn't all bad. Fat Sid, the landlord, was beaming clammily from piggy ear to piggy ear. He caught sight of me and bellowed across the heaving, smoky room with his usual chubbily cordial manner, 'Piss off, you Arsenal wanker.' This *bon mot* tickled him greatly, judging by the accompanying guffaw. Some of his cronies joined in the merriment.

'Only kidding, mate. Haven't seen you for a while. This is for you.' He thrust a pint of Adnams at me. 'On the house!'

'Actually, Sid, I wasn't going to—'

'Drink up, it's my treat!' He stood over me as I gulped down the strong, soupy ale.

'Actually, I was looking for Danny.'

'Go on, finish it!'

I finished it and a second one was put in its place. 'This one's on you. Oh, and so is my gin and ginger beer! Cheers!'

His guffaws disappeared in the general smog of malevolent cheeriness of city-centre Saturday.

I looked round the bar. There was no sign of Danny, but all the reasons why I'd stopped coming to this pub were lined up blearily at the counter. I wove in and out of the various low-lifes looking for Danny. A few dodgy-looking acquaintances of old bought me a drink and I clearly had to buy them one back. No sign of Danny in the beer garden, by the jukebox, in the gents or under the pool table. Sean the Shirt, a shaven-headed, bare-from-the-waist-up ex-con, swigging a pint of cider with a large dash of gin, told me that he'd been speaking to Danny about five minutes ago. That was promising.

'Or maybe longer than that,' the Shirt continued. 'Or was it last night?'

Then I felt a tap on the shoulder. 'What are you doing here?'

An unpleasant chill engulfed me. It was Tony Zanetti. Tony owned a small company that made and distributed ice cream of an allegedly superior quality. 'Ice T', as he was known, had never liked me after an altercation about a girlfriend of his who had ditched him for me. The truth was that she did ditch him, but not for me. A groundless whisper about me and her had, nevertheless, been born and grown into a strapping rumour that was clearly still in good health.

'Ah, Tony, can I get you a beer?' I said as neutrally as possible. I didn't want to sound patronizing. He looked at me through narrow, alcoholically red eyes.

'Don't patronize me. I can buy my own drinks!'

'OK, fine,' I said peaceably.

'No, hang on a minute, I'll have a double Scotch.'

He swallowed the whisky in one gulp and turned to go, then suddenly grabbed my jacket nearly throwing me off balance. 'I haven't forgotten,' he spat loudly in my face.

Fat Sid hurried over. 'OK, Tony, that's enough of that. You can go home now.'

Ice T looked at Sid, then at me, then back at Sid and left the pub. He staggered into the street, treating the neighbourhood to a slurred, halting and uncomplimentary review on the Imperial Arms, its staff and its clientele. Slightly shaken by this episode, I decided to stay in the bar a bit longer and I ordered myself a large vodka.

There was still no sign of Danny but my search for him was no longer uppermost in my mind. It was eleven thirty. I finished my drink and announced to the bar, 'Right, that's me, gentlemen. I've got to be up by four o'clock. I'm going birdwatching!'

This caused no little amusement.

'Well, you'd better have another drink, then,' said Splash O'Brien.

A 'trebles-all-round' moment ensued and at roughly 1 a.m. it was a distinctly wobbly path I took from the bar, out of the pub door and into the street. I suppose, had I been a bit more sober, it might have occurred to me that Zanetti may have been hanging around waiting for me with something other than charity in his heart. But as it was, I stepped into the darkness glowing with good humour and not a care in the world.

TECHNOLOGY

Here's a tip. If you've just been given a new piece of kit like, say, a tripod and spotting-scope, make sure you have a bit of practice at home first: learn how to unpack it, assemble it and use it. Most gadgets nowadays are so simple they don't even come with instructions, or with instructions so minimal as to be fatuous, that say things like, 'Congratulations, you are now the proud owner of a Zeta 88 tripod. Step one: set up the tripod. Step two: enjoy!'

And the trouble with instructions is that they are written by people who already know how to assemble or operate a particular machine, so they skip things like: unpack, plug in, switch on, hit 'user this' or 'function that'. They tell you to hit the network setup icon on the control panel when you're still looking at a blank blue screen and wondering what the hell an icon is (other than a sacred statue in a Greek Orthodox church).

In short, have a little private practice with your new toy and don't unpack it and try to assemble it when you're standing at the edge of a lake in the salt marshes at a bird reserve surrounded by dozens of experienced birdwatchers, who, of course, are experts with all bits of birding kit.

'Don't you think we should have had a little practice at home with this before bringing it straight out to the reed beds?' Tori asked.

We were walking to the site from the car park, proudly carrying our new toy, still in its box, and eager to see birds that were a few counties away.

'No. These things are so simple they don't need instructions,' I said confidently.

'Do you think we should have unpacked it from the box first?'

'No, coz we'll want to repack it straight away after, won't we?'

We stopped on a wooden walkway by the edge of a lagoon in the reed beds. I started to open the box. This was a fiddly job. The cardboard was quite firm and the end of the box seemed to consist of an inordinately complex arrangement of flaps, grooves and slots. I was beginning to tear at one of these flaps when I noticed that I had caught the attention of two passing twitchers laden with paraphernalia.

'I think you're opening the wrong end.' Tori's voice betrayed a little irritation.

'It's only a cardboard box! I'm sure both ends are the same. They're not that sophisticated.'

'That's the bottom. Why don't you open the top?'

'It's taped; that's what the problem is.'

'I'm sure the other end will open more easily.'

'Just a minute!' I started pulling at the tape and shaking the box.

Something happened. There was a plop, a snigger from the twitchers and the box suddenly felt lighter.

Tori was annoyed. 'Brilliant. It's come out of the top and straight into the pond.'

Lesson one: open the box at the right end.

'Well, don't just stand there. Get it out! It's only shallow.'

After twenty minutes of topless sloshing around in the surprisingly deep water of the lagoon, I retrieved the tripod, which fortunately was hermetically wrapped in stout polythene.

'That's not a bad catch. They normally only come out at night,' said a passer-by.

'I thought you was leech-gathering,' smirked another.

Now, tripods are straightforward, aren't they? Extendible legs make them compact and easy to carry. The three legs have two extensions that telescope out on the release of two clips. 'Well, there's one leg done!' I said, standing the tripod up and watching it instantly collapse and fall over.

Lesson two: remember to relock the clips to stop the extensions sliding back inside the main leg.

The tripod was retrieved from the water again and we made a new attempt at getting it to stand up on its own.

'It still keeps falling over,' Tori said with a pained expression.

'Well just extend one bit at a time.'

'That's what I did!'

'But it has to be the same extension. There's no use you extending the bottom extension on one leg while I'm extending the middle section on another leg. That won't work!'

Lesson three: only extend each leg the same amount at a time.

Eventually our new tripod was erect and solid as a rock. In the event, it had only taken us an hour and five minutes to put it up and a lot of that time was taken up fishing around at the bottom of a lake trying to find it.

'Finally got it up then?' asked the same sarky twitcher who had passed an hour earlier, no doubt having done some top-notch, record-breaking bird spotting.

'Oh, well spotted,' I said as disdainfully as I could manage.

'Are you new to birdwatching, then?' This guy was getting on nerves I didn't know I had.

'Not that it's any of your fucking business,' I started.

'Don't start!' hissed Tori.

'We're actually doing market research for *Which Tripod?* magazine. We're testing various models in the field to see which ones are most user-friendly.'

'Alright, didn't mean to annoy you,' the annoying man went on. 'It's just that if you *are* birdwatching, you're going to need something to put on top of that tripod.'

I looked at the tripod. I looked at Tori. I looked back at the annoying bloke.

'Sorry?'

'Well, some binoculars; a spotter; or a telescope.'

It was a bad-tempered trudge back to the car.

'I assumed you had brought the spotting-scope with you!' I snapped.

Tori snapped back, 'You were the one who announced, "I'll get the gear out of the boot."'

'Well, I assumed everything would be in the same box.'

'Why?' She tutted. 'They are two completely separate items. They wouldn't fit in one box anyway.'

'Oh, I see; so when you saw me only carrying one box you didn't think to say, "Darling, that's just the tripod, why don't you bring the spotting-scope, as well?"'

'I wasn't really paying attention to what you were bringing out of the car. I assumed you knew what you were doing!'

Deep breaths all round. 'Well, why did you assume that?'

'Because of something you said, which was, I think: "Don't fuss, dear, I know what I'm doing."'

We were back at the car. We had walked quickly and I was now annoyed and hot; the cold water dribbling from the twice-submerged tripod on my shoulder was welcome.

'Look, let's not spoil the day bickering,' Tori said soothingly, as she opened the boot. 'Let's start the day again. At least we now know how to set the tripod up; we'll just get the spotting-scope and go back and pretend none of this happened.'

'You are lovely,' I said and gave her the kiss of peace.

'Where is it?' she said, pointing into the empty boot.

'What?'

'The spotting-scope.'

'I don't know. What's it got to do with me?' I said guiltily.

'I left the tripod and scope in the hall by the front door. You said, "I'll put the gear in the car."'

'Yes, but you didn't tell me both boxes were required.'

'I didn't think I needed to tell you; I thought it was obvious,' she said, trying to make it seem as if it was my fault.

'Oh, so it's my fault, is it?'

'Yes.'

'I don't recall you saying, "Have you put both boxes, i.e. the tripod and the spotting-scope, in the boot, darling?"'

She tutted a tut for Britain. 'No, but I did say, "Have you put the gear in the boot, darling?" and you said, "Of course, I have!" so definitely and confidently that I didn't dare ask for an inventory of said gear.'

'Right, that's it. Get in the car.' I slammed the boot shut, got in the car and started the engine.

'Where are we going?'

'Well, as it's my fault, I thought I'd better drive the seventy-five miles back home to collect the spotting-scope!'

'Not really?'

'You don't have to come, as it's my fault – you can go to the visitors' centre and look at the next generation of spotting equipment that we'll have to get when our own becomes obsolete.'

'Or lost at the bottom of a lake!' Tori quipped, and I smiled.

'No, I'm not really driving home, but I know somewhere we can go that could make the day. And it doesn't matter if we haven't got the spotting-scope.'

Half an hour later: the day of birdwatching had been saved. Tori and I were friends again and we found ourselves just feet away from a pair of rare, secretive birds. Woodcock.

'Fantastically hard to see, you know. The cryptic camouflage is so accurate. Amazing plumage; looks like a pile of dead leaves but still manages to be beautiful,' I whispered.

'Not that we'll see the feathers today,' Tori said as the waiter approached.

'And who's having the woodcock?'

THERE YOU ARE, DANNY!

I lay in bed staring through tired eyes at the rotating ceiling. I thought hard.

I'd gone to the Imperial Arms to persuade Danny to stop drinking and go home for an early night so we could get up at four for birdwatching. Danny wasn't there and I'd ended up getting drunk and …

Here the memory became a bit ragged at the edges. Did I have a fight with Tony Zanetti? I looked at the clock. 08.30. Oh dear. So we didn't go birdwatching then?

And it was my fault.

I soon became aware of daylight behind the curtains and a fabulous smell of freshly ground coffee. And toast. Heaven. Yes, if I died and went to heaven and found that it was nothing more than waking up with a hangover and having fresh coffee and toast, I wouldn't complain to God.

'Coffee, sweetheart?' It was lovely Tori.

I smiled. She stroked my face and whispered, 'Late-night drinking and birdwatching don't go together!'

'Have I died and gone to heaven?' I asked.

'Yes,' she said comfortingly.

'Ah well,' I sighed, 'show me to Arsene Wenger's throne, then.'

I heard a match being struck and smelled its acrid smoke. I heard somebody inhale and breathe out wheezily. I smelled cigarette smoke and knew that the next voice I heard would be Danny's.

'You OK, mate?'

'Danny saved your life last night, you know.' Tori sounded annoyed now.

'Well, that's not strictly true,' Danny interrupted. 'I suddenly remembered I'd left my car at the Imperial a few nights ago. And, obviously, I'd need it to drive us up to the coast this morning. So I thought I'd wander over to collect it. When I got to the pub, that twat Zanetti was staggering about outside just as you were leaving the bar. The arse looked as if he was about to jump on you so I grabbed him and got a couple of the boys from the pub to help me "neutralize" him.'

'Cheers, mate.' I reached out and shook Danny's hand.

'Then I dropped you back here. Course I realized the twitching was out the window.'

'You're a mensch, as Kramer would say.'

'Don't worry, mate,' Danny went on. 'Plenty more days for the dicky birds!'

'Right, come on then. Breakfast,' Tori said as she stood up. She turned to me and beamed sunnily. 'Hey, some good news, though.'

'What?'

'That's fifty quid you owe me.'

BIRDS ON TELEVISION

Birds and birdwatching on television are very different to birds and birdwatching in real life. I have watched David Attenborough's *Life of Birds* dozens of times. It's a breathtaking piece of work. In one episode there is wonderful footage of a goshawk. Goshawk is *Accipiter gentilis*. It is a stunning bird. A powerful, awesome predator of woodlands. Dark grey-brown above and an unmistakable whitish breast with fine grey barring. Its broad wings with rounded edges and its long rounded tail mean it can fly fast through woodland, retracting its wings to dodge and weave with breathtaking precision though dense trees. It feeds on other birds, rabbits and squirrels, using speed and stealth as its weapons. If it doesn't catch its prey on the swoop, then it can land on the ground where its long legs make it a formidable runner. All this you can see in exquisite detail on David Attenborough's *Life of Birds*, in the episode called 'The Meat-eaters'.

Real life, I warn you, is very different. My experience of spotting a goshawk bears no comparison. Tori and I were staying in Ross-on-Wye. The huge Forest of Dean was minutes away and at that time of year, early March, there was guaranteed very good birdwatching. The loud whisper in the Goodrich Arms was that the goshawks were up and superb sightings were a foregone conclusion. All you had to do was go to a viewing point called New Fancy, point your binoculars to the east and your object lens would be rammed with goshawks.

Four freezing hours we waited on the viewing platform with half-a-dozen doughty twitchers.

'Never seen a goshawk before?' They looked shocked, as if you'd said something world-shattering like, 'I've never seen the "chandelier" episode of *Only Fools and Horses*.'

Then, eventually, a jolly, red-faced man with a greyish beard shouted something barely intelligible and jabbed a finger towards the distant horizon.

'Look, there it is! It's up! Wow. It's the female. She's big. Awesome. Look at that!'

With freezing fingers trying to steady the binoculars and pull focus, we eventually saw it. For a full two seconds, a small dot disappearing rapidly from the white horizon into the dark canopy of conifers.

'Wonderful.'

'What a great spot!' was the general view.

What a tiny spot, I thought.

'Magnificent,' the twitchers agreed, shaking hands and all but opening a bottle of champagne.

'Hope you new boys got that!' they said to us.

'Yes,' I lied. 'The female's bigger than the male then?'

'Oh yes, absolutely.'

'The male's an even tinier nondescript grey dot,' murmured Tori, and we sped off to our cottage to watch *Life of Birds* on the video again.

But you don't need television's state-of-the-art hi-tech natural history documentaries to enjoy birds on television. Tori and I spend many a winter's evening huddled on the sofa together twitching. The lights are low, the screen flickers, there's a drink by our side and pen and paper in our hand. The tense music of *Midsomer Murders* starts, the scene is set …

Barnaby's classic car glides up the winding driveway between the rhododendrons and stops outside the Tudor-beamed farmhouse. He gets out and looks around the impressive garden.

'Chaffinch!' shouts Tori, and I jump.

But she's right. There in the background is the bright, rolling chirrup of the chaffinch. Damn, one–nil to her.

Barnaby reads the sign on the door: *Midsomer Lodge*. He bangs on the door with the heavy wrought-iron knocker.

'Green woodpecker!' Tori shouts. 'Two–nil.'

'That's not fair, I was having a sip of wine!' I splutter. 'I heard it!'

'Ah, well, you need to concentrate on the programme.'

After twenty-five minutes we'd clocked up three chaffinches, a green woodpecker, two yellowhammers, a rook, eight collared doves, a moorhen, an unconvincing sex scene and three murders. After the third advert break, we joined the inspector and Sergeant Troy by a river where a fisherman had stumbled upon the semi-naked body of the new vicar whom none of the villagers had taken to. I was ready.

'Sedge warbler!' I triumphed. 'Nine–eight and I storm into the lead for the first time in the match!'

'Er, hang on a minute,' said Tori, switching the sound off.

'What? That *was* a sedge warbler. Unmistakable!'

'Yes, I heard it.' She looked serious. 'But you said sedge warbler before it started singing.'

'Er …' I wasn't expecting this. 'Well, look, it's clearly set in April. They're down by the river, I thought it was a fair punt that we'd hear a sedge warbler sooner or later.'

'Sooner or later, maybe. But not half a second before it starts singing.'

'Pure luck!'

'You've seen the episode before, haven't you?'

'A long time ago,' I confessed. 'I didn't realize till I saw the floating vicar. That's what reminded me. I remembered there being lots of sedge warblers about.'

Tori huffily switched off the television and the game was declared null and void.

'Don't you want to know who the murderer was?'

'It was the estate agent, wasn't it? I mean—' She stopped mid-sentence.

'You've seen it before as well, you cheat!'

The following night there was a repeat of *Morse*. Hostilities would recommence.

Many apologies to everyone concerned with the productions. But once you know a few birdsongs they will be with you forever. They will forever distract you. Any drama, or comedy, set in rural England in the spring or summer, and they usually are in spring or summer because that's when England can be most attractively sold to America, will be spoiled for you by the twittering in the background. I've lost count of the number of episodes of *Last of the Summer Wine* that have been ruined for me by a wren or song thrush. Oh, and the script and the acting.

HEAVY

A shell landed close by. The blast sounded shockingly close. I was assured that it was way off and told to calm down. The tanks were busy today. The few seconds between the boom of the shell being fired and the dull explosion as it landed were long and anxious. Was this the stench of war? The choking smell of ordnance discharge I had expected, but all around us I breathed in the smell of freshly turned soil; I thought about the trenches and wondered if this was the real stench of war. I trusted that those men knew what they were doing.

Another heart-stopping boom. I jumped.

'Here they come now,' someone said and we heard the approaching engine of a jeep. A soldier shouted over to us, 'All clear; thanks for waiting!'

We drove on.

What a strange location Salisbury Plain is, a striking variety of habitats for all sorts of diverse creatures. Rabbits, hares, foxes, badgers, deer, game birds, larks, pipits, buzzards, harriers, buntings, finches and the British Army go about their business side by side.

On this day we were looking for a rather special bird.

Some birds are more interesting than others. No, that's not true. What am I saying? Some birds interest *me* more than others. I suppose that's it.

I walk past ducks every day. I hear crows every day. Most days I can hardly move for wood pigeons. They're all interesting birds.

The crow family is devilishly savvy. Wood pigeons shouldn't be disregarded just because they're so good at breeding. And the poor mallard is stunning really, but it's just so common. And tame. You have to swing a well-aimed boot at one before it even considers waddling away. Without being in the 'duck-is-a-duck' school of birdwatching, it's tempting not to spend too much time and effort on them. You have a stretch of water, you'll get duck on it; mallards definitely, and OK a few others: teal, wigeon, gadwall and garganey, perhaps even an American wigeon, but they're all rather 'ducky'. And geese. They're more 'goosey' than 'ducky', but the same thing goes. Easy to see, geese, and they hang around in huge gangs. Swans the same.

And seagulls are all, to a lesser or greater extent, a bit samey. White and grey and loud and definitely 'seagully'.

Perhaps I should have been more excited when I saw my first great bustard.

Now, here is a quite amazing creature. The world's heaviest flying bird and at one time very much a part of the British countryside. This beast of a bird has a pale blue-grey head, white underparts and ruddy plumage, heavily barred with black, and an often cocked fantail. In breeding plumage the male develops bizarre, strangely human, large, white, moustachial whiskers. These features and its size made it very attractive to collectors. Being attractive to collectors is not a good thing for a bird. Being stuffed and mounted in a glass case in someone's drawing room are not ideal breeding conditions for a bird. This generously breasted bird, so reminiscent of the turkey, was also more than welcome on the dining table. Changes in agricultural practices as well as human persecution would have contributed to its decline, but whatever the causes the last known breeding pair of this once abundant British bird was resident in Suffolk in 1832. The name 'bustard' or 'bistard' was first recorded in the 1300s. It shares the morpheme 'tard' with its scientific name, *Otis tarda*. From Greek and Latin this should mean something like 'the slow bird with funny little ear tufts', but there is nothing particularly slow (or late, or tardy, or retarded) about this huge bird. For its size, it runs and flies quite powerfully. It certainly looks no dimmer than most 'game' birds. *Tarda* may be an even older Celtic or Basque word, the meaning of which no one knows, or if they do know, they're not telling.

Currently, the Great Bustard Group is running a reintroduction programme on Salisbury plain. Chicks hatched in Saratov in Russia are released into a huge holding pen, where they can eat and forage in safety until they're ready to fly off on their own. Each bird has a colour-coded, numbered wing-tag for easy identification, and some have radio transmitters so that their whereabouts can be checked. It's an exciting project and depends a lot on the general public who are encouraged to report any sighting of the bird, noting, at least, the colour of the wing-tag. And the great bustard is not a bird you'd mistake for any other bird, so the general public will be in no doubt that it has seen something special. This is more than an escaped turkey. But there again it does look a bit turkey-like. And it has that general ground-dwelling game-bird look to it, so, as I said, on seeing one in the wild my face registered the sighting with a lesser-than-expected 'wow factor'.

It happened when I was filming for the BBC's *Saving Planet Earth*. I was looking at three species under threat: the European eel, the barbastelle bat and the great bustard. I was being driven over the plain in a Land Rover by David Waters of the Great

Bustard Group; there was a camera fixed on the outside of the vehicle, pointing back through the open passenger window at me. There was no hiding place. I had to be careful: no looking at my watch, reading the paper or yawning. The last was the most difficult as I'd just consumed two and a half pints of Great Bustard Ale in a pub near Stonehenge called, of course, the Great Bustard Inn.

It was a clear day and we were following the faint bleeps of the radio transmitter on our receiver; it was getter louder. Somewhere not too far away was a great bustard.

'That signal's getting stronger, David, does that mean we're getting closer?' I asked with the dim fatuity expected of television presenters nowadays.

'It does indeed, Rory. Keep your eyes peeled.'

'You bet,' I said, struggling against the overwhelming desire to unpeel them. 'I can't wait to see my first bustard,' I said, sounding like a twat, which I believe is also the job of most TV presenters now. Like all ground-dwelling birds, great bustards are hard to see, despite their size. David had advised me to look out for the long, grey neck above the stalks of the oilseed rape.

'Wow, look, look, there! Over there! Amazing!' I shrieked with genuine excitement. I grabbed my binoculars and trained them on the magnificent bird not ten yards away: large, elegant, soaring close to the ground, pale grey and white like a huge, malevolent seagull, its wings held in a shallow 'V', the dihedral. It gently swooped out of sight behind the hedge.

'That was brilliant,' I said, turning to David. 'The first one I've ever seen!'

The bustard man turned towards me with a mild rebuke, 'That was a hen harrier, Rory.'

'I know. Wasn't it fantastic?'

The producer who was watching the footage from my camera without sound on a monitor about a mile away was very impressed.

When we met up with him later, he said, 'That was great. Wonderful reaction from Rory when he saw the bustard. Genuine excitement!'

'We didn't see a bustard,' David said. 'It was a hen harrier.'

A pause.

'Oh well,' said Peter, the producer, 'we'll get a shot of a bustard and cut in Rory's reaction to the harrier. That'll look fab.'

DANNY AND THE
SIMILARITY OF WADERS

'Bloody hell, there's hundreds of the buggers!'

Danny was looking out across the salt marsh from the hide at the huge numbers of birds assembled there.

'Er, can you moderate your language, please!'

A prissy couple of birding spinsters in the hide objected to his beginner's exuberance.

'You must excuse him.' I turned to them reassuringly, 'He's a beginner. Just started; full of enthusiasm.'

They tutted and walked out.

'Right, Dan, lesson one: waders.'

'I haven't brought any, mate, I've only got my jeans.'

'Don't worry, you'll grow out of puns like that, Dan, eventually. Even I did. Tits, peckers, shags: all those. A wader is a wading bird. They tend to hang around together and they're quite similarly marked so when you see a huge number like this it's easy to think they're all the same, but there are probably twenty or so different species out there. And we're lucky it's late spring because they're in their breeding plumage. In the winter they are all identical. Identically dull. So, because they wade, they tend to have long legs; usually a long bill for poking around in mud and sand. Sometimes curled down like a curlew, occasionally turned up like an avocet, which is that white one with black bits.'

'That's a lovely bird!' He began to set up his camera.

'And what you'll notice also is that waders are very obliging photographic subjects. They pootle about in the water for hours, hardly moving. They'll pose for you, Danny. You can't fail to get a brilliant photo of a wader!'

'Wanna bet?' chuckled Danny, taking out a cigarette.

'You're not going to smoke in here, are you? You'll get arrested!'

'There's just you and me. Come on, mate!'

'If anyone comes in, I'm not with you.'

He puffed away as he assembled the telephoto lens of his camera.

'At least you haven't bought a bottle of Scotch.'

'Ta-ra!' With a flourish, he produced a hipflask from his jacket pocket.

'I'm sure we're breaking all sorts of twitching rules, you know.'

I took a burning swig of whisky and conceded that this was fun.

'Party time,' he enthused. 'All we need now is some birds! Look, there's some. Ha ha ha. Sorry, mate. That's the last time I do the bird pun.'

We settled down to some mild twitching and Danny turned out to be a keen learner.

'So what's that one on that lump of mud?'

'That's a dunlin.'

'Is that common?'

'Very common. It's the wader's wader. It's the SI unit of waderness. It's a good one to know well because you can use it as a yardstick to identify other waders.'

'So what are we looking for to identify it as a dunlin?'

'Well, size of course. About eight inches. Its beak: longish, black, tapered, slightly decurved.'

'Hey,' Danny interrupted. 'Remember that time you couldn't get your computer working and you rang me up and asked me if I could sort it out?'

'Probably.'

'And I said, "Is it booted up at the moment?" And you said, "What the fuck are you talking about, Danny?" And I said, "Booted up! Switched on! Running. Everybody knows what booted up means." And you said, "I don't know what it means so everybody doesn't know what it means so don't use jargon. Don't assume the person you're teaching knows anything about what you're talking about."'

'Yes, that sounds like me,' I admitted.

'Well, what the fuck does *decurved* mean, then?'

'Oh, I do apologize. Curved downwards. These are adults, just about in their breeding plumage. So black patch on their belly, with dark streaks above on the breast. Back like all waders looks dull but close up is quite a nice arrangement of chestnutty-brown and black and cream.'

For the first time in my life I felt 'wise'. A strange feeling. I was a schoolteacher. A mentor. I was a wise elder imparting my hard-earned knowledge to a keen, uneducated youngster. I quite liked it. It made me feel important, a feeling I realized I was unused to.

'*Calidris alpina* is the scientific name, if you're interested.'

'No, I'm not. Don't get all schoolteachery on me.'

'Sorry.'

'Yes, I see what you mean. The longer you look at it, the prettier it gets. Good: that's one I've learned. Dunlin. What are those two by that wooden post?'

'Dunlin.'

'Oh yes, so they are. And that one there?'

'Dunlin.'

'Don't tell me, that big group on the island: dunlin?'

'Correct.'

'That's not a dunlin though, is it?'

'Where?'

'Four o'clock from that wooden post. About ten feet away?'

I turned my binoculars nonchalantly in the direction Danny indicated and gave the bird a casual look.

'Yeah, dunlin. That lot are all dunlin!'

'But it's slightly smaller.'

'Hard to tell through binoculars.'

'And it's more ruddy and hasn't got an obvious black belly patch.'

I said, 'Dunlin', again firmly but had another look anyway. 'Blimey, it's a little stint. You're right; well done!'

'You see! Dunlin, my arse. You don't know what you're talking about!'

I was slightly annoyed that I hadn't been more thorough in my identification, so I thought I'd score a cheap point.

'Yeah, but what's its scientific name?'

Danny furrowed his brow and took in a sharp breath as if he was seriously thinking about attempting an answer.

'Er ... little stint? How about *Calidris minuta*?'

This shocked me. This was my territory. Not Danny's. I'm the only person allowed to know all the Latin names for British birds!

He started laughing and pointed to a large coloured chart on the wall behind me showing all the common waders, their English and scientific names.

'Jesus, what's that smell?'

Danny had flung a cigarette end into the dry strawy corner of the hide and it had caught light. Splashing whisky on it didn't exactly dowse the flames but after a few minutes' jumping and stamping, the fire was out.

'For God's sake, Danny, we're going to end up in jail at this rate!'

After that little shock we passed the time pleasantly, and within a few hours Danny could confidently identify dunlin, redshank, oystercatcher, avocet, ruff, knot, lapwing, golden plover, grey plover, curlew, little stint and a shelduck. The other ducks were still those quacky things and the seagulls remained seagulls. But his knowledge had grown admirably and there were some superb-looking photographs on the way. We got back to the car. Loaded it up and drove out of the reserve in search of an old-fashioned pub for a pint and an ornithological debrief. As we drove away from the coast we travelled up a slight hill and I looked in the mirror at the expanse of reed beds and marshes. To my horror, roughly in the direction of where we'd been, a large dark plume of smoke was arising. Something was on fire.

DULL AND DRAB FEMALES

A summer's evening. A river. Ducks, geese, swans and that ubiquitous pair of wild water chickens: the moorhen and the coot.

Coot with its signature matt black plumage and spotlessly white bill and facial shield. Bald as a coot. The coot, of course, is not bald in the human sense of hairless. Neither is the United States' sacred bald eagle. But then bald originally meant 'white'. A bald person's head was white, that is, pale, compared to a person with hair. I was musing on these things as Tori and I sat at a quayside bar. It was also a great place for other, non-avian, animate objects.

Look at those delicious creatures. Girls out on the town. Rolling, wiggling and bouncing firmly and sweetly. Their scant clothes hanging on to their bodies as if mostly by accident. A single man's dream.

And I was sitting there with my wife sipping a flat lager.

'Isn't this lovely?' Tori asked.

'Perfect,' I assented.

'Then why are you looking so damned miserable, then?'

Before I had time to make up my answer, I noticed that walking towards us were two generously proportioned girls so scantily clad they seemed to be wearing their bodies on the outside of the clothes. Tori, who had noticed the target of my intent stare, turned to me and said, 'I know what you're thinking: whatever possesses some girls to come out dressed like that? Who's going to look at them? The state of them! Appalling.'

'Yes, you're right, sweetheart; my thoughts entirely.'

It certainly does not happen in bird world. It's a truth universally acknowledged among birders, though probably denied by a lot of them, that the bird they really want to see is the adult male. The adult male in full breeding plumage. Not the duller, drabber female. These words are not mine. Look in any bird book and the language is the same:

'Next to the brilliant male, the female is rather plain.'

'The female is smaller and duller.'

'Female is a rather drab version of the male.'

'The female is similar to the male but the colours and marking are weak and washed-out looking.'

'Female drab.'

'Female plainer with fewer streaks.'

'Female plainer with more streaks.'

'Female browner all over, with less pronounced markings and a generally drab look.'

The point can be illustrated by several common species that even the bird-not-watcher will recognize.

The mallard duck: every pond, lake, river estuary, harbour or puddle will have a mallard. The male with his shimmering bottle-green head, white neck ring, clean yellow bill and flashy purple-blue wing-bar, and a dull brown female paddling behind.

The blackbird; female a brown bird.

The greenfinch; female not green.

The chaffinch; female a dull version of the male.

The sparrowhawk: male slate-bluey-grey above and barred orange beneath; female greyish bars beneath and dull, dark brown above.

The golden oriole: male truly fabulous, startling yellow; the dullish green female doesn't stand a chance against a stud coloured like that.

And as for the ruff … In spring, the male doesn't bear thinking about. A bizarre, broad feathery collar that can be black, white or reddish-orange. Forgive me, but it's bordering on the ludicrous. Especially for a British bird. No competition from the duller, drabber, plainer, dingier, mousier, more washed-out, lacklustre female.

'Woah, wait a minute now, Rory,' I hear you cry. 'What about the grey phalarope?'

Alright, yes, I'll let you have that one. The grey phalarope male is duller and drabber than the female, which is, in the summer, a rather fetching brick-orange. And the dreary male of this species is the one that incubates the eggs and rears the chicks.

Come on, male grey phalarope memo to self: 'Must be more brightly coloured.'

But the rule of thumb is largely true, and in species that have drab males, the man-birds make up for it by having louder or more intricate songs.

It didn't seem fair somehow, back in human-world, on a summer's Friday evening in Mojo's cocktail bar. Surrounded by sublime and exotic beauty, there was I, the dullest and drabbest of dull, drab males, drably and vainly leering over the dreary rim of his dull beer glass. And I don't think standing up and delivering a loud, intricate song was going to help.

A punt full of hen-party-goers had pulled up alongside the quay. Most of them in T-shirts and bikini bottoms. They climbed on to the quayside and started cavorting, free from care and sobriety. I couldn't take my eyes off them. Tori nudged me and pointed towards the river.

'Moorhens are quite nicely marked when you see them close up, aren't they?' she said.

I nodded. 'You took the words out of my mouth!'

DANNY PUTS ONE OUT

After some reprehensibly bad driving round single-track country lanes, Danny arrived at a pub so inhospitable looking it would be guaranteed to be free of twitchers. There were two cars in the car park. One without wheels and one without doors.

'This is our kind of place!' said Danny, lighting up a cigarette. 'I can't imagine any birdwatchers come here.'

'I can't imagine any humans come here. Listen, why don't you just not smoke for a bit. You've done enough damage already today.'

We walked into the tiny public bar.

It was packed with birdwatchers who stopped talking as one and turned towards us. It was so unwelcoming, I thought one of them might come up and tie the dartboard round my neck.

I've never really done 'jauntily' that well, but I took a deep breath and made an attempt, starting with, 'Evenin' all.'

Much to our relief they nodded non-committally and got back to their conversations.

We squeezed into a gap at the bar to order a couple of pints, bisecting a worrying dialogue about 'the fire' at Titchwell.

Danny and I exchanged glances of the 'uh oh better not hang around here too long' variety. We were staggered that news of a not very big fire about ten miles away that probably only started half an hour earlier could have reached this remote watering-hole before us. That's Norfolk for you: big county, small place.

'I heard there was a couple of blokes in a hide drinking whisky and smoking. Not birders. Up from London, I expect. Probably staying at the Hoste in Burnham Market with them showbiz types,' said one.

'Two pints of the local bitter please,' Danny said cheerily to our host.

'That's off,' he said glumly.

'Looks like it,' Danny replied, pointing at a glass on the bar. The victualler was unimpressed.

'Two lagers, then. Thirsty work this twitching, eh?'

The entire room looked us up and down. 'See anything special?' asked someone.

'A fire,' Danny said.

'Yeah,' I added, 'we thought it might be a phoenix.'

'I know all about the fire,' a man at the bar said, fixing his knowing eyes on us.

It was a worrying moment that lasted longer than moments should.

'Er, do you know how it started?' I asked tentatively.

'Course, I know how it started!' he blurted.

Another worrying moment, at least as long, if not longer, than the last worrying moment.

'I started it myself. Some of them old reeds and dead wood is no use to man nor beast, you got to burn it. Away from the reserve though.'

'Of course.' Danny and I nodded with enthusiasm, endorsing the local's good countryside practice. Relieved by the knowledge he was not about to be arrested for arson, Danny's confidence grew and he instigated some jolly banter with the other customers.

'OK, any of you twitchers ever seen a dunlin?'

There were a few dismissive snorts from around the room.

'What about a curlew? Any of you heard of one of them?'

'Is this your first day birding then?' asked the barman.

'How dare you, sir! I was born in a nest and raised by ruffs.'

A voice from the corner shouted, 'Have you seen a little crake?'

'No,' answered Danny, 'when did you last have it?'

The landlord had apparently tired of our presence in his establishment and pointed at the two half-full glasses in front of us.

'I expect you chaps want to drink those pints up and leave the premises now, don't you? I expect you two are staying up at the Hoste as well, aren't you, with your London friends. S'pec you'll want to get back up there soonest, won't you?'

'Yeah, well, we just stopped off for one,' I said draining my glass.

Danny did the same, with a parting, 'Bloody nice meeting you chaps. Take care now.' And as the door closed behind us he went on a bit louder, 'Hope this pub never burns to the ground. Could cause up to three quids' worth of damage.'

We were out in the car park.

'So, back home?' Danny said.

'No fear,' I said. 'That miserable git has given me an idea. Let's go to the Hoste.'

Years earlier on a colourless November afternoon, Tori and I had been driving round North Norfolk after an abortive bird-watching session. As frequently happens in that place at that time of year, the sea, the sky and the land had drained into an icy monochrome as daylight faded and the flocks of huddled waders had become part of the mottled background. That evening, sunset had been called off at short notice and the sky was as slatey in the west as it was in the east. We drove through one anonymous village after another. The houses were blind, the streets were empty and the occasional string of Christmas lights in a window merely emphasized the bleakness.

Then we drove into Burnham Market.

The town was ablaze with light, music and laughter. The pale yellow façade of a pub called the Hoste Arms dominated a pretty village green whose tiny brook reflected the dazzling main street, bustling with excitement and smiles. This was an oasis. A lavishly tasteful, old world Las Vegas in the desert of winter Norfolk. It seemed like a mirage. But we stopped. We stayed. We went back over and over again and it became our base-camp for birdwatching and much more besides.

'This place is bloody excellent, mate,' enthused Danny, drooling as his eyes passed along the array of real ales and real barmaids.

We fell in with a fairly bad crowd, which was fairly good, and had a very good time, which was very bad. I phoned a jealous and incredulous Tori to say that we had been forced to stay at the Hoste in Burnham Market that night, due to fire in one of the hides at Titchwell bird reserve.

I introduced Danny to an acquaintance of mine who was a photographer in London, who was coincidentally doing some freelance work for a natural history magazine. Danny and he talked a load of apertures while I got in some mild womanizing practice just in case I'd have to come out of retirement and do it again for real one day.

In a corridor on the way back from the gents I passed a glass case containing a stuffed bird. Judging by the date on the case, it was a genuine antique and a testament to the Victorians' mania for taxidermy. This bird was another resident of the soggy world of reed beds and accordingly it was clothed in another mottled, feathery symphony of browns, blacks, creams and rusts; but a spectacular symphony, none the less. I'd never seen one this close up but, then, few people had.

'Hey, Danny, I've just seen a little crake.'

'I was wondering where that had got to!'

SEXUAL DIMORPHISM

Boys and girls are different. No, it's true. And there are more male then female birdwatchers. And there are more men than women in pub-quiz teams. Men like the names of things. They like learning lists. Why should this be? What happened to us fearless hunters who once risked death on a daily basis to stalk dangerous prey and bring home meat for the table? The hunting stopped, that's what happened. By and large women made the home and reared the children. It could be argued that their role has changed less over the centuries. But what of the alpha hunter male? Hunting was about knowing the land, mapping it, learning the names of places, recognizing what was prey and what was food, the names of both, the behaviour of both. It was about looking into the distance. The hunter had to dominate the world, he had to control it; to control it, he had to know it. Knowing or not knowing meant surviving or perishing. So, the modern, sedentary, castrated male hunter twiddles his thumbs and idles away his time cataloguing facts. Is not the pub quiz an elaborate ceremonial version of hunting, a coded and symbolic assertion of the hunter male's dominance over his environment and, indeed, over his rival males? We have gone from scanning the landscape, spotting our quarry, ambushing it and tearing it apart to knowing who won the FA Cup in 1979, which of Henry the VIII's wives survived him or which common bird is *Strix aluco*.

This is not a sexist generalization but based on experience. I'm not rerunning a tired cliché of the sort that claims that 'girls can't read maps' nor 'catch a cricket ball'. I am familiar, of course, with these theses. And when it comes to lists of seemingly unconnected names and numbers, do men do it better because they care more?

Or maybe it's to women's credit that they care less. The female likes and knows the big picture, the general picture, and is not bogged down or preoccupied by tiny details. How far is that mountain away from here? Is that animal spoor a wildebeest or leopard? How long would it take me to run to that tree? Is that plant poisonous? Which is the only Beatles' song with the word 'peanuts' in it?

Girls want to cut the crap and get to the good bit. I am touched when I hear girls talk about a night out. The conversation could go like this:

'I met this bloke in the pub last night ...'

'Yeah ...'

'And he walks over and he starts chatting me up ...'

'No? What was he like?'

'Well, he wasn't bad. Quite hot actually.'

'Really?'

'Yeah, but he didn't realize that I knew him.'

'What?'

'I know who he is. And I know his girlfriend!'

'Noooo! Get away ...'

And so it goes on. An interesting tale of intrigue. I fancy that if two men embarked on a similar conversation, it might go like this:

'I met this girl in the pub last night.'

'Which pub?'

'Lamb and Flag.'

'Where's that?'

'Corner of Conway Street.'

'Oh I know. Used to be the Moon and Sixpence.'

'That's the one.'

'What's it like nowadays?'

'Good. Nice drop of Young's. Keeps his beer well.'

There are differences between males and females in the birding world too. Put bluntly: boys like birds of prey and girls like warblers. I'm well aware that generalizations are clumsy tools and can be unfair and misleading, but my limited observations tell me that boys like raptors and girls like BJs. (Brown jobbies, if you must know. Or LBJs – little brown jobbies, in twitching parlance.)

You can understand this superficially. Raptors attack things and rip them to shreds or carry them off somewhere and rip them to shreds later. And they have all the equipment that goes with this: huge powerful talons, hooked bills and fabulous eyesight, which means they have big eyes in a perpetual frown. A piercing glare that seems to say, 'What are you looking at, fuck-face?'

Boys like this.

The LBJs, which are mainly warblers, are tiny, slim, secretive birds usually with amazing songs. They are pale beneath and brown above. Sometimes they are streaky brown above and pale beneath. Sometimes they are streaky brown above and streaky pale beneath. Rarely, though, streaky pale beneath and not streaky brown above. They are, in short, cute birds.

Girls like this.

But I don't think this is the heart of the matter. LBJs take a lot of care, patience and hard work to see. Boys do not like this. LBJs skulk and hide deep in trees, bushes, hedges and reeds. Boys can't be bothered with all that nonsense, even though, as a girl will tell you, the bird, when you finally see it, is beautiful, delicately marked and superbly individual, not just a little brown job.

Raptors, on the other hand, are easy. They perch openly, alert and busy. The glide, hover or soar, in full view of everything, except, of course, some unlucky mammal on the ground. If there is a red kite about, you will see it. And spectacular it is. There is absolutely no effort involved in finding a red kite in the sky and watching its lofty magnificence for hours. A piece of twitching piss.

Boys like this.

Warblers, on the other hand, are tricky. Well, for a start, pick up a book of British birds and look in the index under warblers. There are forty-two entries. Most people have probably never heard of any of them, though those with a little country knowledge, or maybe pub-quiz knowledge, may have heard of these:

The whitethroat: a pretty bird that used to be widespread and resident in this country, and now visits from April onwards. In the olden days country people used to call them Peggy. 'Morning, Peggy Whitethroat,' they'd say. I've no idea why. Next time I'm in the olden days, I'll ask a country person. The whitethroat takes it name from the colour of its throat. Which is? Anyone? White! Very good. It often sings its scratchy but musical song perched openly when its white throat is unmistakable. Its scientific name is *Sylvia communis*, meaning 'common forest dweller'. It is not as *communis* as it once was, nor particularly forest-dwelling, but it does give its name to a whole bunch of similar birds, the 'sylvia warblers', one of which the whitethroat is usually paired with in books. Another well-known bird:

The blackcap: as you probably can tell from its name, this bird has *not* got a white throat. Like all warblers this one has a lovely song, bright and clear, getting louder and faster. Its scientific name is *Sylvia atricapilla*, which means 'forest dweller with a black cap'.

The chiffchaff, one of my favourites already mentioned, is the little bird with the memorable two-tone song. The chiffchaff is virtually identical to the **willow warbler**, its twin, you could say, but the tiny, dull, greeny-brown willow warbler's song could not be less identical. An ascending trill becoming a cascading warble, fading away but finishing with a slight flourish.

'They are very similar but both beautiful in their own sweet way,' Tori assured me.

'If you say so,' I added cursorily.

'Birds of prey are obvious. They're too easy to see.'

'I like easy,' I said, hoping to put the matter to rest.

'They're just there. Alone in the sky. It's as if they're shouting, "Hey, look at me, I'm a bird of prey!"'

'In my book, that's good.' I puffed my chest out and added, 'We hunters have a special bond!'

There was a short, unkind snigger from my side. It was early evening and we were 'stalking' a sedge warbler at the edge of a field by the river.

'Look at that!' She pointed at the small bird. A small brown bird. Streaked. The sedge is streaked and, through binoculars, rather engagingly marked. Its song, if you can call it that, is a loud, fast, excitable mix of trills, clicks, squeaks and whistles. Apparently, according to those with lots of time and sound-recording equipment on their hands, the sedge warbler has never been known to make the same noise twice.

'Hey, look,' shouts Tori. 'It's parachuting!'

And it parachutes. It does a short song flight from its perch in the undergrowth, then glides back down again.

It is lovely. And this parachuting business is quite impressive. We watched it 'parachuting' a few more times. On the third one, there was a sudden, loud, high-pitched squeak.

A dark angular blur shot past us.

A sparrowhawk.

No more sedge warbler.

'That's what I call a bird!'

Tori pulled a dismissive face and walked off.

DANNY AND THE BLACKBIRDS

It was a nice, cosy suburban bedroom. But very fifties. Too much fabric. Curtains, bedspreads, seat covers, cushions, woollen flower-pot covers. And too many flowers in the patterns. And all the colours too dark. It gave the impression the room was caving in on us. We were being drowned in rhododendrons and suffocated with mauve. Despite the attempted homeliness, this place had no heart to it. The bedroom did not smell of bedroom. It smelled of hospital. Disinfectant and anaesthetic. The uneasy smell of chemicals that hide disease and mask death. Danny lay awkwardly upright on too many flowery bolster pillows. He was clearly in shock. His white eyes were bulging. The blueness of his thin lips was empha-sized by the grey pallor of his face. The dryness of his throat made his voice grate, and a sudden strange noise caused panic. Was he trying to speak or was he choking?

I looked at the doctor. 'Do something then!' The man looked blank. 'Come on, for Christ's sake! You're the doctor!'

The doctor returned a horrified stare at me. 'I'm not a doctor,' he stammered. 'I'm a man wearing a white coat.'

What did he mean by that? Was he surrendering responsibility?

'Has he had painkillers? Have you given him painkillers? He needs something. Urgently!' I was having difficulty getting their attention.

'There's something in his throat. Look, he's got something stuck there down his mouth, down the back of his gullet,' said one of the medical students.

'It's a feather. A black feather! I know what ...' The doctor thrust his hand in Danny's mouth, extracted a small black feather and immediately spit, phlegm and sticky clots of blood spewed from Danny's lips.

The man wearing the white coat shook his head. 'We're going to have to open him up.'

I was afraid it would come to this. 'The whole chest?'

'Yeah, cut through the ribcage, get that out of the way and slice into the lungs.'

He sounded matter-of-fact and detached.

'How long will it take?' I asked.

'Not long at all,' he said. 'Very quick, in fact. Watch this!'

I couldn't believe what happened next. The doctor produced a long-bladed knife and rammed it into Danny's sternum and split his chest. It plopped open with a warm hiss. The escaping air reeked of urine, damp straw and animal filth. And then we saw them: free now from the cage of his ribs, four-and-twenty blackbirds. Large slimy crows? Crows deformed by an oil-slick? Or perhaps mutant cormorants covered in coal-black grease. Unable to see beyond a gummy squint, unable to move beyond a pitiful spasm, unable to crow beyond a rasping rattle. This was the nest of the birds of death.

I picked one up. 'Danny, what sort of bird is this?'

'Is it a dicky bird?'

'That's not good enough; I want the scientific name. I want the Linnean binomial!'

'I can't stand this,' said Danny getting out of bed.

'Where are you going?' I asked.

'Pub, mate. Must have a beer. And fags, mate. Got to get a snout.' And he disappeared.

We sat together in the pub. 'And that's how it ended?' I asked.

'That was how it ended.' Danny looked quite shaken, but he managed a smile. 'But you, you bastard, asking me for the Latin names for birds after my body had been cut open.'

I hoped that I would never do that in real life. 'And what would Dr Freud have to say about a dream like that?'

'It's got to be about smoking, hasn't it?' said Danny reluctantly.

'Er ... well, it's quite possible.'

'If I'm going to keep having dreams like that, I'm going to be too scared to go to sleep.'

'What are you going to do about it, then?' I asked.

'I'm going to have to seriously consider giving it up.'

'What, smoking?'

'No, sleeping!'

FIRST OF THE YEAR

A friend of mine, who is resident in an exotic faraway Eastern place, once said to me, 'What's odd about England is the seasons. How do you put up with things changing all the time?'

To me, the question seemed incomprehensible; almost sacrilegious. How does he put up with every day being the same tedious round of rain, sweltering sun, humidity, rain and so on?

'I always know what the day is going to be like,' he boasts.

And is that a good thing? Is that not like being in a prison? Does that not turn each day's weather into a routine, a drudgery? The subtle change to the landscape as the seasons pass is surely one of the unrivalled pleasures of the English countryside. The snowdrops, crocuses, daffodils and the tentative pale greens as winter gives way to spring and the gentle days of May bursting with blossom and ... but you already know. I don't need to tell you. Keats and Wordsworth would have been lost without the four seasons. And as for poor old Vivaldi!

I once told my children that birdwatching was nothing like trainspotting because, unlike trains, birds do not follow a timetable. But they do, of course.

As any countryman will tell you, our bird life is locked into the timetable of the seasons and the accompanying changes. We have resident birds that do different things at different times of the year: singing to find a mate, mating, nest-building, frenzied food gathering as the young arrive, the young fledging and maybe another bash at breeding.

Then we have the visitors. A whole different set of birds arrives in spring, autumn and winter. It is a pleasure to see or hear the song of a new arrival; some birds that have come from as far as South Africa turn up on a favourable breeze to feed and breed in England.

They arrive bringing delight, but they also bring mystery. Birds migrate so they are always near an abundant food source, but why do they fly so much further than they need to? Swallows winter in South Africa, fly to us for the summer to breed and then return. But why here? I have seen swallows in Aberdeen in the summer. They've come from South Africa to find food to sustain their breeding, but on the way they have flown over Central Africa, which has more than enough food for them. And Greece, Italy, Spain, France. Loads of flying insects in all those places. No disrespect, but why the hell Aberdeen? And their navigational abilities defy belief; they are the stuff of NASA's dreams. The cuckoo, born here in English woodland, flies south to find a mate. The couple returns here to leave their egg in the nest of an unsuspecting pipit or warbler. The staggering mystery is how did the cuckoo find its mate? Brought up by its small brown surrogate parents, a cuckoo had never seen another cuckoo before.

The unexplained does not diminish our joy at seeing or hearing the first of the year. It is an annual pleasure that Tori and I share. In our house, there's a tangible excitement as March and April approach.

Who will get the first chiffchaff?

Blackcap?

Sedge warbler?

Swallow?

This is so much a case of a pleasure shared, a pleasure doubled.

This is a true point of connection; something you share with some-one you love; a connection with that person and a very concrete connection with the seasons, with nature, with the world.

I mention the cuckoo because it is the most identifiable arrival. People would write to the national press to boast 'first of the spring'. Frederick Delius, Bradford's most famous musical son, wrote 'On Hearing The First Cuckoo In Spring', which surprisingly consists of more than two notes.

And one swallow doesn't make a summer but it certainly means the end of winter. I love the fact that this phrase is now so fossilized in our language that scarcely a sporting weekend goes by without some report using the cliché. 'Middlesbrough may have won three on the trot but one swallow doesn't make a summer.' Or: 'One swallow doesn't make a summer, the Red Sox are still bottom of the league.'

Our summer visitors are not exactly clockwork, but it's amazing how close to the same date they arrive each year. Because the chiff-chaff has such a recognizable song and its arrival is usually around the time of my birthday (St Patrick's Day, but keep it to yourself, I don't like a lot of fuss), I always note my first hearing of it. For me and Tori this is very special, *the* moment that winter is over.

And how about this? In 2003, 2004 and 2005 I heard my first chiffchaff on the same date. The 15th of March. I wonder if Julius Caesar heard one on that fateful day? In 2006 it was much later, the 22nd of March. In 2007 it was the 19th. It was about ten in the morning and I was walking down a tree-lined street in town when I heard it. I phoned Tori at work straight away. Standing right under the chiffing and chaffing little bird, I said, 'Listen to this,' and pointed the phone towards the tree. 'Did you hear it?'

'I can't hear you. There's a lot of traffic noise.'

'Listen. Can you hear it? Isn't it amazing?'

'I can only hear a bus, I think, or a lorry.'

'Wait, I'll hold the phone up as high as I can ... there, did you hear it then?'

'Sorry, darling, you're breaking up.'

'What did you say?'

'Listen, we'll have to speak later. It's all crackly.'

'But did you hear it?'

'Sorry what was that?'

'Did you hear it? First of the year!'

'Hello? Are you still there?'

'Hello ... I think I've lost you.'

'Hello? ... Hello? ... Look, I'll call back later.'

So I waited till she got home. I couldn't wait to tell her. 'Sorry about this morning,' she said as soon as she walked in the door. 'I couldn't hear anything you were saying.'

'Don't worry, I said. 'It's just—'

She interrupted me straight away.

'Oh, guess what! I heard a chiffchaff this morning. First of the year. Just before you phoned me, in fact.'

'I heard one as well!'

'Liar,' she mocked.

'That's why I phoned you.'

'Yeah, right!'

She's lying. I know she is. 'Oh and something else,' I add. 'I saw a swift!'

'Blimey, that's amazing! That is early. I'm impressed. Where did you see that?'

'Er ...' I mumble, 'on a repeat of *Bergerac*.'

DANNY, THE PUPIL
AND THE TEACHER

'Redshank,' exclaimed Danny, pointing at the water's edge.

And so it was.

It had been nearly a year since I introduced Danny to twitching. Nearly causing a major fire in a bird reserve and having nightmares about terrifying growths in his chest had not noticeably made him cut down on smoking, but he had retaken up his old hobby of photography with a commendable zeal that was earning him money and taking him over Europe and beyond.

'Yes, that's a redshank.'

I was tempted to act the real twitcher and say, 'Yes; or is it a spotted redshank?' even though I knew it *wasn't* a spotted redshank but still wanting to show off that I knew there was such a thing as a spotted redshank and that they were a little bit tricky to tell apart. And not just showing off my expertise but to remind Danny of the teacher–pupil relationship I had with him when we were birding, and to reinforce our respective roles.

'Well done, Danny.'

'Don't "well done" me, young man!' Danny retorted, semi-jokingly. 'Didn't I photograph one last time we went out?'

'So you did.'

Danny coughed. He coughed again. And then again and I thought he was not going to stop.

'Sorry, mate. Bloody fags. So what did little Tori think of them?'

'She loved them.'

In fact she'd said, 'Blimey, these are fantastic pictures.' Danny had printed off the digital originals on to high quality photographic paper. 'Amazing shot of an avocet.'

'Not difficult to photograph waders though,' I'd said.

'That's a bit unkind; this dunlin is amazing!'

'Yes, or is it a little stint? No, you're right, it's a dunlin.'

'He has a good eye.'

'Yeah, well at least one part of his body is good.'

Tori looked reproachfully over the top of her reading glasses. 'Sounds like you're jealous.'

'Eh?'

'You were the one who wanted to get Danny out birdwatching. Now he's quite keen, you don't like it.'

'That's not true.'

'Just because he's uses a camera and you use binoculars, you don't like it. You think it's a branch of photography rather than pure, immaculate twitching.'

'Not at all. I'm pleased for him. He's out in the fresh air, not smoking and drinking … as much.'

Though Tori had a point. A little tiny bit of a point, anyway. I was imparting my superior bird knowledge to Danny and he was turning it into photography, which was already his hobby. And it was also a subject I knew nothing about. In fact, I loathed photography: surely one of the world's most overrated talents, if that's not too generous a description. I always thought the gift of the world-class photographer was to be somewhere where something was worth photographing and to have his camera with him. Anything above and beyond that seemed to be pretentious bollocks. Though

I didn't want to annoy or upset Danny by voicing this opinion. It dawned on me that perhaps the bit I liked about birdwatching with Danny was the '*après*'. Danny was good at '*après*': eating, drinking, talking rubbish, swapping obscene reminiscences, having a huge laugh and making fools of ourselves in mixed company. The photography aspect of our expeditions had made it more serious for him and less fun for me.

'Thing is,' said Danny as we walked toward the lake. 'Thing about photography is that there's nothing to it. Being a good photographer just means being in the right place at the right time and having a camera with you. The rest is pretentious bollocks.'

'Mmm.' I pretended to muse on this. 'I'm sure a lot of people would disagree with you.'

'Stuff 'em.'

We were at Rutland Water, about sixty miles north of Cambridge. When I was a little boy, in the days when you had to learn things at school, everybody knew that the smallest county in England was Rutland. For a long time it was subsumed into Leicestershire but the plucky Rutlanders had agitated for it to be restored to its former tiny glory. So now it was Rutland again, with the pretty town of Oakham as its capital; a beacon of hope for rapidly disappearing Britain. Rutland Water was built in the seventies when I was still a student panting after the most beautiful girl in the world. It was originally called Empingham Reservoir and had been created to supply water to the East Midlands. It is an impressive site and one of the largest man-made reservoirs in Europe.

'Now, look, Danny, follow my finger there. What do you see?'

'Water.'

'Er ... correct; keep watching – something's about to appear.'

There was a plop and a dark, toy-duck-shaped bird bounced to the surface.

'Recognize that?'

'Oh yes, that's another one I photographed at Titchwell. Oh, it's er ...'

'If I said *Tachybaptus ruficollis* to you, what would you say?'

'I'd say cut out the bloody showing off and remind me what it is!'

'Little grebe.'

'Oh yes, I remember. Hang on. I don't think it is, you know.'

'It is, Danny, trust me.'

'I spent about an hour developing those photos; the little grebe didn't have a red eye and those funny yellowy feathers on the side of the head. Not that I remember anyway.'

I looked at the bird closely though the binoculars and saw that there was something odd about this little grebe, but I put it down to a seasonal plumage variation.

'It's probably some seasonal plumage variation.'

'Oi, mate!' Danny was calling out to a passing birder. 'What's that little black ducky thing down there?'

I'm sure this was another severe breach of twitching etiquette. The stranger looked Danny up and down suspiciously as if he were the sort of person who'd set fire to hides with fag ends. He gave the bird a brief going over with his scope.

'It's a black-necked grebe.'

'Not a little grebe, then?' Danny asked.

'No, a little grebe doesn't have that bright red eye and those yellow ear tufts.'

'One–nil to Danny!' he shrieked annoyingly.

'*Podiceps nigricollis*,' I announced, limply trying to get back some self-respect and pixie points.

Tori laughed at this anecdote. 'It's not a race: who sees the most birds, who sees the most species, who sees the rarest one. It's not a competition to see who knows the most Latin names for birds.'

'Well, I'd win that. Hands down.'

'Tch, there you go again! He's learnt a lot from you, what's wrong with you learning from him? There's nothing wrong with that. Don't be so proud. You don't have to save face all the time. Be wrong occasionally. I know you're not used to it but give it a go.'

'How dare you say I'm not used to being wrong? I've been wrong eleven times. Twice in the same year. 1982, it was.'

'You may joke, but you don't like to be shown up, do you?'

'Nonsense. Alright then,' I said, reaching for the nearest bird book. 'I'm going to show you a picture of a bird and you tell me what it is.'

Reluctantly Tori went along with this. I turned to the black-necked grebe. I covered up the name and turned the book towards her.

'What's that?'

'It's a black-necked grebe,' she said instantly.

'Exactly. Black-necked grebe. Just what I thought.'

STARLING

A spring day on the coast. I am with a hardy old countryman and birders surveying the estuary and its inhabitants.

'Look at that. Huge flock of dunlins,' say I.

'A fling.'

'Sorry?'

'A fling. That's what you say for dunlin. A fling of dunlin, not a flock.' And notice he says 'dunlin', singular, not 'dunlins' as I did.

'And a large group of pintails, as well.'

'Knob,' says countryman.

I pause to work out whether this is a comment about me and my ignorance of collective names for birds, or the collective name for pintails.

'It's a knob of pintail.'

'Oh, of course.' I press on tentatively. 'Is that not a flock of guillemots?'

'No, that's a bazaar of guillemot.'

'And what about those thrushes?'

'A mutation.'

'Linnets?'

'A parcel.'

'And what about that flock of shelducks?'

'A dodding of shelduck.'

'Well, I never.'

I should perhaps inform you that this dialogue never actually took place. You know this, first, from the odd collections of species: would I really be able to see a bazaar of guillemot from the same point I could see a mutation of thrush or a parcel of linnet?

Collective nouns, eh? Can you really be doing with them?

Compilers of pub quizzes apart, is anyone remotely interested in them? Who on earth would use them in everyday conversation?

A 'swarm of bees' or a 'den of thieves' is passable, but a 'siege of herons'? A 'cadge of peregrines'? I ask you! Some of them have a vague logic. A 'ballet of swans', for example. An 'ostentation of peacocks' makes sense. But does it imply that the peacocks have to be adult males with their tail feathers fully extended and fanned? Can you have an ostentation of baby peacocks? Or what about the females, the peahens? Is it a 'self-effacement'?

But what is more worrying: who bothered to make them up? Who the hell thought it necessary to have a different collective noun for each bird species? And besides, answer me this. If a 'dodding' can only be of shelduck, why would you ever say a 'dodding of shelduck'? And not just 'dodding'? Eh? See: not so clever now, Mr Collective-noun-inventor!

Having said that, I will own up a strong affection for one or two. If you've ever watched a group of goldfinches sociably tripping from bush to bush, singing its trilling, chattering, liquid song and flashing its patches of black, yellow and bright red, then you cannot argue with this flock being called a 'charm'.

A charm of goldfinch. Perfect.

And what about 'a parliament of owl'? Those wise-eyed, grey faces, deep in thoughtful debate on matters weighty and solemn. (Not that at any time in our history would we associate 'parliament' with wisdom or serious, thoughtful debate, but you get the idea.)

And as for crows: huge, brooding, smart and powerful. A 'murder of crow' and an 'unkindness of raven' are spot on.

I also have a soft spot for a 'murmuration of starling', because a murmuration is something special. When you see one, you'll know; and you'll never forget it. A murmuration is a dramatic display of the majesty, power and mystery of the bird world. People who think 'birds' are boring are stopped in their tracks.

The memory of one November afternoon over a city park will stay with me for ever. Not for the birds, particularly, but for the people. A sun was disappearing over the horizon leaving a narrow strip of gold on the edge of a sky, which was the colour of slate. Dog-walkers, families and children, strolling lovers, late shoppers, all stood with open mouths on the footpath as a giant, fluttering ball of starling wheeled and shimmered above them. A cloud of birds, a thousand strong, like a massive shoal of black fish, swirling in all directions with perfect coordination. The onlookers were bewitched, awed, and even a little scared, by the alien spectacle.

Yes, a murmuration of starling; I'll buy that. Better than a 'plump of moorhen', definitely.

DANNY AND THE
BIRDS OF EAST AFRICA

This lilac-breasted roller is a stunning bird. I have enough difficulty finding the superlatives to describe our own British specials,
like the humble kingfisher, so the hyperbole needed to convey the
magnificence of an East African bird like the lilac-breasted roller is
truly beyond me. It can only be described by the words: 'Go to
East Africa and see one.'

'Any idea what this champion is?' Danny had said, laying the
photograph neatly down on the table in front of us.

'Wow,' said Tori on the intake of breath. 'That's a beaut.'

'Yes, pretty,' I admitted. 'No idea what it is, though. But I bet
it's a bird you photographed in East Africa.'

'Spot on,' Danny laughed. 'It's a lilac-breasted roller. And
this one?'

Another slickly professional photograph was offered unto us.
This one again depicted a bird with predictably superb markings.
Impossibly coloured as only tropical birds can be. A huge irides-
cent flash of turquoise on its cheeks and neck, bright orange
breast and a snowy-white rump. Its head, black with a staring
white eye, and its beak, slightly curved and stabby, gave it the look
of a starling.

'It's superb,' enthused Tori.

'Looks like a starling in fancy dress,' I unenthused.

'Well, what about that? It's a superb starling!' chuckled Danny.
'Now what's interesting about that piccie is that I shot it with a

Canon EOS-IDs Mark II with a Canon EF lens 300mm f/2.8 IS plus 1.4x converter.'

'Ooh, Danny, you're blinding us with science now,' Tori said rather kindly. 'Boring us without science' was how I was going to put it.

'No, but what I was going to say was this: the interesting thing about the two photos—'

'Careful of incontinent use of the word "interesting", Danny!'

'No, it's just that the starling, that superb little feller, was shot on film. Ilford XP2 with an Olympus OM-1N. I was wondering if you could see any difference in tone or quality or anything.'

I ummed for a bit and said, 'I think I'd need to know a bit about the apertures, shutter speeds and focal lengths first.'

'Well, actually,' he started, then realized I was being sarcastic and stopped, looking genuinely deflated. He lit a cigarette and Tori reached for the next photograph. It showed a pretty bird with a snow-white breast and head, perilously perched on a branch covered in huge thorns.

'That looks like a shrike,' Tori said.

'A northern white-crowned shrike,' Danny confirmed.

'It's on a good tree for impaling its prey,' I said, and Tori reminded me of our first ever sighting of a shrike, a great grey shrike, in Lanzarote. It was our first holiday together in the early, nervous days of our relationship, and I remember needlessly worrying that the habits of the shrike might be too bloodthirsty for her.

The glossies kept coming; on each one some wonder bird from another continent. Bigger, more bizarre and more brightly coloured. After half an hour we'd 'ooh-ed' and 'aaah-ed' our way through Somali bee-eaters, red and yellow barbets, African paradise flycatchers, spotted morning thrushes, sooty chats, pin-tailed wydahs and a whole host of drongos. My respect and admiration for Danny's work was made grudging by a slight irritation I couldn't really put my finger on.

'You weren't very enthusiastic about his photos,' Tori said as we lay in bed later.

'I was. I thought they were fab.'

'You didn't show it. You should be pleased. You pestered him to go birdwatching with you and he did. He gets really good at it and into it through photography, and gets paid by a magazine to go round the world photographing birds. I'd have thought you'd be delighted.'

I blew out a deep breath in the direction of the ceiling and tried to think honestly.

'Well, the thing is with Dan that we do different things now. We're both busier than we used to be so there isn't time for the crack we used to have; you know, just going out on the town, on the piss, to football, womanizing.'

'What womanizing?' Tori cut in hard.

'Well, that was mainly Danny's department. Obviously.'

Tori was not completely satisfied with this. 'Because you've already got a lovely woman you're devoted to!'

'How did you find out about her?'

'Ha ha.'

'No, but it was a laugh at first,' I went on. 'Twitching with Danny. A few hours in the bushes then a night on the piss. Now he's gone all serious about it.'

Tori forced out a snide guffaw. 'Well, that's rich. I thought you were the serious birding bore trying to get your best mate to join your club. Was he only allowed to join on your terms then? Has he broken the rules by becoming more interested and serious about it than you?'

She was right. I had started it and it was fun having Danny as the new boy, as my private pupil.

'Do you resent the fact that you got him these shoots abroad?' Tori said, cuddling up to me.

'No, not all,' I said, truthfully. But another truth was beginning to dawn. I was interested in birdwatching in Britain. I would be exhilarated to see a British rarity. A black redstart or a golden oriole. It seems almost to be cheating to go to a far-off country where birds like a Lewin's honeyeater or a cobalt macaw or a streamer-tailed humming bird are two a penny.

'Where's the skill in going to Java and seeing a Java sparrow?'

'Oh I see,' said Tori in best *Advocatus diabli* mode. 'If you want to be a birdwatcher, you can only do it in the country you live in?'

'Not really. If we go abroad, we always take our binoculars just in case, but we don't go abroad precisely in order to bird-watch, do we?'

'We could do, though. And what's wrong with people who do?'

Nothing, of course. I was unsure now what I thought. I knew that I was pleased the exotic birds, and indeed the dull ones, of other countries existed, and I was pleased that people would travel to see them and photograph them, but I was pleased not to be one of them, and I was pleased to carry on doing casual birdwatching in Britain with our small but varied collection of birds, not all of which I'd seen by far.

Since Tori and I had been living together, I'd seen less of Danny and all my friends. But that is normal and to be expected. I thought we'd spend more time together if he came birding with me occasionally. It worked, but now that he was seriously into it through the photography, I hardly saw him at all. He felt the same way, I think, which is why one day he surprised me by inviting me on a trip to the Gambia.

'He's said I should go with him on his next trip: a photo-shoot in the Gambia,' I told Tori.

'That's great. Will it be expensive?'

'He wants to pay. Not him personally but the job. He thinks he owes me.'

'Ah, that's lovely. You must go.'

'I'm not sure I want to.'

'You've got to go.'

It was a nice offer, but for whatever reasons I did not really want to go. Tori seemed touched by the whole idea. 'Why don't you go, just for Danny? You've done a lot for him. It would be nice.'

I shook my head. 'I don't think I'd enjoy it if I was doing it just to please him. I don't think he'd enjoy it either.'

'Amazing birdlife I bet. And I'm sure you'll be in a luxury hotel.'

'Probably.'

'With a bar and womanizing facilities.'

I laughed. 'For Danny, of course.'

I came up with several excuses as to why I couldn't go. The hassle of rearranging work, the administrating of flying, my loathing of airports and the tedium of air travel, the mosquitoes, missing my daughter's birthday and an Arsenal home game, but the truth was that this was his thing and not my thing, and while I was pleased for him, I didn't want to go.

'That's a real shame, mate.' He seemed genuinely disappointed. This made me feel awkward. He started coughing so much I could almost feel the scratching pain in my own chest.

'A change of climate will do you good. You go off and have a great time.'

'You'll be sorry.'

'Maybe, I will.'

And he was right.

I would be sorry.

HERON

But sometimes the best birdwatching moments are not watching a bird, but *seeing* a bird. You haven't planned a trip, you're not in some exotic location, you haven't chosen the time of year or the place and you haven't got any complex gadgetry with you. You're just out for a walk in the country as Tori and I were, one early summer's evening. We were taking a short cut by a bend in the river across a lane thick with nettles and cow parsley. We weren't exactly being silent and our thrashing through the undergrowth disturbed a heron, which took off scarcely a yard in front of us.

Have you ever seen a heron? You probably have. It's a bit of a one-off bird. Or should that be a two-off bird, because, to my mind, there are two herons: there's the standing heron and the flying heron.

A grey heron standing by the edge of a pond or river is a mesmerizing sight. Its trance-like stillness is hypnotic. Is it moving? Yes, imperceptibly, it moves. Staring into the water for its prey, which it grabs with a lightning strike from a spring-loaded neck. It's one of those creatures that makes you think ah, that's why God gave us slow-motion photography.

But a gift to the apprentice birdwatcher. Easy to see. Tall, elegant and boldly marked: beautiful blue-grey wings with black tips, a black cap elongated into a plume at the back of the neck and a white breast with little black streaks on its neck. And its beak: pinkish, orangey-yellow and … can I avoid saying dagger-like? No. Its beak is like a dagger. Go and look at one; that beak was designed for 'dagger' clichés.

And when you see one flying, or taking off close by, as Tori and I did that night, then you know straight away that you have *seen something*. It's a stop-you-in-your-tracks moment. What is that huge bird, you think. Big, broad, scoopy wings struggling to get itself off the ground. Away it goes, massive against the sky with its yes, dagger-like head tucked into its shoulders and its long legs dragging behind. I always think, when I see one, especially this close, that it must be the biggest bird in Britain, but I *know* that the mute swan is. But still I wonder.

My friend Mannie is in no doubt.

He has hugged one.

'Have you ever hugged a heron?' he asked me once.

'Er, no … funnily enough I haven't. I've kissed a frozen chicken, does that count?'

'No, hug a heron when you get the chance.'

Now, Mannie is an experienced wildlife cameraman and has filmed many birds all over the world; if there's anyone I know with good reason to hug a heron, it'd be him.

'There's nothing to a heron,' Mannie continues. 'You think they're going to be massively chunky and heavy, but not a bit of it. Insubstantial. Feeble. Shandy lightweights'

'So definitely not as big as a swan then?' I venture.

'Ooh no! And I beg of you: never hug a swan!'

I won't, Mannie.

But people don't like herons. Well, people with fishponds don't like herons. Little garden ponds stuffed with carp and gold-fish are very attractive to herons. A lot of fish in one small area. It's like a buffet, all you can eat for £1. 99, or whatever that is in heron. So owners of fishponds go to extreme lengths to deter them. Some get a life-size and life-like model of a heron and stick it next to their pond. They can look quite nice, but not as nice as a heron. Some use an air-rifle.

My friend Howie who lives near the coast in Lancashire has a beautiful fishpond with some lovely rare fish in it. He quite liked herons; he liked all creatures, in fact; he had three cats and a small dog. His neighbour liked birds too. Well, he liked pigeons; only pigeons, racing pigeons. So he didn't like herons; or cats and dogs for that matter.

'Here, Howie,' said the neighbour, proffering the air-rifle. 'Any time, it's yours, pal.'

'What for?'

'Bloody herons. I've seen 'em sat on the edge of your pond. Eyeing up your fishies. And I wouldn't put it past them to have a go at my birds an' all. I've lost a couple recently, you know.'

'No, thanks, I don't need a gun,' Howie said meekly.

'Well, don't worry; I'll be keeping an eye out.'

Over the next year and a half, Howie's pond was unmolested by herons.

And so were his neighbour's birds.

But Howie's cats disappeared one by one.

And his little dog.

'Bloody herons!' said the neighbour. Unconvincingly.

Vermin, then, to many, the graceful and dagger-like heron. But in our history a lot of birds have been considered vermin, and not just the ones you might think. There are records from England in the sixteenth and seventeenth century that bear bleak witness to man's fondness for destroying his fellow creatures. Birds as varied as cormorant, osprey, eagle, kite, green woodpecker, dipper, jay, starling, house sparrow and bullfinch were considered vermin and people could earn good money catching and destroying them. What made them vermin? Interfering with man's provisions, we assume: attacking game, and farmed fish, and cereals and fruit.

But what of the heron? The dagger-headed fish-murderer? Why is his name not on the list of vermin?

Aha. An interesting reason, with man, of course, again calling the shots.

In the Middle Ages, falconry was at its most popular. Popular with the royals and nobles, that is. Falconry was a very expensive pastime. Edward 'Longshanks' the First who almost single-hand-edly rid Britain of wolves, and tried to do the same with the Scots and Welsh, was passionate about hawks. When one of his birds was ill he not only paid to have it specially looked after but had a waxen image of the bird made so it could be offered at the shrine of St Thomas de Cantilupe in Hereford Cathedral. Most castles, palaces and noble houses would have a master falconer and numerous falcons, which were kept in cages round the back of the building. These were called 'mewes'. Later the 'mews' were larger buildings for horses and later still they were converted into townhouses for yuppies. The falconers (who were called 'austringers' if they were using 'accipitrines' – true hawks – rather than falcons) had to train their birds to hunt and this required some 'live' action.

Obviously inexperienced hunting birds could not start straight away on fast-flying game birds or fleet-footed rabbits and hares, so they had to practise on birds that were not too demanding. A large, slow bird, maybe, that could not hide away easily. And a bird that was not much use for anything else. The heron, of course. So the verminous grey man of the river became suddenly non-verminous.

Indeed, it became protected! Protected by the king so the king could practise killing it.

But from its years of being target practice for falcons, the herons learned something too. A peregrine falcon over the reed beds could easily knock out a standing heron, so when there's a falcon about, the great grey bird invariably flies low over the water, as close to the surface as it can, knowing that no falcon is going to be able to attempt a high-speed dive at it without risking crashing into the water.

And one of my favourite things about the heron is in the cooking of it. I don't mean that I like eating heron; I've never eaten one, nor would I; of course, we have it on good authority from Mannie, the wildlife cameraman who has hugged a heron, that there is not much on them. But before you cook a heron, or indeed any wild game, you need to prepare it. And dating from the early sixteenth century there are specific terms for jointing beasts of the field, air and water.

Apparently, one 'thighs' a woodcock.

A pike should be 'splatted', and in the unlikely event your fish supper consists of a porpoise, this should be 'undertranched'.

A peacock should be 'disfigured', and a heron, my favourite, should be 'dismembered'. It would be nice to answer the phone and say, 'Sorry, I can't speak just now, I'm dismembering a heron.'

Tori and I watched the undismembered heron fly off. Such an impressive flight too: the rhythmic flap of the wings so broad and so slow. This felt like a proper birdwatching moment; the sunset turned the sinuous river into a dazzling golden serpent zigzagging through the dusky reeds and we were alone with the great grey bird. So simple and calm.

SCAVENGERS

But I do go abroad occasionally. And I do look at the birds. I once worked briefly in India, a country with a daunting number of superb bird species. I hadn't gone there to watch birds but to do a tedious job I did not enjoy. Bombay is a miserable place. Or perhaps a place of misery. I know that being brought up in English cities and English countryside is not a good preparation for places like Bombay. I know we judge things differently here and I know all about culture shock, but, nevertheless, to me Bombay was grim. Or was the misery inside me and I was projecting it on to my surroundings? Anyway, I was looking for something to lift my spirits. I looked to the sky.

Wow! What the hell is that?

A bird with the proportions and swagger of an eagle but the slim grace of a swallow.

A kite.

A black kite. Right over the middle of this vast, teeming Indian city.

And another next to it.

And another. And ... against the glaring white sky, I could see the magnificent kite silhouette of thousands of individual birds.

'Kites!' I exclaimed to the local driver.

'Pariahs,' he said. 'Pariah kites.'

That's not nice, I thought. 'Pariah.' The lowest caste. In fact, even lower than that. No caste at all. The social outcast. Such a beautiful bird.

'They are vermin,' he went on. 'Pests. Worse than rats,' and he finished by spitting out the word 'scavengers'.

This was always the way. Hyenas? Horrible creatures, scavengers, you know! Herring gulls? Nasty birds; scavengers, of course! Sharks, evil things, they mostly scavenge, you know!

Poor scavengers. Why such bad press? A lion is alright because it hunts and kills zebras and eats as much as it can. That's fine, apparently. Then along come those filthy scavengers, hyenas, jackals, vultures. What is the suggestion: are they lazy? Can't be bothered to chase their own antelopes? No, hyenas are doing all they can do, surely; all that nature intended them to do, which is be hyenas. The scavengers are vital to any eco-system. Could we not say: bloody lions! They kill a load of wildebeest, leave tons of it uneaten, just lying about the place, being messy and stinking to high heaven; thank heavens for those nice hyenas and vultures who come and clear up every last morsel.

I was captivated by the pariah kites above the teeming, steaming, choking streets of Bombay.

In Britain we have the red kite. A stunner. I remember my first. Where the M40 cuts a spectacularly white gorge through the chalky Chilterns in Buckinghamshire, I saw the magnificent bird swoop in to land on a footbridge. I would defy anyone not to look up and gaze at this masterpiece. A large but graceful bird, deep chestnut-red, greyish head and the distinctive and unmistakable forked tail, constantly twisted like a rudder throughout its elegant flight. Their presence on the M40 is a success story. Will the kite go back to its medieval status of irritating pest? Possibly, but for now it's a beauty; a birdy masterpiece. Definitely the best thing about the M40. Though there's really good a John Lewis at High

Wycombe. The numbers in that area now are truly impressive and, if you're not the driver, they make the motorway journey from London to Birmingham a delight.

Why the extinction? Why, man, of course. Birds of prey interfere with other birds. Other birds that man wants for himself for food (and in some cases for hunting, as well). And there is something so obvious about a bird of prey. They are attractive. One of the things they attract is attention. The attention of farmers, hunters and game-keepers. So the red kite was wiped out. But go back to the time before the shotgun and it's a different story. In medieval London, the kite was at the peak of its scavenging menace, boldly swooping to grab the food out of people's hands.

In those days to call someone a kite was an insult. Not just a bird but a low-life. Shakespeare called London the 'city of crows and kites' where 'kites' could easily have referred to the cockney populace. Hamlet, in referring to the 'bloody, bawdy villain' Claudius, says:

> *But am I pigeon-livered, and lack gall/ to make oppression bitter.*
> *Or 'ere this/*
> *I should have fatted all the region's kites /with this slave's offal.*

But the beautiful red kite is back. Its success is staggering. They're everywhere. Soon they may once again be as common as they were in the times of Shakespeare and Chaucer. People are already feeding them junk food in their back gardens. A few individual birds in Wales clawed the species back from extinction – since then there have been re-introduction schemes in many places, including the Chilterns.

I was watching one as I drove on the outskirts of Milton Keynes one spring evening: so pleasing to the eye; such a dashing reminder of the energy and vigour of life.

'It would be a shame to lose you again,' I said to the bird. I don't know why but my thoughts turned to Danny.

GOODBYE

A beautiful summer's day. The sun overhead in a spotless sky meant there were no dark corners for the shadows to hide in.

'What a terrible day,' I said to Tori as we looked over the golden reeds to the dark blue band of sea beyond. 'Doesn't it ever rain in this country?'

'It's lovely. I know it doesn't feel right but I think we should be glad.'

I had promised Danny that when he got back from his travels we would have a nostalgic trip to Norfolk: a little bit of birdwatching and a huge helping of eating, drinking and merriment at the Hoste Arms in Burnham Market. Tori was with us this time so it would not be a 'boys' night out' but this *was* a rather special occasion.

'Where's Danny?'

'He's still in the car. I'll go and get him.' She turned to go.

'He's missing the birds. And they're his favourites. Dicky birds. Get him out here quick!'

High summer is not a great time for serious birdwatching. The partners have been found, the nests have been built, the mating has been done, eggs laid and hatched, the hyperactive feeding of voracious chicks is over, the fledglings have left and the parents have nothing much to do now except to moult the finery of their breeding plumage and survive till the circus of life rolls back into their town. Above the reed heads the momentary flitting of nameless warblers was obvious. An occasional swallow, swift or martin would twitter by in a dark flash, and the distant white specks of some reliably ubiquitous seagulls were visible with the accompaniment of shrieking laughter and bad-tempered wailing.

Danny would have once thought a day like this spent in the countryside looking at nature was a waste. A day like this was for iced drinks and scantily clad girls followed by a warm twilight of music, laughter and mischief. But we all change.

Danny had changed a lot since I last saw him three months ago as he left for the Gambia, struggling into Heathrow under the weight of suitcases, camera gear and his worsening hacking cough.

'Here we are,' Tori announced sadly.

The ashes were in a small ornate urn. Tori's hands were shaking as she handed it to me. Ashes. How painfully apt.

A small brown bird flew up from the reeds in front of us and immediately disappeared.

'Hey, what was that?' Tori asked, her excitement not disguising the tears in her voice.

'A dicky bird,' as Danny would say.

The sun went behind a cloud. I shivered. I looked up. There were no clouds. It was just my thoughts getting dark.

'Alright then, here goes,' I said, and took the lid off the urn and flung its contents as hard and high as I could. As the ashes emptied out, the soft, westerly summer breeze picked up the blue-grey cloud of dust and floated it gently off towards nothingness and Brancaster.

ROCKIN' ROBIN

Stormcock. What a great word! The old name for the mistle thrush. A larger, greyer and tougher version of the song thrush, but with a similar talent for singing. This hardy bird had often been observed perched high in the wind and rain, pouring its tuneful heart out into the teeth of a gale. It gets its common name from its predilection for mistletoe. Its fondness for this particular plant makes me think its popular name should be something like 'kissing bird' or 'kiss-cock'. Neither of these suggestions has yet been taken up by the birding community.

'Hey, Jon,' I said enthusiastically, 'what about *Stormcock*? You know, Roy Harper? Play something from that. You must have heard of it. It's a classic. Only four tracks and one of them lasts thirteen minutes.'

Jon was nowhere to be seen. He was sitting on the sofa a few feet away but he was nowhere to be seen. He was deep in his electronic fortress. The Xbox controls at his feet snaked towards the television, which every few seconds blared out the same request to 'choose a weapon'. I turned it down. Jon didn't notice, he was sitting with the electric guitar on his lap, legs crossed and feet resting on the amp. He was wearing headphones and, for extra isolation, his woolly hat was pulled right down over the rims of his sunglasses.

'You're just so fucking annoying, Jon,' his loving sister chimed in.

'What about "Fly Like An Eagle" by the Steve Miller band?' I suggested. Jon nodded, but I think that was a coincidence.

'"Bird On A Wire" by Leonard Cohen?'

Louise looked imploringly to heaven. 'Come on, Dad, we'll never regain contact if you want him to play Leonard Cohen. Anyway, there are songs not to do with birds, you know.'

'Name one.'

She came straight back with, '"Dirty", Christina Aguilera?'

'OK, that's not about birds, but it's sung by a bit of ruff.'

A big tut. 'That's just lame, Daddy!'

'Hey, Jon, do you know "The Chicken Song"?'

A loud twangy minor chord rang out; it throbbed with reverb, chorus, sustain and 'why don't you two just get out and leave me alone?'

'OK, Jon,' I said picking up my coat. 'Me and Lou are going shopping. We'll be an hour or so. See you later. Are you warm enough, by the way? You've only got three sweatshirts and a hoodie on.'

Another dismissive twang rattled the amp and we left.

The deal was that I'd take Louise shopping provided we could walk into town the long way round: the scenic route; the pretty way.

'You mean the birdwatching way?' she had correctly surmised, and we ambled round the meadowy outskirts of the city and were rewarded with a skylark singing high up in the clouds.

'Beautiful. Hear that!'

Louise looked around, back and front, up and down. 'What is it?'

'It's called the invisible bird.'

'I can't see it.'

'Well, there you are, you see.'

She was intrigued to pin it down but this one was invisible in the whiteness. I told her this bird was special but made the mistake of telling her it was also rather dull and streaky brown, and while the shops were open she wasn't going to wait to see one drop back to earth.

'In Victorian times, they used to eat them, you know.'

'Ugh, that's gross! Anyway there can't be much meat on them.'

'No, there isn't. You'd need about twenty for your pie. And then you'd have to bung in loads of stuff like bacon, beef and onions.'

'Mmm, sounds lovely; apart from the skylark. Would you eat one?'

Children have an uncanny knack of putting you on the spot.

'Er ... good question, Lou!'

'You're always going on about how wondrous skylarks are, how they're endangered and all that, but would you eat one? You eat other birds: chickens, pheasant and loads of creepy stuff. What about a skylark?'

'Ah, I know,' I said, pretending I'd suddenly had a flash of inspiration, 'a merlin!'

'What do you mean, "a merlin"?'

Good, she hadn't noticed I was evading the question.

'The merlin is a small bird of prey; looks like a little pigeon. They're really neat. In the day when the aristocracy hunted, the men had peregrines and the women had merlins. In royal circles, the merlin was the lady's falcon. Anyway, *they* eat skylarks. Their favourite prey, and I'll tell you something interesting ...'

'Can't wait!'

' ... if the lark stops singing and drops down for cover, the merlin nearly always gets it, but sometimes the lark carries on singing, even louder, and rising as the merlin approaches it, as if to say, "Don't mess with me, pal!", and then the merlin leaves it alone.'

'Cool,' said Lou, 'So, answer me, would you eat a skylark?'

'Oh hell, I suppose so; if there was no other food and I was starving and desperate. God knows how I'd catch one, though.'

'You could borrow the Queen's merlin!' She smiled and I held her hand. We hurried up a bit and scared a pair of chaffinches off the path in front of us, and Louise listened indulgently as I told her about how chaffinches were hunted and captured for singing contests. The male has a loud song, which it repeats over and over again all day long. In the late nineteenth century, men would catch them and cage them in dingy pubs, place bets on which would sing the longest or repeat its song the most times. The contests produced a lot of money and no little crime. Good singers changed hands for substantial sums. 'It was quite cruel, I should imagine, and it's against the law now to trap birds like chaffinches.'

Louise betrayed the tiniest hint of interest. 'Where do you get all this weird shit from?'

'Oh, you know; I read it in books, mainly.'

'So people actually write books about all this birdy stuff? And some people read it?'

'Apparently … Hey, Lou, stop! Keep still.'

We were crossing a small square of park lined with large old trees. The grass had just been mown. This is the ideal setting for a green woodpecker. I have seen them here before and out of habit I always look. And there was one. Just a greenish lump in the distance, unless you knew what you were looking for. Despite their name, the green woodpecker spends most of its time on the ground looking for ants, which it scoops up with a long, sticky tongue.

'You wait here,' I said to Louise, leaving her on the path as I tiptoed in long, slow strides towards the bird. The nearer I got, the slower and more precise my movements got. I was near enough to see every detail of the marvellously coloured creature. One tiny move at a time now, I edged closer and closer. I was playing statues as I came within a couple of yards of it as it busily stabbed the neat lawn. One step too many and it yaffled away to the trees, showing off its fine yellow rump.

'Wonderful!' I turned back to my daughter. Two or three passers-by had stopped to watch my curious, slo-mo dance, and next to them my gorgeous sixteen-year-old Loulou was twisting and squirming with excruciating embarrassment.

A tour of clothes shops seemed to help her over the trauma of seeing her father behaving like a headcase in the busy broad daylight of a city Saturday.

We got back from town to find that Jon, too, had returned from the planet he was on earlier. He seemed very keen and lively.

'Hey, Dad, listen to this!' He picked up the guitar and announced, 'Some birdsong for you.'

His nimble fingers glided effortlessly up and down the fretboard as he played an almost note-perfect version of the Beatles' 'Blackbird'.

'That's amazing, Jon! All it needs is a foot-tap and a real blackbird singing in the background.'

I was impressed but a little miffed. I taught him to play that. And *I* can't play it.

AT LAST

Tori was beginning to look intently into the reeds. 'That was something a bit special. Something I've never seen before.'

'It was an LBJ. A little brown jobbie. Or a "lousy blow job" in Danny's words.'

'We should have brought the binoculars.'

The dull bird I had just dismissed suddenly appeared again and perched for a tantalizing instant on a reed stalk.

'That wasn't a warbler.' She seemed quite insistent. 'I can't believe we didn't bring our binoculars.'

'Well, we haven't got our bins because we didn't come here to birdwatch, did we? We came here for Danny.'

She looked away.

'I know, I know. That bird was different, though.'

'Was it an Indian harpy eagle?'

She aimed a reproachful schoolteacher's face in my direction. 'No!'

'A Madagascar firefinch?'

'I'm not playing this game.'

'A construction site crane?'

She put her hands to her ears and shut her eyes tightly.

'A fireside chat? A bit of a lark? A three-point tern?'

'You need Danny here to laugh at your drivel.'

I sighed. 'Oh, what's the point?'

'Well there's not much around. It's summer and the birds aren't up to much, are they?'

'No, I mean what's the point of birdwatching? Death makes you think things like that, doesn't it?'

A sudden breeze stroked the reed heads, causing a ripple of light and shade to glide over the marsh.

'There's exactly the same point to birdwatching now as ever. Death has never changed the point of something!'

'So, what is the point of birdwatching?'

Tori sighed. 'What's the point of anything?'

'True; go on, tell me.'

She tutted, but not too unkindly. 'Why don't you ask your kids? Didn't you say that either everything has a point or nothing has a point? And even if everything is pointless, it doesn't mean to say you don't have to do it, or you can't enjoy doing it.'

I looked out across the reed beds to the sea and sky. Yes, I probably had said those things. 'Death is bound to stop you in your tracks and make you think oh, what's the point, we're all going to die.'

'That fact that we're all going to die surely means there's even more of a point to doing anything.' Tori's magical words derailed my train of thought.

'Actually, talking of death, what are we going to do about Danny?'

'What do you mean, what is there to do?'

'Well, we've done our duty, haven't we?'

Tori looked puzzled. 'Explain.'

'Well,' I said, 'we've got rid of his cat, as requested, scattering the ashes in a long, touching and sacred ceremony – which, incidentally, he was too wussy to attend.'

'Well, he was upset.'

'I don't know why. He resented that cat and every penny he spent on its banana sandwiches.'

'No, the thing is this: deep down, he didn't want to lose his last reminder of Diana, the one and only love of his life. He couldn't bear to say goodbye.'

'I think you and me deserve some just you and me time together.'

Tori shook her head. 'We can't just abandon him in Norfolk. Anyway, we're supposed to be having a memorial lunch in the Hoste together. Strictly non-vegetarian.'

'True.'

We headed back to the car park.

'At least the car's not going to reek of fags,' she said.

'True. He hasn't smoked since he left for the Gambia. He's done well.'

'Nicotine stained fingers crossed.'

'You know what,' I said, putting my arm around her, 'I think I've watched enough birds. Let's do something else. We can always do it now and again. Not every day, every week or whatever. We don't have to upgrade our spotting-scope. We don't have to get on the rare-sighting paging network. Let's just go out for a walk and see what flies across our path. But I don't feel like being a "keen" anything at the moment.'

'OK, what shall we do instead?' asked Tori. 'I mean, what would you *like* to do? What have you never ever done that you'd like to do before you die?'

'Fuck a black girl.'

'Apart from that? Anything sensible? Any pastimes you fancy? Ballroom dancing?'

'No fear. That is sad!'

'Hey, steady on, Mr Ballroom-Dancing's-Sad. Remember what your children said about birdwatching.'

'Yeah, that's true.'

'And anyway, ballroom dancing's sexy now. *Strictly Come Dancing*'s a hugely popular show.'

'I hated that.'

'Yeah, but I haven't heard that they've commissioned *Strictly Come Birdwatching*.'

She was right. Not even Bill Oddie in a gold, sequinned, skin-tight ballgown was going to sell twitching to the masses. No prime ministerial candidate would be clamouring to be photographed birdwatching, instead of shaking hands with babies or having the Arctic Monkeys round for tea. There was no doubt about it that there was something cool-proof, sexy-proof about birdwatching. Perhaps that's why it appealed so much to me. It was so unconnected to the false, glam, empty, tawdry, superficial world of 'cool'. It had just about come within nodding distance of 'right-on' status by clinging to the current mania for things wildlifey, conservationalist and save-the-planety. But joining a local nature club or ornithological group was not going to replace speed-dating as an effective way of meeting potential life-partners.

'Anyway, is birdwatching really our hobby? When did it become a hobby as opposed to just something we'd do occasionally when we were out walking in the countryside?'

'When you bought me the spotting-scope and tripod,' I answered confidently.

'Which we've never used. Apart from dropping it in the water. So it's never really been our hobby then?'

She was right again. I kissed her and said, 'I hate the word "hobby", anyway. It sounds like what people did in the fifties.'

Tori did mock indignation 'I was still in nappies in the fifties!'

'So was I. Being in nappies was obviously one of the most popular hobbies back then.'

Tori sighed one of those big sighs of life that people who were born in the fifties did a lot of in 2007. We fell silent and surveyed the pretty summer landscape.

As it was a bad time of the year for birdwatching, there were not many twitchers about. No hearty 'good mornings' interrupted our closeness and privacy.

'The trouble with birdwatchers is they're people,' I said as Tori put her hand in mine.

'Well, a lot of them are,' she said, holding me back to look at a little brown jobbie flitting among the reeds.

'It'll be a sedge warbler,' I said, trying to walk on.

'No, this was very different.' She seemed quite certain.

'But look at this. An empty bit of the North Norfolk coast. No people, just land, sea, sky and birds.'

'Well, two people. You and me.'

'One person: you!'

'Eh?'

'Well, I can't see me.'

'Oh, I see, do you want me to go so you can be alone with nature?'

'No, I want you here all the time.'

'Ah, thank you.' She squeezed my hand.

'But just don't stand where I can see you.'

She let go of my hand to point into the reeds. 'There it is again.'

I was not that interested. 'Yes, that's the second time I haven't seen it now.'

'It's not a sedge warbler!'

We sat down on the grass bank and faced the expanse of reeds.

She nudged me hard. 'I knew it; we should have brought the binoculars.'

'We're not twitching though, are we? We're just being. Just walking in the country. Being with each other. We can still look at birds.'

'But we'll never see what that thing was unless we have the bins!'

I shook my head. 'I don't care. It was a small brown bird. Yes, I'm sure it is beautiful and unique and all that and I bet it has an interesting scientific name. But I'm happy not to see it. Or find out what it is. I like a bit of mystery.'

'OK.' She rested her head on my shoulder. 'Do you really want me here all the time?'

'Of course. You're the only girl I ever wanted to share my life with; you know that.'

'I'm sorry about JJ.'

'We've been over that loads of times; what happens, happens.'

So much had happened between now and that remote moment when JJ left my life that it took a real effort to recall it. Of course, she was engaged to be married. I didn't ask her about her private life because I was frightened of losing what we had. And she didn't tell me about it because she didn't want to lose what we had. Every time she didn't tell me about it, and every second I didn't ask her about it, it got harder for both of us. I was sure I knew what I wanted; she was sure she didn't know what she wanted. We had an unspoken pact that would lead us as close to each other as was possible. It was doomed. As shocking and upsetting as it was, it was not an act of cruelty. It was an act of kindness, of generosity, of love. At least every moment leading up to that last moment was. We were very young and had that infernal curse of the very young, which is not knowing how very young they are. What makes remembering the days of JJ so difficult now is not remembering her or the events, it's remembering me and trying to work out, to confirm, that that person was in fact me. But for the next twenty-five years, life, in that annoying little way that life has, bombarded me in each waking minute with shocks, disappointments, surprises and delights. And things turned out for the best. No, things turned out better than 'for the best'.

Tori's voice seemed to come from miles away. 'I bet I know what you're thinking about.'

'You'll be right.'

'I'm sorry.'

'Stop saying "I'm sorry"; it wasn't *your* fault! It was just the situation. What happened to that bird you were tracking?'

'It's still in there, somewhere.' She turned to me, pulled my head towards her and kissed me firmly.

'That was an unexpected pleasure. You couldn't have done that wearing binoculars!'

'I wouldn't have done it if I'd been wearing binoculars. I'd have been finding out what that bird is.'

'A sedge warbler.'

'It's not a sedge warbler!' She held her hands up to her eyes and made little round imaginary binoculars and squinted into them. 'Ah that's better. Right, where are you, little bird?'

I hugged her and she put her arm round me.

'JJ's a stupid name anyway.'

I laughed. 'Tori's not great, is it? Sounds a bit right wing!'

'But it *is* my name,' she reminded me. 'Well, my middle name is Victoria and Tori is its most agreeable abbreviation.'

'True; I couldn't go out with a Vicky!'

She laughed. 'Apart from that Welsh girl in the Love Bar. She was called Vicky.'

'You know what I mean. I wasn't having a relationship with her.'

'Would you if she'd changed her name?'

'No. Well, I might have if she'd changed her face and her personality.'

'That's not nice!'

'Sorry, Vicky.'

'Victoria, to you.' And then she added, 'Juliet Victoria Jameson, in fact.'

'Yes, I can see why you chose "JJ".'

She smiled a smile that wanted to be something else and looked away. I turned her face back towards me and she was crying.

'Oh my lovely.' I kissed her as if it were our first kiss ever. Though, as our first kiss ever was twenty-five years earlier, I hope this one was better.

'Come on, let's not go down that road again. We made it, didn't we?'

'Yes,' she nodded, 'we made it.'

'Divorce, agony, pain, disaster, more agony, alcohol, crisis, torture, more alcohol and we've even survived being twitchers. We made it, JJ!'

Through a tear, she smiled the smile to end all smiles. Then she glanced up.

'Look, there it is! Wow.'

I looked and there it was. A bird neither of us had seen before. Perched obligingly in the open and easily visible to the naked eye. A pretty bird, too. Not a sedge warbler. An impressive, long-tailed, orangey-brown bird, with black and cream wings, a pale, blue-grey head and black 'moustaches' either side of its bill.

It was unmistakable.

'Ah, that's sweet,' said Tori. 'It's a reedling.'

'A what?'

'A reedling.'

'I've never heard of a reedling. No such bird!'

She scoffed. 'It's a bearded tit. Reedling's another name for a bearded tit!'

'Oh I see. Why did you say reedling?'

'I didn't want to say "bearded tit" in case you made a puerile joke.'

'Moi?'